# Faith & Reason Made Simple

(Training for the 21$^{st}$ Century Christian Believer)

# RICK McGOUGH

Copyright © 2019 Rick McGough

All rights reserved.

ISBN: 9781793081049

"Scripture quotations taken from the New American Standard Bible® (NASB),
Copyright © 1960, 1962, 1963, 1968, 1971, 1972, 1973,
1975, 1977, 1995 by The Lockman Foundation
Used by permission. www.Lockman.org"

## Table of Contents

| | |
|---|---|
| Faith & Reason Made Simple Part 1 – (With Blanks) | 1 |
| Faith & Reason Made Simple Part 1 – (Without Blanks) | 7 |
| Faith & Reason Made Simple Part 2 – (With Blanks) | 13 |
| Faith & Reason Made Simple Part 2 – (Without Blanks) | 19 |
| Faith & Reason Made Simple Part 3 – (With Blanks) | 25 |
| Faith & Reason Made Simple Part 3 – (Without Blanks) | 37 |
| Faith & Reason Made Simple Part 4 – (With Blanks) | 49 |
| Faith & Reason Made Simple Part 4 – (Without Blanks) | 57 |
| Faith & Reason Made Simple Part 5 – (With Blanks) | 65 |
| Faith & Reason Made Simple Part 5 – (Without Blanks) | 73 |
| Faith & Reason Made Simple Part 6 – (With Blanks) | 81 |
| Faith & Reason Made Simple Part 6 – (Without Blanks) | 91 |
| Faith & Reason Made Simple Part 7 – (With Blanks) | 101 |
| Faith & Reason Made Simple Part 7 – (Without Blanks) | 111 |
| Faith & Reason Made Simple Part 8 – (With Blanks) | 121 |
| Faith & Reason Made Simple Part 8 – (Without Blanks) | 131 |
| Memory Cards & Additional Resources Available | 141 |

Note to User – This manual was created to be used with the 8 session video series entitled "Faith & Reason Made Simple". There are notes with blanks to be filled in for each session and notes with the blanks already filled in for each session. You are encouraged to use the notes with blanks while viewing the sessions and fill in the blanks as you go. It is important to notice that you also have notes with the blanks already filled in so you can fill in any blanks you miss while viewing the sessions. For full benefit of the training series you will want to use the memory cards shown at the end of this manual. You may also want to purchase a copy of the book "Faith & Reason Made Simple" that this training series is based upon. Downloadable Memory Cards (for free), the video series on DVD or Flashdrive, and the book, "Faith & Reason Made Simple" are all available online at LOCALCHURCHAPOLOGETICS.ORG

# FAITH & REASON MADE SIMPLE — Part 1

## (Introductory Material & The Scientific Flaws of the Theory of Evolution)

### Part 1 – Intro. Material & The Six Scientific Flaws of the Theory of Evolution

> 1 Peter 3:15 NASB  but sanctify Christ as Lord in your hearts, <u>always *being* ready to make a defense to everyone who asks you to give an account for the hope that is in you</u>, yet with gentleness and reverence;

### What Is Apologetics and Why Do We Need Apologetics?

* The word "apologetics" comes from 1 Peter 3::15 where the Greek word "Apologia" is used and is translated as "to make a defense". Apologetics is not an apology for our faith but rather a defense of our faith!

* Apologetics deals with not just what we believe but also _____ we believe these things to be true!

* Apologetics deals with _____ as opposed to just proclaiming!

* Often, people outside the Christian faith accuse Christians of having _____ faith. The Christian faith is actually supported, or confirmed by many lines of rational evidence. Studying apologetics helps the believer to understand and express these lines of evidence.

* Apologetics is often a necessary part of evangelism in America today (and in other nations), because we now live in a culture that is "humanistic", "skeptical", non Judeo-Christian in foundational worldview, and "post-christian".

* Ravi Zacharias has said, "What I believe in my _____ must make sense in my _____!"

* Faith and _____ fit together!   (Acts 17:1-3 – Paul reasoned with them from the Scriptures)
      (Note also that Paul took a different approach in Acts 17:22-24 when he spoke with
      people who did not have an Old Testament background than he did in Acts 17:1-3
      when he was speaking with those who did have knowledge of the Old Testament.)
* The gospel has not changed but our starting point in sharing it must change when we are trying to reach people who are questioning if we are created and if the Bible is the Word of God.

> Acts 17:1-3 NASB  Now when they had traveled through Amphipolis and Apollonia, they came to Thessalonica, where there was a synagogue of the Jews.  (2)  And according to Paul's custom, he went to them, and for three Sabbaths reasoned with them from the Scriptures,  (3)  explaining and giving evidence that the Christ had to suffer and rise again from the dead, and *saying,* "This Jesus whom I am proclaiming to you is the Christ."

## Definition of "reason"

"A faculty of the mind by which it distinguishes truth from falsehood, and good from evil, and which enables the possessor to deduce inferences from facts or from propositions." (related to "logic")

## Definitions of "faith"

1. (From Easton's Bible Dictionary) – "**Faith is in general the persuasion of the mind that a certain statement is true. Its primary idea is trust. A thing is true, and therefore worthy of trust. It admits of many degrees up to full assurance of faith, in accordance with *the evidence on which it* rests**"

## Note – Faith rests upon _____!

2. (From Webster's Dictionary) – "**The assent of the mind to the truth of a proposition advanced by another; belief, or probable evidence of any kind.**"

3. (From Hebrews 11:1) – "**Now faith is the substance of things hoped for, the evidence of things not seen.**"

Faith is very much related to _____. - (Faith is not blind but is based on, and is made strong by supporting evidence that confirms that which is believed.)

"All truth is given by revelation, either general or special, and it must be received by reason. Reason is the God-given means for discovering the truth that God discloses, whether in His world or His Word. While God wants to reach the heart with truth, He does not bypass the mind."
Jonathan Edwards (Leader of the 1st Great Awakening in America)

\* Like Goliath in David's day, the giant of intellectualism and skepticism challenges and intimidates the body of Christ today, attempting to cripple believers of all ages with fear. Just as David understood that "greater is He that is in us than he that is in the world", so we must understand this powerful truth and not shrink back in fear. When we equip ourselves with apologetic truths it is like David collecting the stones for his sling. It is critical in this hour that churches, church leaders, Christian parents and grand-parents, as well as believers of all ages prepare themselves to face the Goliath of our age! The Bible is clear that when we defend our faith we are to do so with gentleness and reverence so we are not arming ourselves to hurt others but rather to keep our faith strong and to help others come to faith in Christ!

# Are Science & The Bible Against Each Other?

The Bible & _____ are not against each other.

Many evolutionary scientists and professors say that you cannot be a legitimate scientist if you do not believe in Darwinian Evolution. This is a form of intimidation and propaganda. Dr. John C. Sandford is a great example of scientists who do not believe in Darwinian Evolution but who have contributed much to the world by the science they have been involved in. (Of course, most of the pioneers of science believed in God as creator as well. This is actually what often motivated them to study the world scientifically.)

1980 - 1998 Assistant– Then Associate Professor of Horticultural Sciences at Cornell University

Honorary Adjunct Associate Professor of Botany at Duke University

Sanford has published over 70 scientific publications

Sanford is an inventor with more than 32 issued patents

At Cornell Sanford and colleagues developed the "Biolistic Particle Delivery System" or so-called "gene gun"

He has founded two biotechnology companies

Author of "Genetic Entropy & the Mystery of the Genome"

**Dr. John C. Sanford**
American Plant Geneticist
Advocate of Intelligent Design
Young Earth Creationist

**Example - Brilliant Scientists Who Believe in Creation**

It is certainly true that there are many examples of tremendous scientists in the past and in the present who believe in the Bible and in creation. It is also true that many scientists around the world question the validity of the Darwinian Theory of Evolution as an explanation of the complexity of life seen today. Note the example below from the website www.dissentfromdarwin.org. The list of over 900 scientists, many from leading universities around the world, can be downloaded from the site.

A SCIENTIFIC DISSENT FROM DARWINISM — **Signed by Over 900 Scientist Thusfar!**
www.dissentfromdarwin.org

### A SCIENTIFIC DISSENT FROM DARWINISM

*"We are skeptical of claims for the ability of random mutation and natural selection to account for the complexity of life. Careful examination of the evidence for Darwinian theory should be encouraged."*

**What is Science?** "a systematically organized body of knowledge on a particular subject.
**For something to be truly scientific it must be _____, demonstratable and repeatable.** (Note – Evolution is not observable, demonstratable or repeatable.)

In order to understand how the issue of creation vs. evolution fits within scientific study we need to understand that there is a difference between **Operational (or Observable) Science** and **Historical Science**. Historical Science involves ideas and theories about the past and does not involve empirical evidence that can be demonstrated and repeated in a laboratory. (The theory of evolution does not deal with Operational Science but rather with Historical Science.)

## What is Naturalism?

(Those who deny creation as a possible answer for origins do so because they are committed to Naturalism)

"Naturalism is a system of which the salient characteristics is the exclusion of whatever Is spiritual or _____ ."

By declaring that anything beyond the natural realm cannot be considered in science as an answer for how things are as they are, naturalism eliminates creation as a credible explanation to how things came to be, no matter how much the scientific evidence points to a creator or designer.

Applying Naturalism to the scientific study of origins is like trying to solve the math equation "2+2=?" with "4" being eliminated as a possible answer before trying to solve the question.

Dr. Richard Lewontin (Formerly of Harvard University) acknowledges the effects of naturalism on the pursuit of knowledge and understanding of origins and why life works as it does.

> "Our willingness to accept scientific claims that are against common sense is the key to an understanding of the real struggle between science and the supernatural. We take the side of science in spite of the patent absurdity of some of its constructs, ... because we have a prior commitment, a commitment to materialism. ... It is not that the methods and institutions of science somehow compel us to accept a material explanation of the phenomenal world, but, on the contrary, that we are forced by our a priori adherence to material causes to create an apparatus of investigation and a set of concepts that produce material explanations, no matter how counter-intuitive, no matter how mystifying to the uninitiated. Moreover, that materialism is absolute, for we cannot allow a Divine Foot in the door."

Richard Lewontin, Billions and billions of demons (review of *The Demon-Haunted World: Science as a Candle in the Dark* by Carl Sagan, 1997), *The New York Review*, p. 31, 9 January 1997.

**Summary of introductory points** – Christians need apologetics in the skeptical culture we now live in. Creation is attacked and evolution is promoted in our culture, not by scientific evidence, but by propaganda, intimidating accusations and deceptive definitions.

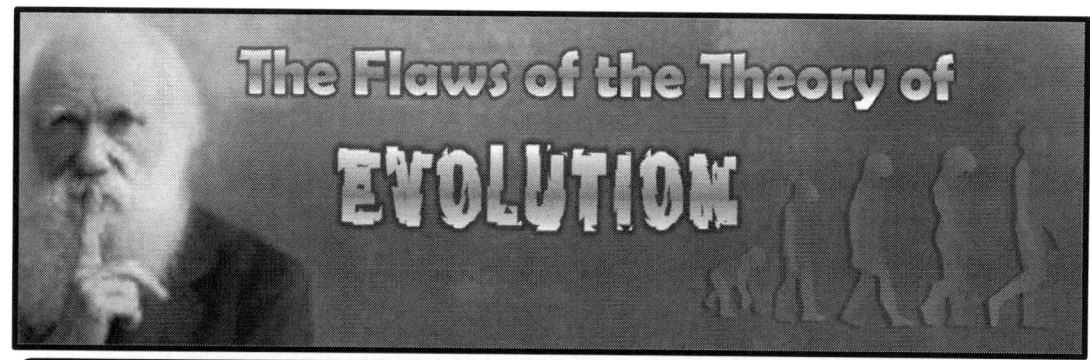

## The 6 Scientific Flaws of the Theory of Evolution

### 1. It Violates the 2nd Law of Thermodynamics

The 2nd Law of Thermodynamics states that the amount of usable energy within any closed system always decreases. (Things move from _____ to chaos, not from chaos to _____) (The 2nd Law of Thermodynamics is also referred to as "_____") (An increase in entropy is an increase in chaos and a decrease in order.)

Examples of entropy (or the 2nd Law of Thermodynamics) can be seen all around us. Some examples are dying stars, the deterioration of metal and wood products, the deterioration of living animals, the deterioration of our own bodies, the deterioration of the human genome, etc.

The theory of evolution depends upon the idea that total chaos (a huge explosion) has become increasingly ordered without any outside assistance. (This idea violates true science.) Some evolutionists attempt to explain this away by saying that the earth is not a closed system. This does not explain away the problem at all though because the Law of Thermodynamics impacts the entire universe, not just the earth.

In order for the 2nd Law of Thermodynamics to be overcome not only is an outside production source of energy needed, but a way of harnessing and utilizing the inflowing energy is needed. All of this involves design.

**Explosions do not create orderly things, they destroy things!**

### 2. It Violates the Law of Biogenesis

The idea of "Spontaneous _____" or "life coming from non-life" has been proven to be false. Research by scientists such as Dr. Louis Pasteur has established the Law of Biogenesis and confirmed that life only comes from life! The theory of evolution states that life came from non-life here on earth billions of years ago.

An example of this evolutionary claim can be seen in the documentary movie made for the discovery channel entitled "Mankind Rising". Here is a summary of the movie's explanation of how life came to exist on the earth between 4 billion and 3.5 billion years ago.

> Life came to exist upon the earth through a chain of events that defy the laws of probability. Though no one knows exactly how or where life began it couldn't have happened without water. Water was probably delivered here by asteroids or comets. The water was teeming with chemicals and organic compounds. The chemical soup was struck by lightning at just the right place, at just the right time, causing the chemical's atoms to join up in a precise sequence, creating a bundle of genetic material. By chance, a blob of oily material surrounded some of the combined organic compounds, enabling them to become the first cell. Now the newly formed genes send out messages, chemical instructions, and 3.5 billion years ago they do something extraordinary, they copy themselves. This cell becomes the first ever living thing. (Taken from "Mankind Rising" documentary)(Available on YouTube)

As you can easily see, this explanation of the origin of life upon the earth is contrary to what the Law of Biogenesis reveals to us through scientific research. It is also easy to see that this explanation of the origin of life is filled with vast amounts of speculation and critical unanswered questions such as where did the chemical instructions come from (now seen in DNA) that would have allowed the cell to replicate itself.

Even many evolutionists, such as Dr. Francis **Crick**, the co-discoverer of the DNA double helix structure, have acknowledged that life is much too complex at the cellular level to have come about from non-life here on earth. In his book "Life Itself: Its Origin and Nature" Crick explains that the complexity of life at the cellular level reveals that life did not evolve from non-life here on earth. He proposes "Directed Panspermia" as an alternative possibility. He says, "Given the weaknesses of all theories of terrestrial genesis, directed panspermia (the deliberate planting of life on Earth by _____ ) should still be considered a serious possibility."

Another confirmation that the theory of evolution's claim that life evolved from non-life is false can be seen in the immense complexity of proteins, the building blocks of life. A protein contains a string of amino acids aligned in a precise order. There are 20 amino acids used in the building of proteins so it is easy to calculate the mathematical probability of a protein being linked together by chance. The chances of a protein with just 1 amino acid would be a 1 in 20. A protein with 2 amino acids would be 1 in 20 x 20 or 1 in 400. For 3 amino acids the chances are 1 in 20 x 20 x 20 or 1 in 8,000. You can see how this works. Proteins have many more amino acids than this though. The chances of a simple, relatively small protein with 150 amino acids assembling by chance would be 1 in $10^{164}$. That is a 1 with 164 zeros behind it. To understand how big this number is consider that there are believed to be $10^{80}$ atoms in the entire universe. To get from $10^{80}$ to $10^{164}$ you have to multiply by 10, 84 times! It gets even more improbable though. The average size of the thousands of different types of proteins in the human body is about 300 amino acids long, not 150! As you can see, the idea of life randomly coming from non-life is nonsensical. Life had to have a designer!

Textbooks that teach evolution pass over this enormous problem for the theory of evolution with simple statements such as this one found on page 346 of the Miller and Levine High School Biology textbook used at the high school my sons attended. *"Hey, what's going on?" you might exclaim. If we just said that life did arise from nonlife billions of years ago, why couldn't it happen again? The answer is simple: Today's Earth is a very different planet from the one that existed billions of years ago."*

So the Theory of Evolution violates the 2$^{nd}$ Law of Thermodynamics and it violates the Law of _____. Four additional scientific flaws are covered in part 2 of the seminar.

# FAITH & REASON MADE SIMPLE — Part 1

### (Introductory Material & The Scientific Flaws of the Theory of Evolution)

## Part 1 – Intro. Material & The Six Scientific Flaws of the Theory of Evolution

> 1 Peter 3:15 NASB  but sanctify Christ as Lord in your hearts, <u>always *being* ready to make a defense to everyone who asks you to give an account for the hope that is in you</u>, yet with gentleness and reverence;

## What Is Apologetics and Why Do We Need Apologetics?

* The word "apologetics" comes from 1 Peter 3::15 where the Greek word "Apologia" is used and is translated as "to make a defense". Apologetics is not an apology for our faith but rather a defense of our faith!

* Apologetics deals with not just what we believe but also **why** we believe these things to be true!

* Apologetics deals with **reasoning** as opposed to just proclaiming!

* Often, people outside the Christian faith accuse Christians of having **blind** faith. The Christian faith is actually supported, or confirmed by many lines of rational evidence. Studying apologetics helps the believer to understand and express these lines of evidence.

* Apologetics is often a necessary part of evangelism in America today (and in other nations), because we now live in a culture that is "humanistic", "skeptical", non Judeo-Christian in foundational worldview, and "post-christian".

* Ravi Zacharias has said, "What I believe in my **heart** must make sense in my **mind**!"

* Faith and **reason** fit together!   (Acts 17:1-3 – Paul  reasoned  with them from the Scriptures)
    (Note also that Paul took a different approach in Acts 17:22-24 when he spoke with
    people who did not have an Old Testament background than he did in Acts 17:1-3
    when he was speaking with those who did have knowledge of the Old Testament.)

* The gospel has not changed but our starting point in sharing it must change when we are trying to reach people who are questioning if we are created and if the Bible is the Word of God.

> Acts 17:1-3 NASB  Now when they had traveled through Amphipolis and Apollonia, they came to Thessalonica, where there was a synagogue of the Jews. (2) And according to Paul's custom, he went to them, and for three Sabbaths reasoned with them from the Scriptures, (3) explaining and giving evidence that the Christ had to suffer and rise again from the dead, and *saying,* "This Jesus whom I am proclaiming to you is the Christ."

## Definition of "reason"

"A faculty of the mind by which it distinguishes truth from falsehood, and good from evil, and which enables the possessor to deduce inferences from facts or from propositions." (related to "logic")

## Definitions of "faith"

1. (From Easton's Bible Dictionary) – "**Faith is in general the persuasion of the mind that a certain statement is true. Its primary idea is trust. A thing is true, and therefore worthy of trust. It admits of many degrees up to full assurance of faith, in accordance with *the evidence on which it rests*"**

### Note – Faith rests upon evidence!

2. (From Webster's Dictionary) – "**The assent of the mind to the truth of a proposition advanced by another; belief, or probable evidence of any kind.**"

3. (From Hebrews 11:1) – "**Now faith is the substance of things hoped for, the evidence of things not seen.**"

Faith is very much related to **reason**. - (Faith is not blind but is based on, and is made strong by supporting evidence that confirms that which is believed.)

"All truth is given by revelation, either general or special, and it must be received by reason. Reason is the God-given means for discovering the truth that God discloses, whether in His world or His Word. While God wants to reach the heart with truth, He does not bypass the mind."
**Jonathan Edwards (Leader of the 1st Great Awakening in America)**

\* Like Goliath in David's day, the giant of intellectualism and skepticism challenges and intimidates the body of Christ today, attempting to cripple believers of all ages with fear. Just as David understood that "greater is He that is in us than he that is in the world", so we must understand this powerful truth and not shrink back in fear. When we equip ourselves with apologetic truths it is like David collecting the stones for his sling. It is critical in this hour that churches, church leaders, Christian parents and grand-parents, as well as believers of all ages prepare themselves to face the Goliath of our age! The Bible is clear that when we defend our faith we are to do so with gentleness and reverence so we are not arming ourselves to hurt others but rather to keep our faith strong and to help others come to faith in Christ!

# Are Science & The Bible Against Each Other?

The Bible & **Science** are not against each other.

Many evolutionary scientists and professors say that you cannot be a legitimate scientist if you do not believe in Darwinian Evolution. This is a form of intimidation and propaganda. Dr. John C. Sandford is a great example of scientists who do not believe in Darwinian Evolution but who have contributed much to the world by the science they have been involved in. (Of course, most of the pioneers of science believed in God as creator as well. This is actually what often motivated them to study the world scientifically.)

1980 - 1998 Assistant– Then Associate Professor of Horticultural Sciences at Cornell University

Honorary Adjunct Associate Professor of Botany at Duke University

Sanford has published over 70 scientific publications

Sanford is an inventor with more than 32 issued patents

At Cornell Sanford and colleagues developed the "Biolistic Particle Delivery System" or so-called "gene gun"

He has founded two biotechnology companies

Author of "Genetic Entropy & the Mystery of the Genome"

**Dr. John C. Sanford**
American Plant Geneticist
Advocate of Intelligent Design
Young Earth Creationist

**Example - Brilliant Scientists Who Believe in Creation**

It is certainly true that there are many examples of tremendous scientists in the past and in the present who believe in the Bible and in creation. It is also true that many scientists around the world question the validity of the Darwinian Theory of Evolution as an explanation of the complexity of life seen today. Note the example below from the website www.dissentfromdarwin.org. The list of over 900 scientists, many from leading universities around the world, can be downloaded from the site.

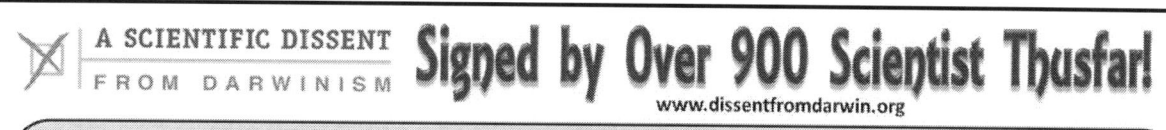

A SCIENTIFIC DISSENT FROM DARWINISM — **Signed by Over 900 Scientist Thusfar!**
www.dissentfromdarwin.org

**A SCIENTIFIC DISSENT FROM DARWINISM**

*"We are skeptical of claims for the ability of random mutation and natural selection to account for the complexity of life. Careful examination of the evidence for Darwinian theory should be encouraged."*

**What is Science?** "a systematically organized body of knowledge on a particular subject.
**For something to be truly scientific it must be <u>observable</u>, demonstratable and repeatable.**
(Note – Evolution is not observable, demonstratable or repeatable.)

In order to understand how the issue of creation vs. evolution fits within scientific study we need to understand that there is a difference between **Operational (or Observable) Science** and **Historical Science**. Historical Science involves ideas and theories about the past and does not involve empirical evidence that can be demonstrated and repeated in a laboratory. (The theory of evolution does not deal with Operational Science but rather with Historical Science.)

## What is Naturalism?

(Those who deny creation as a possible answer for origins do so because they are committed to Naturalism)

"Naturalism is a system of which the salient characteristics is the exclusion of whatever Is spiritual or **supernatural** ."

By declaring that anything beyond the natural realm cannot be considered in science as an answer for how things are as they are, naturalism eliminates creation as a credible explanation to how things came to be, no matter how much the scientific evidence points to a creator or designer.

Applying Naturalism to the scientific study of origins is like trying to solve the math equation "2+2=?" with "4" being eliminated as a possible answer before trying to solve the question.

Dr. Richard Lewontin (Formerly of Harvard University) acknowledges the effects of naturalism on the pursuit of knowledge and understanding of origins and why life works as it does.

"Our willingness to accept scientific claims that are against common sense is the key to an understanding of the real struggle between science and the supernatural. We take the side of science in spite of the patent absurdity of some of its constructs, ... because we have a prior commitment, a commitment to materialism. ... It is not that the methods and institutions of science somehow compel us to accept a material explanation of the phenomenal world, but, on the contrary, that we are forced by our a priori adherence to material causes to create an apparatus of investigation and a set of concepts that produce material explanations, no matter how counter-intuitive, no matter how mystifying to the uninitiated. Moreover, that materialism is absolute, for we cannot allow a Divine Foot in the door."

Richard Lewontin, Billions and billions of demons (review of *The Demon-Haunted World: Science as a Candle in the Dark* by Carl Sagan, 1997), *The New York Review*, p. 31, 9 January 1997.

**Summary of introductory points** – Christians need apologetics in the skeptical culture we now live in. Creation is attacked and evolution is promoted in our culture, not by scientific evidence, but by propaganda, intimidating accusations and deceptive definitions.

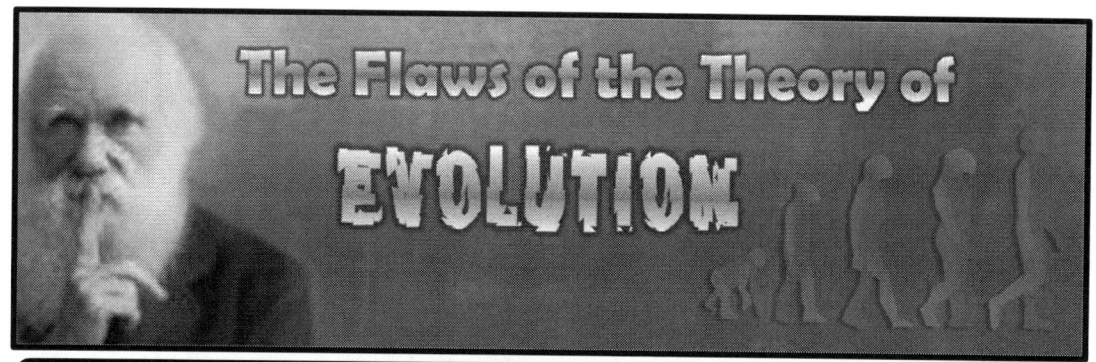

## The 6 Scientific Flaws of the Theory of Evolution

### 1. It Violates the 2$^{nd}$ Law of Thermodynamics

The 2$^{nd}$ Law of Thermodynamics states that the amount of usable energy within any closed system always decreases. (Things move from **order** to chaos, not from chaos to **order**) (The 2$^{nd}$ Law of Thermodynamics is also referred to as "**entropy**") (An increase in entropy is an increase in chaos and a decrease in order.)

Examples of entropy (or the 2$^{nd}$ Law of Thermodynamics) can be seen all around us. Some examples are dying stars, the deterioration of metal and wood products, the deterioration of living animals, the deterioration of our own bodies, the deterioration of the human genome, etc.

The theory of evolution depends upon the idea that total chaos (a huge explosion) has become increasingly ordered without any outside assistance. (This idea violates true science.) Some evolutionists attempt to explain this away by saying that the earth is not a closed system. This does not explain away the problem at all though because the Law of Thermodynamics impacts the entire universe, not just the earth.

In order for the 2$^{nd}$ Law of Thermodynamics to be overcome not only is an outside production source of energy needed, but a way of harnessing and utilizing the inflowing energy is needed. All of this involves design.

**Explosions do not create orderly things, they destroy things!**

### 2. It Violates the Law of Biogenesis

The idea of "Spontaneous <u>Generation</u>" or "life coming from non-life" has been proven to be false. Research by scientists such as Dr. Louis Pasteur has established the Law of Biogenesis and confirmed that life only comes from life! The theory of evolution states that life came from non-life here on earth billions of years ago.

An example of this evolutionary claim can be seen in the documentary movie made for the discovery channel entitled "Mankind Rising". Here is a summary of the movie's explanation of how life came to exist on the earth between 4 billion and 3.5 billion years ago.

> Life came to exist upon the earth through a chain of events that defy the laws of probability. Though no one knows exactly how or where life began it couldn't have happened without water. Water was probably delivered here by asteroids or comets. The water was teeming with chemicals and organic compounds. The chemical soup was struck by lightning at just the right place, at just the right time, causing the chemical's atoms to join up in a precise sequence, creating a bundle of genetic material. By chance, a blob of oily material surrounded some of the combined organic compounds, enabling them to become the first cell. Now the newly formed genes send out messages, chemical instructions, and 3.5 billion years ago they do something extraordinary, they copy themselves. This cell becomes the first ever living thing. (Taken from "Mankind Rising" documentary)(Available on YouTube)

As you can easily see, this explanation of the origin of life upon the earth is contrary to what the Law of Biogenesis reveals to us through scientific research. It is also easy to see that this explanation of the origin of life is filled with vast amounts of speculation and critical unanswered questions such as where did the chemical instructions come from (now seen in DNA) that would have allowed the cell to replicate itself.

Even many evolutionists, such as Dr. Francis **Crick**, the co-discoverer of the DNA double helix structure, have acknowledged that life is much too complex at the cellular level to have come about from non-life here on earth. In his book "Life Itself: Its Origin and Nature" Crick explains that the complexity of life at the cellular level reveals that life did not evolve from non-life here on earth. He proposes "Directed Panspermia" as an alternative possibility. He says, "Given the weaknesses of all theories of terrestrial genesis, directed panspermia (the deliberate planting of life on Earth by aliens) should still be considered a serious possibility."

Another confirmation that the theory of evolution's claim that life evolved from non-life is false can be seen in the immense complexity of proteins, the building blocks of life. A protein contains a string of amino acids aligned in a precise order. There are 20 amino acids used in the building of proteins so it is easy to calculate the mathematical probability of a protein being linked together by chance. The chances of a protein with just 1 amino acid would be a 1 in 20. A protein with 2 amino acids would be 1 in 20 x 20 or 1 in 400. For 3 amino acids the chances are 1 in 20 x 20 x 20 or 1 in 8,000. You can see how this works. Proteins have many more amino acids than this though. The chances of a simple, relatively small protein with 150 amino acids assembling by chance would be 1 in $10^{164}$. That is a 1 with 164 zeros behind it. To understand how big this number is consider that there are believed to be $10^{80}$ atoms in the entire universe. To get from $10^{80}$ to $10^{164}$ you have to multiply by 10, 84 times! It gets even more improbable though. The average size of the thousands of different types of proteins in the human body is about 300 amino acids long, not 150! As you can see, the idea of life randomly coming from non-life is nonsensical. Life had to have a designer!

Textbooks that teach evolution pass over this enormous problem for the theory of evolution with simple statements such as this one found on page 346 of the Miller and Levine High School Biology textbook used at the high school my sons attended. *"Hey, what's going on?" you might exclaim. If we just said that life did arise from nonlife billions of years ago, why couldn't it happen again? The answer is simple: Today's Earth is a very different planet from the one that existed billions of years ago."*

So the Theory of Evolution violates the 2nd Law of Thermodynamics and it violates the Law of Biogenesis. Four additional scientific flaws are covered in part 2 of the seminar.

# FAITH & REASON
## *MADE SIMPLE*

### Part 2

### (The Scientific Flaws of the Theory of Evolution, Cont.)

## Review From Part 1 – The Scientific Flaws of the Theory of Evolution 1 & 2

#1 – The Theory of Evolution Violates the 2nd Law of Thermodynamics

#2 – The Theory of Evolution Violates the Law of Biogenesis

## Part 2 – The Remaining 4 Scientific Flaws of the Theory of Evolution

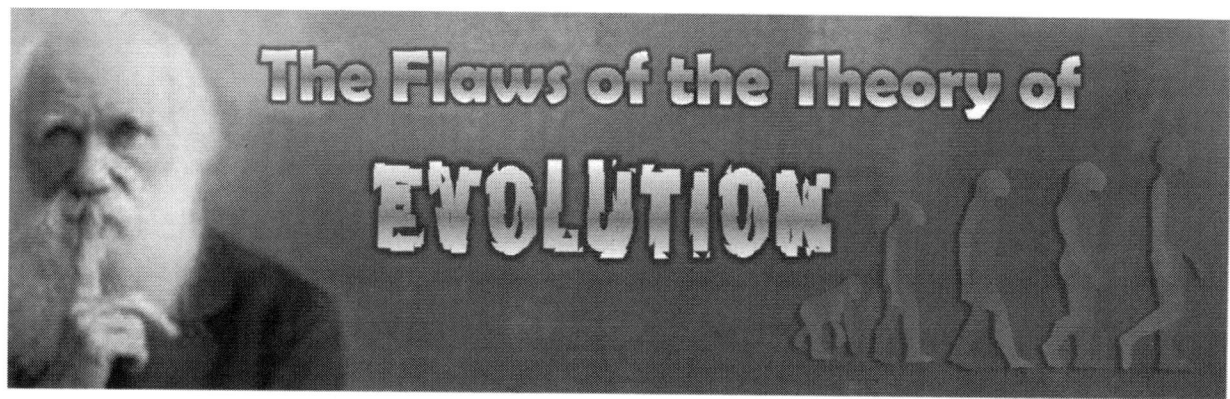

### #3 - The Theory of Evolution Purposely Confuses "Microevolution" which is adaptation within a kind of creature, with "Macroevolution" which is one kind changing into a completely different kind of creature over time.

Microevolution, or adaptation within a kind is scientific and Scientist who believe in Creation acknowledge the reality of adaptation within a kind. Macroevolution, or one kind turning into a completely different kind of creature over time has _____ been observed in the past or in the present and is not scientific.

Evolutionists point to examples like _____ turning into different types of _____ and bacteria turning into other types of bacteria as their proof that Darwinian Evolution is scientific. Probably the most used examples of microevolution in textbooks and other evolutionary materials to supposedly illustrate that the theory of evolution is true are Darwin's _____. Darwin observed various finches on the Galapagos Islands and noted that their beaks changed over generations as their environment changed. He proposed that these small changes over a short period of time could account for very large changes over a very long period of time. It is important to note that the finches Darwin observed never became anything other than finches and that their beaks wavered back and forth, depending upon conditions. There are many examples of "wiggle room" within the DNA that the creator has placed within various living things. This "wiggle room" does not illustrate macro-evolution, one kind turning into a different kind of creature.

The fact that textbooks and other evolutionary materials continue to use examples of "micro-evolution" to illustrate the supposed reality of "macro-evolution" is very telling. If there were examples of "macro-evolution" available textbooks would certainly be using them to illustrate their point.

## #4 – The Theory of Evolution Violates the Evidence that is Found in the Fossil Record

If evolution had occurred as the theory states, there should be millions (or billions) of _____ life forms found in the fossil record but there are not. Even the few supposed transitional fossils that evolutionists have referred to have often been proven to not be transitional life forms at all, or have, in some cases even been proven to be frauds.

Note that Darwin himself acknowledged the lack of transitional fossils in the fossil record in his day.

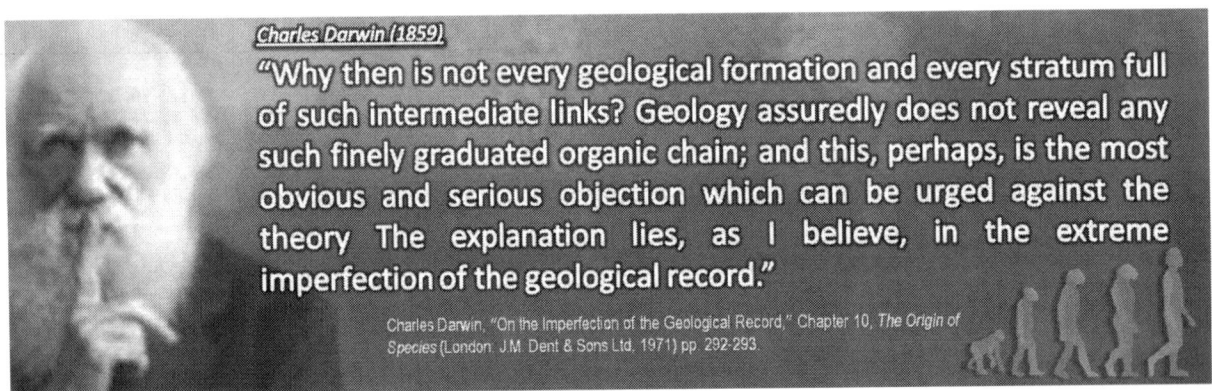

The fossil record has not changed since Darwin's day in regard to the lack of _____ fossils, which are sought as evidence that Darwinian evolution has occurred in the past. Note the following quotes by evolutionary scientists acknowledging the lack of transitional fossils.

**"Well, we are now about 120 years after Darwin and the knowledge of the fossil record has been greatly expanded ... The record of evolution is still surprisingly jerky and, ironically, we have even fewer examples of evolutionary transition than we had in Darwin's time." Dr. David Raup**
D. Raup, "Conflicts Between Darwin and Paleontology," Field Museum of Natural History Bulletin 50(1), 1979, p.25.

**Dr. Stephen Jay Gould – Harvard University**
"All paleontologists know that the fossil record contains precious little in the way of intermediate forms; transitions between major groups are characteristically abrupt."
S.J. Gould, "The return of hopeful monsters," *Natural History* 86(6), 1977, p24.

"The absence of fossil evidence for intermediary stages between major transitions in organic design, indeed our inability, even in our imagination, to construct functional intermediates in many cases, has been a persistent and nagging problem for gradualistic accounts of evolution."
S.J. Gould, "Is a New and General Theory of Evolution Emerging?", Paleobiology 6(1), 1980, p. 127.

'The extreme rarity of transitional forms in the fossil record persists as the trade secret of paleontology. The evolutionary trees that adorn our textbooks have data only at the tips and nodes of their branches ... in any local area, a species does not arise gradually by the gradual transformation of its ancestors; it appears all at once and "fully formed."'
Stephen Jay Gould, Evolution's erratic pace, Natural History 86(5):14, May 1977.

<u>Collin Patterson (Senior Paleontologist – British Natural History Museum (1979)</u>
" ... I fully agree with your comments on the lack of direct illustration of evolutionary transitions in my book. If I knew of any, fossil or living, I would certainly have included them .... Yet Gould and the American Museum people are hard to contradict when they say there are no transitional forms. ... I will lay it on the line – there is not one such fossil for which one could make a watertight argument."
C. Patterson, Personal letter to L. Sunderland, April 1979, as quoted in *Darwin's Enigma* (Green Forest, AR: Master Books, 1984) p. 89

**Note the findings of a very recent research project referred to on "phys.org"**

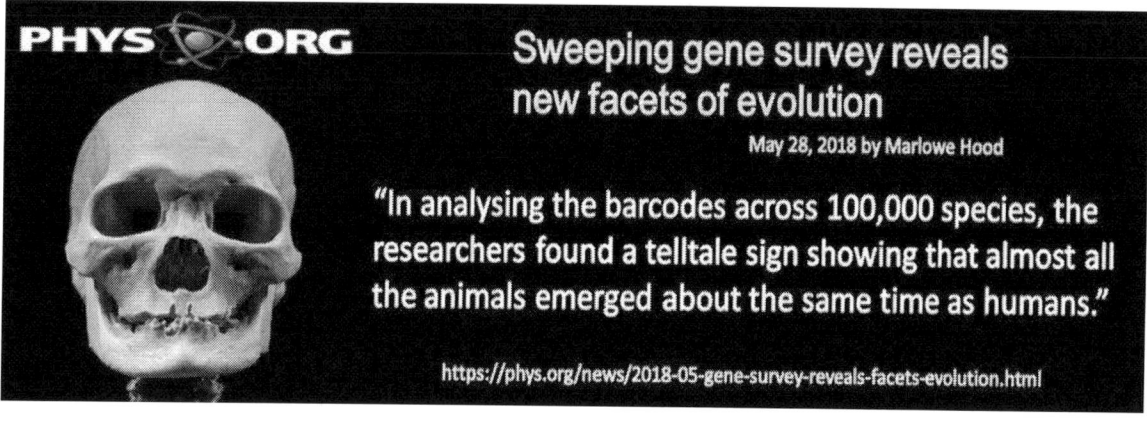

The same research also revealed the following. "And yet—another unexpected finding from the study—species have very clear genetic _____, and there's nothing much in between. ... The absence of "in-between" species is something that also perplexed Darwin, he said."

15

In an attempt to produce transitional fossils some have produced fraudulent fossils such as "Archaeoraptor" and "Nebraska Man" to make

their case for evolution. "Archaeoraptor" was a supposed example of a _____ dinosaur. This fossil was proven to be a pieced together fraud by Dr. Timothy Rowe at Texas University. Nevertheless, it was still used by some to give the appearance that dinosaurs began to grow feathers as they evolved into birds. N o true feathered dinosaurs have ever been found. "Nebraska Man" was a supposed link between ape and human. The entire supposed upright walking link between ape and man was developed from a single tooth that was later proven to be the tooth of an extinct pig!

## #5 – The Theory of Evolution Violates the Fact That Mutations Do Not Increase Genetic Information

The theory of Evolution says that genetic _____ bring about beneficial changes that are then selected by natural selection to bring slow but continual evolutionary changes within creatures.

In fact mutations are almost always _____ & are almost always involve a decrease in genetic information.

Note the following quote from Dr. John Sanford, who is an expert in genetics and the inventor of "the gene gun"

> **The Human Genome is Deteriorating!**
> **Mutations Do Not Add Genetic Information & Value**
> (Taken from "Apologetics Press" online article)
>
> Indeed, "beneficial" mutations are so exceedingly rare as to not contribute in any meaningful way. Sanford concludes that the frequency and generally harmful or neutral nature of mutations prevents them from being useful to any scheme of random evolution.
>
> http://apologeticspress.org/APContent.aspx?category=9&article=4670

Dr. John C. Sanford
Author of
"Genetic Entropy & the Mystery of the Genome"

There is a famous YouTube video of an interview with Dr. Richard Dawkins where he is asked if he can give an example of a genetic mutation or an evolutionary process which can be seen to increase the information in the genome. Dr. Dawkins attempts to think of an example. After a long, awkward pause he asks that the video tape be stopped. When the videotaping is resumed he gives an explanation as to why we should not expect to see such examples. At no point is he able to give an example of a mutation which has been seen to increase the genetic information in creature's genome.

# #6 – The Theory of Evolution is Contrary to the Order, Beauty & Design We Find Throughout the Known Universe

No matter where we look in the universe things appear to be _____ with purpose. They are orderly and often beautiful. Even some evolutionists acknowledge that things appear to be designed, but they say they are not designed. They come to this conclusion not by evidence, but because of their preconceived religious view, holding to naturalism and humanism.

> Romans 1:20 NASB  For since the creation of the world **His invisible attributes, His eternal power and divine nature,** have been clearly seen, being understood through what has been made, so that they are without excuse.

Based on Romans 1:20 we would expect to see marvelous, precise design features everywhere we look! Examples within created things that show great design rather than random, unguided evolutionary processes -

Protein synthesis – As we discussed in part 1, each protein consists of many _____ _____ connected in perfect order. There are 20 different amino acids that can be chosen from, for each link of the protein chain. That means that the probability of the protein chain being correct by chance would be figured by considering a 1 in 20 chance for every amino acid in the chain. For example, if a protein consisted in just 1 amino acid, the chances of the correct amino acid being in place would be 1 in 20. If the protein consisted of 2 amino acids the chances of both amino acids being in the correct order would be 1 in 20 times 1 in 20, or 1 in 400. For a protein with 3 amino acids the chances would be 1 in 8,000.

This type of probability can be compared to spelling specific words by randomly selecting scrabble letters from a huge pile which contains an equal number of each of the 26 letters of the alphabet. To spell the word "chance" by random chance the possibility can be figured by multiplying 26 x 26 x 26 x 26 x 26 x 26, which would give you a 1 in 308,915,776 chance. Attempting to spell out the Lord's prayer with scrabble letters in this random chance way would create an improbability that rules out chance as a possibility!

The average protein in the human body has 300-375 amino acids lined up in a precise order. Consider that for a simple protein of just 150 amino acids to be sequenced correctly by chance, the odds would be 1 in 10 the $164^{th}$ power. So, as you can see, _____ are an example of the exquisite design that God has used in creating the universe that we live in. These kinds of exquisite designs rule out evolution as a viable explanation for life.

There are many other examples of these design features that we can see throughout the universe, whether we are looking into the vastness of space, or into the tiny microscopic world where proteins and amino acids are found.

Also consider –
* The design of Male & Female  (Could they have evolved at precisely the same moment?)
* The Finely Tuned _____
* The Earth which has been created to be Inhabited (Isaiah 45:18)
* _____ _____ on the Earth

We will look at many of these examples, and more, in parts 3 & 4 as we look at evidences of a creator.

> Summary – The 6 Scientific Flaws of the Theory of Evolution
> (It will be beneficial to memorize these 6 points)

**The Flaws of the Theory of Evolution**

1 – Violates the 2nd Law of Thermodynamics
2 – Violates the Law of Bio-Genesis
3 – Purposely Confuses Micro-Evolution w/Macro Evolution (New Kind)
4 – The Fossil Record Contradicts Evolution
5 – Mutations Do Not Bring Increased Information
6 – Evolution Contradicts the Order, Design, Beauty & Information We Observe

To download memorization cards that will assist you in remembering these 6 scientific flaws of the Theory of Evolution go localchurchapologetics.org. The cards are free! There are also cards for the 8 levels of evidence of a creator, the 8 areas of evidence that the Bible is the Word of God, and for the areas of evidence showing that Jesus Christ is Who the Bible says He is. With a little bit of effort you can memorize the main points of this seminar and use them in conversations with others.

## (The Scientific Flaws of the Theory of Evolution, Cont.)

## Review From Part 1 – The Scientific Flaws of the Theory of Evolution 1 & 2

#1 – The Theory of Evolution Violates the 2$^{nd}$ Law of Thermodynamics

#2 – The Theory of Evolution Violates the Law of Biogenesis

## Part 2 – The Remaining 4 Scientific Flaws of the Theory of Evolution

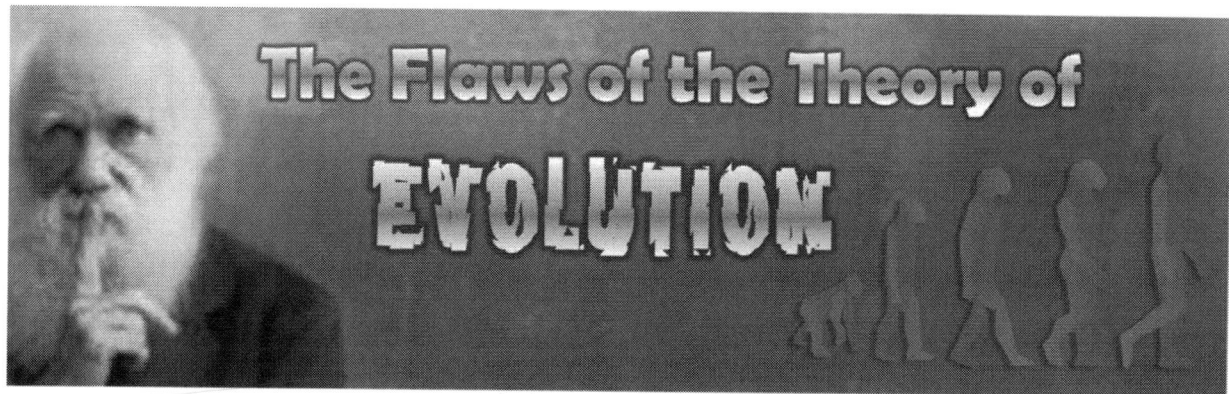

### #3 - The Theory of Evolution Purposely Confuses "Microevolution" which is adaptation within a kind of creature, with "Macroevolution" which is one kind changing into a completely different kind of creature over time.

Microevolution, or adaptation within a kind is scientific and Scientist who believe in Creation acknowledge the reality of adaptation within a kind. Macroevolution, or one kind turning into a completely different kind of creature over time has **never** been observed in the past or in the present and is not scientific.

Evolutionists point to examples like **fish** turning into different types of **fish** and bacteria turning into other types of bacteria as their proof that Darwinian Evolution is scientific. Probably the most used examples of microevolution in textbooks and other evolutionary materials to supposedly illustrate that the theory of evolution is true are Darwin's **finches**. Darwin observed various finches on the Galapagos Islands and noted that their beaks changed over generations as their environment changed. He proposed that these small changes over a short period of time could account for very large changes over a very long period of time. It is important to note that the finches Darwin observed never became anything other than finches and that their beaks wavered back and forth, depending upon conditions. There are many examples of "wiggle room" within the DNA that the creator has placed

within various living things. This "wiggle room" does not illustrate macro-evolution, one kind turning into a different kind of creature.

The fact that textbooks and other evolutionary materials continue to use examples of "micro-evolution" to illustrate the supposed reality of "macro-evolution" is very telling. If there were examples of "macro-evolution" available textbooks would certainly be using them to illustrate their point.

## #4 – The Theory of Evolution Violates the Evidence that is Found in the Fossil Record

If evolution had occurred as the theory states, there should be millions (or billions) of **transitional** life forms found in the fossil record but there are not. Even the few supposed transitional fossils that evolutionists have referred to have often been proven to not be transitional life forms at all, or have, in some cases even been proven to be frauds.

Note that Darwin himself acknowledged the lack of transitional fossils in the fossil record in his day.

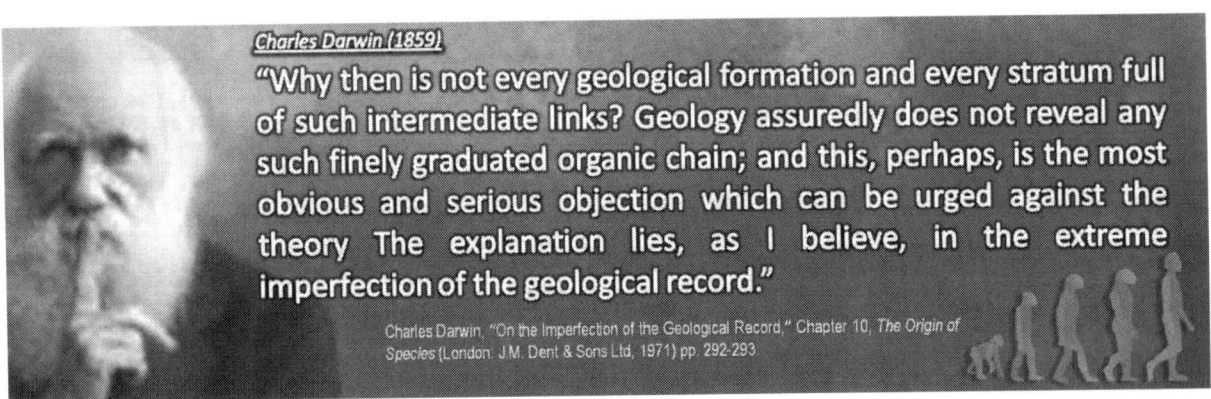

The fossil record has not changed since Darwin's day in regard to the lack of **transitional** fossils, which are sought as evidence that Darwinian evolution has occurred in the past. Note the following quotes by evolutionary scientists acknowledging the lack of transitional fossils.

"Well, we are now about 120 years after Darwin and the knowledge of the fossil record has been greatly expanded ... The record of evolution is still surprisingly jerky and, ironically, we have even fewer examples of evolutionary transition than we had in Darwin's time." Dr. David Raup
D. Raup, "Conflicts Between Darwin and Paleontology," Field Museum of Natural History Bulletin 50(1), 1979, p.25.

**Dr. Stephen Jay Gould – Harvard University**
"All paleontologists know that the fossil record contains precious little in the way of intermediate forms; transitions between major groups are characteristically abrupt."
S.J. Gould, "The return of hopeful monsters," *Natural History* 86(6), 1977, p24.

"The absence of fossil evidence for intermediary stages between major transitions in organic design, indeed our inability, even in our imagination, to construct functional intermediates in many cases, has been a persistent and nagging problem for gradualistic accounts of evolution."
S.J. Gould, "Is a New and General Theory of Evolution Emerging?", Paleobiology 6(1), 1980, p. 127.

'The extreme rarity of transitional forms in the fossil record persists as the trade secret of paleontology. The evolutionary trees that adorn our textbooks have data only at the tips and nodes of their branches ... in any local area, a species does not arise gradually by the gradual transformation of its ancestors; it appears all at once and "fully formed."'
Stephen Jay Gould, Evolution's erratic pace, Natural History 86(5):14, May 1977.

<u>*Collin Patterson (Senior Paleontologist – British Natural History Museum (1979)*</u>
" ... I fully agree with your comments on the lack of direct illustration of evolutionary transitions in my book. If I knew of any, fossil or living, I would certainly have included them .... Yet Gould and the American Museum people are hard to contradict when they say there are no transitional forms. ... I will lay it on the line – there is not one such fossil for which one could make a watertight argument."
C. Patterson, Personal letter to L. Sunderland, April 1979, as quoted in *Darwin's Enigma* (Green Forest, AR: Master Books, 1984) p. 89

**Note the findings of a very recent research project referred to on "phys.org"**

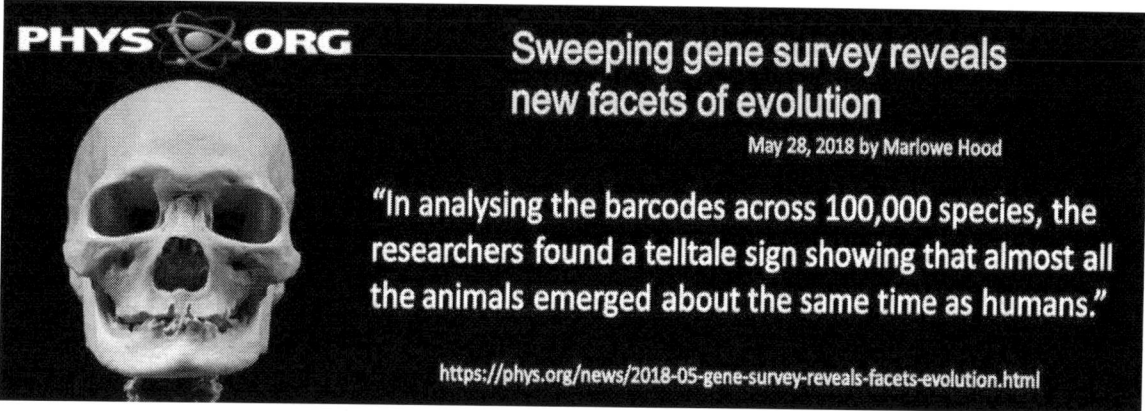

The same research also revealed the following. "And yet—another unexpected finding from the study—species have very clear genetic **boundaries**, and there's nothing much in between. ... The absence of "in-between" species is something that also perplexed Darwin, he said."

In an attempt to produce transitional fossils some have produced fraudulent fossils such as "Archaeoraptor" and "Nebraska Man" to make

their case for evolution. "Archaeoraptor" was a supposed example of a **feathered** dinosaur. This fossil was proven to be a pieced together fraud by Dr. Timothy Rowe at Texas University. Nevertheless, it was still used by some to give the appearance that dinosaurs began to grow feathers as they evolved into birds. N o true feathered dinosaurs have ever been found. "Nebraska Man" was a supposed link between ape and human. The entire supposed upright walking link between ape and man was developed from a single tooth that was later proven to be the tooth of an extinct pig!

## #5 – The Theory of Evolution Violates the Fact That Mutations Do Not Increase Genetic Information

The theory of Evolution says that genetic **mutations** bring about beneficial changes that are then selected by natural selection to bring slow but continual evolutionary changes within creatures.

In fact mutations are almost always **harmful** & are almost always involve a decrease in genetic information.

Note the following quote from Dr. John Sanford, who is an expert in genetics and the inventor of "the gene gun"

**The Human Genome is Deteriorating!**
**Mutations Do Not Add Genetic Information & Value**
(Taken from "Apologetics Press" online article)

Indeed, "beneficial" mutations are so exceedingly rare as to not contribute in any meaningful way. Sanford concludes that the frequency and generally harmful or neutral nature of mutations prevents them from being useful to any scheme of random evolution.

http://apologeticspress.org/APContent.aspx?category=9&article=4670

Dr. John C. Sanford
Author of
"Genetic Entropy & the Mystery of the Genome"

There is a famous YouTube video of an interview with Dr. Richard Dawkins where he is asked if he can give an example of a genetic mutation or an evolutionary process which can be seen to increase the information in the genome. Dr. Dawkins attempts to think of an example. After a long, awkward pause he asks that the video tape be stopped. When the videotaping is resumed he gives an explanation as to why we should not expect to see such examples. At no point is he able to give an example of a mutation which has been seen to increase the genetic information in creature's genome.

# #6 – The Theory of Evolution is Contrary to the Order, Beauty & Design We Find Throughout the Known Universe

No matter where we look in the universe things appear to be **designed** with purpose. They are orderly and often beautiful. Even some evolutionists acknowledge that things appear to be designed, but they say they are not designed. They come to this conclusion not by evidence, but because of their preconceived religious view, holding to naturalism and humanism.

> Romans 1:20 NASB  For since the creation of the world **His invisible attributes, His eternal power and divine nature,** have been clearly seen, being understood through what has been made, so that they are without excuse.

Based on Romans 1:20 we would expect to see marvelous, precise design features everywhere we look! Examples within created things that show great design rather than random, unguided evolutionary processes -

Protein synthesis – As we discussed in part 1, each protein consists of many **amino acids** connected in perfect order. There are 20 different amino acids that can be chosen from, for each link of the protein chain. That means that the probability of the protein chain being correct by chance would be figured by considering a 1 in 20 chance for every amino acid in the chain. For example, if a protein consisted in just 1 amino acid, the chances of the correct amino acid being in place would be 1 in 20. If the protein consisted of 2 amino acids the chances of both amino acids being in the correct order would be 1 in 20 times 1 in 20, or 1 in 400. For a protein with 3 amino acids the chances would be 1 in 8,000.

This type of probability can be compared to spelling specific words by randomly selecting scrabble letters from a huge pile which contains an equal number of each of the 26 letters of the alphabet. To spell the word "chance" by random chance the possibility can be figured by multiplying 26 x 26 x 26 x 26 x 26 x 26, which would give you a 1 in 308,915,776 chance. Attempting to spell out the Lord's prayer with scrabble letters in this random chance way would create an improbability that rules out chance as a possibility!

The average protein in the human body has 300-375 amino acids lined up in a precise order. Consider that for a simple protein of just 150 amino acids to be sequenced correctly by chance, the odds would be 1 in 10 the $164^{th}$ power. So, as you can see, **proteins** are an example of the exquisite design that God has used in creating the universe that we live in. These kinds of exquisite designs rule out evolution as a viable explanation for life.

There are many other examples of these design features that we can see throughout the universe, whether we are looking into the vastness of space, or into the tiny microscopic world where proteins and amino acids are found.

Also consider –
* The design of Male & Female  (Could they have evolved at precisely the same moment?)
* The Finely Tuned **Universe**
* The Earth which has been created to be Inhabited (Isaiah 45:18)
* **Living Creatures** on the Earth

We will look at many of these examples, and more, in parts 3 & 4 as we look at evidences of a creator.

> Summary – The 6 Scientific Flaws of the Theory of Evolution
> (It will be beneficial to memorize these 6 points)

**The Flaws of the Theory of Evolution**

1 – Violates the 2nd Law of Thermodynamics
2 – Violates the Law of Bio-Genesis
3 – Purposely Confuses Micro-Evolution w/Macro Evolution (New Kind)
4 – The Fossil Record Contradicts Evolution
5 – Mutations Do Not Bring Increased Information
6 – Evolution Contradicts the Order, Design, Beauty & Information We Observe

To download memorization cards that will assist you in remembering these 6 scientific flaws of the Theory of Evolution go localchurchapologetics.org. The cards are free! There are also cards for the 8 levels of evidence of a creator, the 8 areas of evidence that the Bible is the Word of God, and for the areas of evidence showing that Jesus Christ is Who the Bible says He is. With a little bit of effort you can memorize the main points of this seminar and use them in conversations with others.

 # FAITH & REASON
## *MADE SIMPLE*
### Part 3

## (Scientific Evidence That Confirms God Created Us)

### Review of Parts 1 & 2 – The Scientific Flaws of the Theory of Evolution

 **The Flaws of the Theory of Evolution**

1 – Violates the 2nd Law of Thermodynamics
2 – Violates the Law of Bio-Genesis
3 – Purposely Confuses Micro-Evolution w/Macro Evolution (New Kind)
4 – The Fossil Record Contradicts Evolution
5 – Mutations Do Not Bring Increased Information
6 – Evolution Contradicts the Order, Design, Beauty & Information We Observe

\* To download free memory cards for these 6 points go to localchurchapologetics.org

## Scientific Evidence That Confirms That God Created All Things

What would we look for in science that would point to a creator? We would look for 2 things! We would look for _____, because design always points to a designer. We would also look for usable, ordered _____, because usable, ordered information always points to a source of intelligence.

To help us remember these 8 areas of scientific evidence that confirm that God created all things we need to remember "_____ to _____". Note how these areas of evidence begin with the biggest thing we know of (The Universe) and end with one of the smallest things we know of (DNA within the nucleus of the living cell).

### "Biggest to Smallest"

1. The Universe (Finely Tuned)
2. The Solar System (Finely Tuned and Ordered)
3. The Earth (Created (Designed) to Be Inhabited)
4. Living Creatures on the Earth (Each with Design Features)
5. The Human Body (Amazingly Designed)
6. The Microscopic World (With Design Features though Very Small)
7. The Human Cell (Incredibly complex & designed)
8. DNA in the Nucleus of the Cell (Vast amounts of usable, ordered information)

Remember, these lessons are not designed to go into great detail but rather to introduce believers to these areas of evidence in a simple way that is easy to understand and remember. You are encouraged to read the book "Faith & Reason Made Simple" that goes along with these lessons and look into the additional resources listed in the appendix at the back of the book. This is a starting point!

As we look at the incredible levels of design at 8 different areas of creation we should remember that the Bible tells us in Romans 1:18-22 that God has revealed Himself to us through the things that He has made. God's invisible attributes, God's eternal _____, and God's divine _____ are all revealed to every human being through the created things around us that God has made. No one has an excuse to not believe in God. The revelation of His existence is easily seen by anyone who looks at the created world with an open mind and heart.

> Romans 1:20 NASB  For since the creation of the world ❶His invisible attributes, ❷His eternal power and ❸divine nature, have been clearly seen, being understood through what has been made, so that they are without excuse.

# #1 - The Finely Tuned Universe

At least 30 physical constants (or laws of physics) are set perfectly in order for the universe to exist and in order for stars and planets to exist.

Examples of the physical _____, or laws of _____ that are precisely set are "The Law of Gravity", "The Speed of Light", "The Cosmological Constant" and "The Ratio of Electron to Protons."

The chart below shows how much precision is involved in the setting of these physical constants or laws of physics. The level of precision rules out chance as an explanation and confirms the designing work of a creator.

## FINE TUNING OF THE PHYSICAL CONSTANTS OF THE UNIVERSE

| PARAMETER | MAX. DEVIATION |
|---|---|
| Ratio of Electrons: Protons | $1:10^{37}$ |
| Ratio of Electromagnetic Force: Gravity | $1:10^{40}$ |
| Expansion Rate of Universe | $1:10^{55}$ |
| Mass Density of Universe | $1:10^{59}$ |
| Cosmological Constant | $1:10^{120}$ |

These numbers represent the maximum deviation from the accepted values, that would either prevent the universe from existing now, not having matter, or be unsuitable for any form of life.

Basically, all scientists have acknowledged the wonder of this fine-tuning. Many, even among those who hold to evolutionary views, have acknowledged that it creates the impression that the universe has a _____. For those who believe in a creator this evidence gives more than an impression of design, but rather, confirmation that God created the heavens and the earth. Note the following quotes:

"A commonsense interpretation of the facts suggests that a superintellect has monkeyed with physics, as well as with chemistry and biology, and that there are no blind forces worth speaking about in nature. The numbers one calculates from the facts seem to me so overwhelming as to put this conclusion almost beyond question."  **Sir Fred Hoyle**

"There is for me powerful evidence that there is something going on behind it all … It seems as though somebody has fine tuned nature's numbers to make the Universe … The impression of design is overwhelming."
Theoretical Physicist, Cosmologist, Astrobiologist - Dr. Paul Davies

"As we survey all the evidence, the thought insistently arises, that some supernatural agency must be involved. Is it possible that suddenly, without intending to, we have stumbled upon scientific proof of the existence of a Supreme Being? Was it God Who stepped in and so providentially crafted the cosmos for our benefit?"
Astronomer – Dr. George Greenstein

Evolutionists acknowledge that this amazing fine-tuning is seen within the universe. Their explanation is found in the "_____" theory which states there may have been millions of _____ produced and this one, out of the millions produced, is by chance, just right. Some have referred to this theory as "The Goldilocks Theory". Dr. Neil deGrasse Tyson has acknowledged that scientists have no _____ to support this theory, but only theoretical and philosophical reasons to believe that a Multiverse exists. It should be obvious to anyone looking at this truth about the universe with an open mind and heart that the universe has been created by an amazingly wise and powerful God!

PSALMS 19:1 – "THE HEAVENS ARE TELLING OF THE GLORY OF GOD; AND THEIR EXPANSE IS DECLARING THE WORK OF HIS HANDS."

## #2 - The Solar System (Wonderfully Ordered)

Note the following facts about our solar system that show evidence confirming design (creation).

1. Our solar system is perfectly ordered. We can know where each of the planets will be in their orbit around the sun, 100 years from now on this date, at this time. Nothing about the _____ of the planets around our sun gives the impression of randomness. It works like clockwork!
2. The makeup of the various planets is not at all the same. Some are gaseous, some are terrestrial, etc. This shows that they do not exist as the result of an explosion billions of years ago.
3. The Gas Giant planets within our solar system are critical for life to exist on the Earth. The gravitational pull of these huge planets protects us from incoming objects.
4. The planets do not all rotate in the same direction. _____, Uranus and Pluto all rotate in different directions from the other planets. Again, this shows that the planets are not the result of an explosion of rotating matter.
5. Some of the moons within the solar system orbit their respective planets in the opposite direction as that of other moons. This again reveals design, not explosion!

The relationship of our _____ to the earth also shows evidence of great design. It is just the right size and orbits at just the right distance from the earth so that it controls the tides of the oceans, which is critical for life, and so that it controls the tilt of the earth at 23 ½ degrees, allowing for the seasons we experience here on earth.

## #3 - The Earth

The ability of a planet to sustain inhabited life forms involves over 75 different parameters. The Earth perfectly meets all of these parameters needed to support living creatures.

The Bible says in Isaiah 45:18 that God created the Earth not to be a waste place, but to be _____.

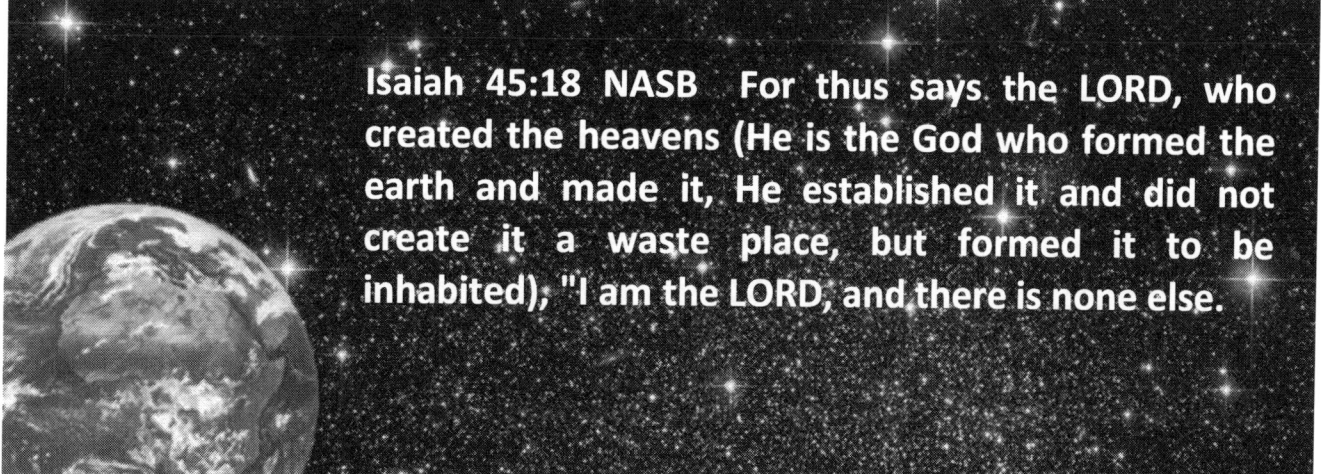

Isaiah 45:18 NASB  For thus says the LORD, who created the heavens (He is the God who formed the earth and made it, He established it and did not create it a waste place, but formed it to be inhabited); "I am the LORD, and there is none else.

Scientists now understand that there are over 75 different parameters that a planet must have in place in order to be inhabited and sustain life. Some actually place the number at around _____, so 75 is a very conservative number. These are very precise parameters that must be met. The earth meets every one of those parameters. There is no other planet known in the universe that meets these parameters. Everything about this gives the impression that the earth has been designed to be inhabited, just as the Bible says.

Examples of these are "being the right distance from the sun", "having the right _____ rate", "having the right atmosphere", "having the right amount of liquid water", "having a moon to control the tilt of the earth and the ocean tide", "having the right _____ field", "having the right thickness of tectonic crust", "having the right amount of seismic and volcanic activity", "having the right amount of soil mineralization", "having the right amount of atmospheric pressure", "located in the right place within the galaxy", etc. The earth is perfectly designed with all of these characteristics to allow for life to inhabit the earth!

Some have estimated that the chances of any planet randomly having all of these qualities, so as to be able to sustain living creatures, would be 1 chance in a million, billion. That would be 1 chance in 1,000,000,000,000,000.

The earth also exhibits a number of amazing features in the way things function and fit together in the grand scheme of things. Consider just a few here.

### 1. – The Hydrological Cycle (The <u>Watering</u> System of the Earth)

We tend to take for granted the watering system here on earth that allows us to live and flourish. If we begin to think about how efficiently it works we will begin to marvel. The water evaporates from the oceans, seas and lakes into the atmosphere. The water condenses and forms clouds. The upper level winds push the clouds across the land. As the clouds mount higher in the atmosphere the water is eventually released in the form of rain, hail, snow or sleet. Crops and other plants are watered so that we can live. Water supplies are replenished. Then, excess water runs back into the rivers, lakes, seas and oceans. The entire process continues over and over, allowing for life.

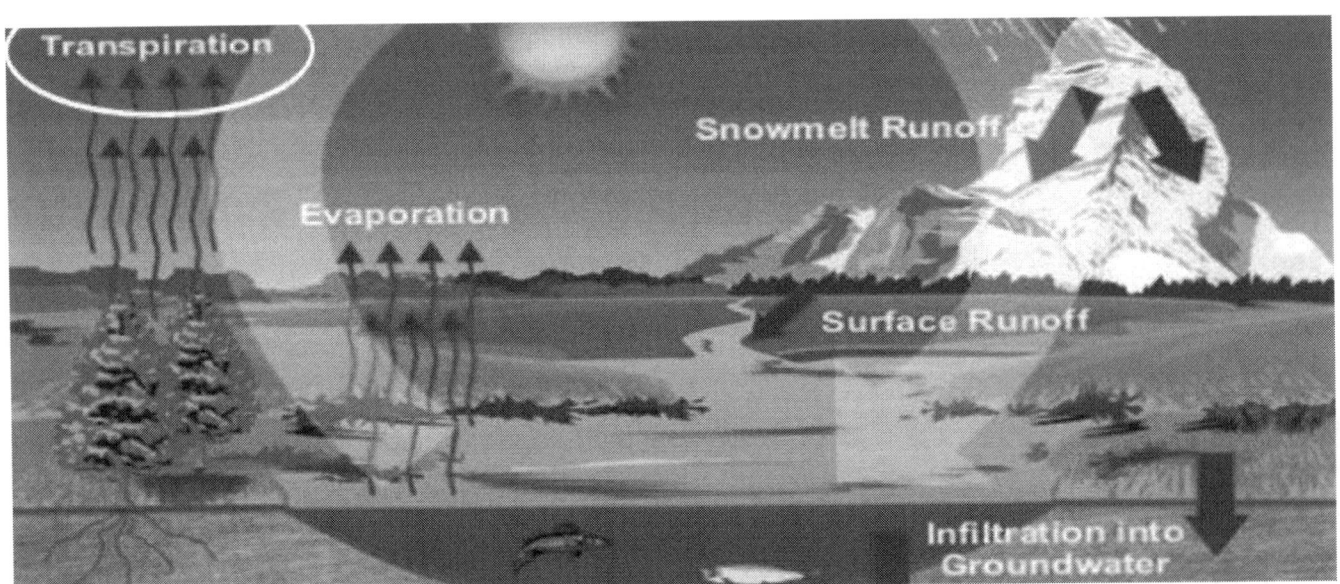

I did some calculations once to determine just how much water this system is moving in order for life to thrive here on earth. I calculated how much water would be released in one thunder storm that released an average of 2 inches of rain over an area 500 miles by 500 miles. That is a pretty good size storm but remember that some storms drop large amounts of rain across the U.S. from the west coast to the east coast, which is about 3,000 miles across. After doing the math I discovered that this storm would drop enough water to create a lake from where I live, just off the Mississippi River, to Chicago, 10 miles wide and 25 feet deep. This would be by far the largest lake in the state of Illinois! That's just one storm! Consider that every day this established watering system is dropping vast amounts of water all around the world, allowing life to flourish on the earth! It truly is amazing!

One Rainstorm distributing an average of 2" of rain over an area 500 miles by 500 miles would drop enough water to create a lake from the Quad Cities to Chicago 10 miles wide and 25' Deep

A major part of the hydrological cycle is something called "transpiration". This is what we call it when plants sweat. Just as we define our sweating as perspiration, so we define plants sweating as transpiration. I have come to understand that if this were not a reality we would all be dead. Trees of course are the biggest contributors to transpiration, although other plants transpire as well. On the underside of a tree's leaves there are tiny pours that open and close, depending on the weather conditions, allowing water vapor to exit the tree. The process itself is marvelous! The efficiency of the process is amazing! As an example of how efficient this process is consider that on a hot summer day a Maple Tree will transpire 50-60 gallons of water per hour!!! A Weeping Willow tree will transpire up to 80 gallons per hour!!! Now consider how many trees there are in the world, along with corn fields, flowers, grassy yards, etc. The plants use the moisture to live and then send it back to be recycled. What a design!!!

Example of "Transpiration"
Maple Tree
(50-60 Gallons Per Hour)

 Consider the growth of seeds into plants of all types upon the earth. If we simply add soil, sunshine and water to a seed planted in the ground we will see life coming forth in amazing ways. One tiny seed can often times produce a huge tree or some other type of beneficial plant life.

Finally, consider the balance that is created in our atmosphere by living creatures and plants. Billions of people, along with billions of animals breathe in oxygen out of the atmosphere each second of the day, all around the world, and breathe out carbon dioxide. This would seem to be a problem since it would look as though the atmosphere would very quickly be filled with carbon dioxide and void of oxygen. This would be

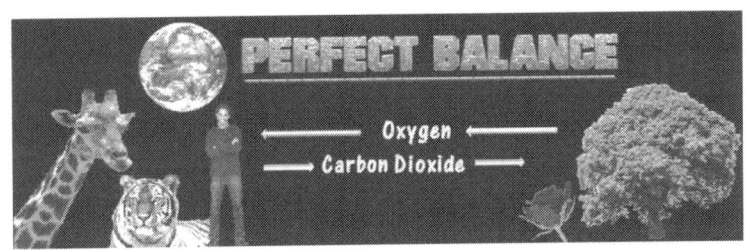

the case if it were not for the wonderful design of God here on earth! The fact is that trees and all other plant life around the world breathe in carbon dioxide to live and breathe out oxygen, creating a perfect balance and keeping the atmosphere filled with all that living creatures and living plants need to live.

Truly the earth exhibits many characteristics that give us confirming evidence of a wonderful Creator!!!

## #4 - Living Creatures on the Earth
### (Each are uniquely and wonderfully designed)

The more that we learn about living creatures that inhabit the earth the more we come to understand that each of them exhibits tremendous design features, both in their structure and in their abilities. Nothing that we find in the living creatures here on earth gives the impression of random chance and unguided processes. They all look wonderfully designed. From insects, to large land animals, to sea creatures of all types we find evidence of design. We could look at the male Beetles that in their larvae form dig holes deeper than their female counterparts in order to allow for the formation of their large pinchers that will form. We could look at Ruminant Animals, such as Cows, Buffalo, and Rabbits with their intricate digestive systems, involving 4 separate stomachs. We could look at all of the remarkable features of the Camel which allow him to be the perfect choice for a travel companion in the dessert. We could look at the Bombardier Beetle, with its ability to shoot an exploding substance from its behind to ward off would be predators. We could look at the Squid's ability to quickly morph into a camouflaged state. We could look at the Salmon's ability to return to the very spot of her birth to lay her eggs after traveling hundreds, or even thousands of miles. We could consider the spider's abilities when it comes to creating a strong and artistic web for a home. There are almost unlimited numbers of creature to consider in which we could find great design features. Here a few examples that illustrate the point well!

### 1 – The Australian Brush Turkey
They make their nest on the ground, a mound 3-6 feet high and 10-15 feet wide. The female places the eggs inside the mound. The male keeps the nest within a degree or two of 91 degrees Fahrenheit, as well as the humidity levels at precise levels, for 7 weeks by placing and removing sticks, sand and leaves in various places. Without this ability by the father, the chicks would not hatch or live. The Brush Turkey's ability is evidence of design!

### 2 - Ear Mites
A certain type of Ear Mite only makes their home in the ear of a moth. These Ear Mites will sometimes make their home in the right ear of the moth and sometimes in the left ear. When the Ear Mites make their home in the ear of the moth the moth will go deaf in that ear. Amazingly, the Ear Mites will never make homes in both ears of the moth, allowing the moth to continue to hear and avoid predators.

### 3 - Monarch Butterflies

Monarch Butterflies primarily winter in mountainous trees found in southern Mexico. They only lay their eggs on Milkweed Plants. In the spring they begin to move north and lay eggs on Milkweed Plants now showing up in Mexico and the southern U.S. After laying her eggs the Monarch dies. The eggs hatch and the new caterpillars eat the Milkweed leaves. They then enter the Chrysalis stage and eventually emerge as beautiful new Monarchs. This generation will live for 6-8 weeks. This process continues throughout the spring, summer and early fall. Monarch will end up in the northern U.S. and in southern Canada by the end of summer. All of this, including what happens during the Chrysalis stage is truly remarkable when examined, but the most amazing fact is that the generation of Monarchs that are born in the northern parts of the U.S. and the southern parts of Canada will migrate back to the very trees that their great-great-great grandma and grandpa lived in last winter. Some will fly across the gulf of Mexico. This generation will live for about _____ instead of the normal 5-8 weeks!

### 4 – Beavers

Beavers are very well equipped for their lifestyle, with transparent eyelids so that they can see under water and a special flap in their mouth to allow them to carry sticks under water with their teeth without swallowing undue amounts of water. Their engineering abilities are remarkable allowing them to quickly build water dams that humans would struggle to build, even with special equipment.

### 5 - Honey Bees

Honey Bees are master engineers, utilizing the honeycomb shape to build their homes. They design each honeycomb chamber with the perfect amount of angle for holding honey and for housing their young. Scout bees communicate to the rest of hive after finding a food source through the use of a special _____. In this way they communicate the direction and distance of the food source as well as how good the food source is. Research has also shown that Honey Bees can figure out the best path to move from flower to flower in large fields to save energy and time. They do this is a very short time. The research revealed that it would take super computers great amounts of time to accomplish the same task.

### 6 – Giraffes

Giraffes are equipped by God with some special design features to accommodate their great height. First of all they have the largest heart of any creature, enabling them to pump blood against gravity all the way up their long neck. Secondly, they have special _____ in their neck that no other creature has which open and close, depending on whether they have their head up or are lowering their head to get a drink of water. Without these valves they would certainly pass out, if not worse whenever they lowered their head and gravity began to work with their powerful heart, instead of against it. Finally, they have a sponge in the top of their head which fills when they have their head lowered so that they will have the proper amount of blood in their head when they stand upright after getting a drink, until the valves open and a new supply of blood reaches their head.

### 7 – Woodpeckers

Woodpeckers have a number of special design features which allow them to hunt for bugs inside of trees very effectively. They have special feet to allow them to cling to the side of a tree for long periods of time. They have special shock absorbers in their necks that no other bird has to protect them as they bang their head against a tree all day. They can open and close their eyelids with every strike to protect them from wood chips. They also have tongues that coil up in the back of their mouths and can be uncoiled to reach bugs within a tree. Their tongue also has a barbed end to stick the bug. Their tongue secretes a sticky substance to help them retrieve the bug. Once their tongue is back in their mouth they are able to secrete another substance to negate the sticky substance, allowing the bug to be swallowed and digested. Woodpeckers are pretty cool!

### 8 – Chickens

When we think about creatures with amazing, unique abilities we may not quickly think about common chickens as creatures with great skills or abilities. A few years ago I was thinking about how God has revealed Himself through the things that He has made and for some reason my thoughts went to chickens. I started thinking about how critical chickens are to our existence. What an amazing food source chickens and the eggs they lay are for each of us! I really think that chickens are a great gift that we should praise God for! We will look for a moment at how critical chickens are to our everyday lives and how uniquely equipped they are to play the role they play in life here on earth.

Consider these facts about birds and their egg-laying abilities and habits.
* Bald Eagle (typically will lay 1-3 eggs per year and approximately 40 in a lifetime)
* Cardinals (2-5 eggs in a clutch – Usually 2 times per year)
* Penguins (It varies among species but generally a maximum of ___ _____ in a lifetime)
* Blue Jays (3-6 eggs each year in a clutch)
* Ringneck Doves (2 eggs per clutch)(a maximum of 16-18 per year)
* Turkeys (Another great food source!)(a maximum of 100 eggs per year)
* Chickens are egg-laying machines. A hen hits puberty only 18-24 weeks after hatching out of an egg herself. It only takes about 26 hours for a hen to make an egg, and she can start producing another one 40-60 minutes later. What's more, hens lay a lot of eggs--up to _____ a year.

Now consider these facts about our consumption of chickens and chicken eggs and you can see how important it is that these birds are uniquely adept at the production of eggs!

* 8 Billion Chickens Per Year are eaten by humans in the United States - Almost 26 per person each year or 1 per person every other week)
* In 2014 Americans consumed an average of 256 eggs per person - That's Over 81 Billion Eggs in just One Year!!!)
* Ask.com reports that Americans consume an average of 25 billion chicken wings each year, including 1.25 billion during Super Bowl weekend alone!)

If there were no chickens think of how it would affect our world! The stats above of just for the United States. It is hard to find stats for worldwide egg consumption. One stat I did see said that in 2002 it was estimated that there were over 53 million tons of eggs produced for consumption worldwide. The numbers truly are mindboggling. Of course chicken eggs are not just a part of our diet when eaten by themselves but are an ingredient in so many things that we cook each day. It is for this reason that I think it is safe to say that if there were no chickens the impact on our world would be catastrophic!

It should not be surprising, since God is a masterful designer, to discover that chicken eggs, which are produced so plentifully for us by these amazing birds, are very, very nutritious. Note the following information from an online article by Dr. Fred Kummerow.

"We've discussed how mother's milk is nature's most perfect food, and Figure 5 shows the egg to be in second place because its amino acid content mimics the levels in mother's milk. Moreover, the egg is also inexpensive and readily available. If you doubled the portion to two whole eggs, these would contain even more essential amino acids than one quart of human milk."

Later in the article he adds, "Although maligned in nutritional recommendations, eggs are the most nutritious and the least expensive protein source in the grocery store. At only 68 calories, one egg provides about 11 percent of your daily protein requirement. Eggs contain a variety of important nutrients including every vitamin, mineral and natural antioxidant that your body needs." He also dispels the myth that eggs are a source of high cholesterol. So the eggs of this bird that is so efficient in the production of eggs are arguably the most nutritious form of food available to us. I do not believe this is a coincidence! We should praise God for this!

There are multitudes of other examples of living creatures that have amazing abilities and features that cannot be explained by random evolution, but are examples of evidence that confirms creation!

Summary – In this session we looked at the first 4 of the 8 levels of evidence for creation.

- **1 – The Finely Tuned Universe**
- **2 – The Order of the Solar System**
- **3 – The Earth (Designed to Be Inhabited)**
- **4 – Living Creatures on the Earth (Each Showing Design Features)**

In the next session we will look at the remaining 4 levels of evidence for creation.

# FAITH & REASON MADE SIMPLE — Part 3

## (Scientific Evidence That Confirms God Created Us)

**CREATION vs. EVOLUTION**

### Review of Parts 1 & 2 – The Scientific Flaws of the Theory of Evolution

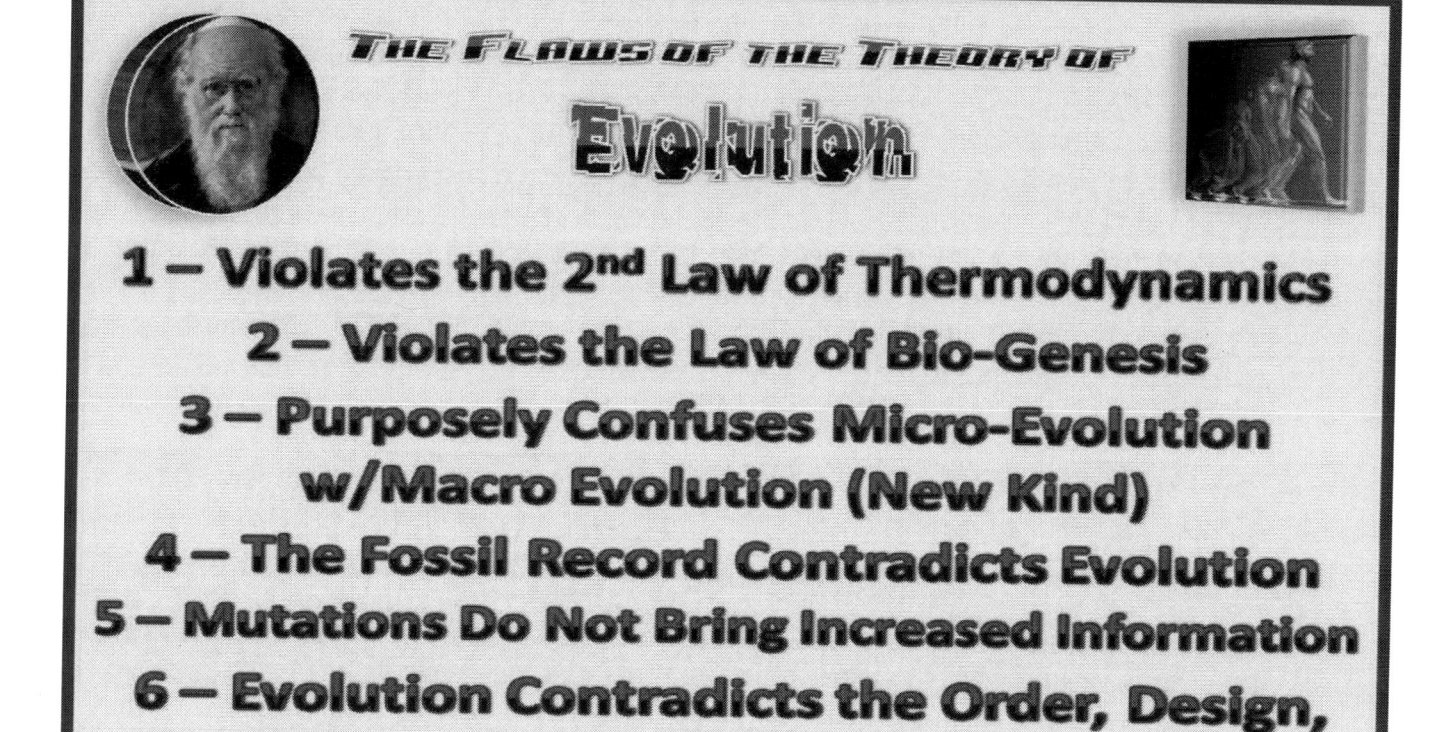

**The Flaws of the Theory of Evolution**

1 – Violates the 2nd Law of Thermodynamics
2 – Violates the Law of Bio-Genesis
3 – Purposely Confuses Micro-Evolution w/Macro Evolution (New Kind)
4 – The Fossil Record Contradicts Evolution
5 – Mutations Do Not Bring Increased Information
6 – Evolution Contradicts the Order, Design, Beauty & Information We Observe

\* To download free memory cards for these 6 points go to localchurchapologetics.org

# Scientific Evidence That Confirms That God Created All Things

What would we look for in science that would point to a creator? We would look for 2 things! We would look for **design**, because design always points to a designer. We would also look for usable, ordered **information**, because usable, ordered information always points to a source of intelligence.

To help us remember these 8 areas of scientific evidence that confirm that God created all things we need to remember "**Biggest** to **Smallest**". Note how these areas of evidence begin with the biggest thing we know of (The Universe) and end with one of the smallest things we know of (DNA within the nucleus of the living cell).

## "Biggest to Smallest"

1. The Universe (Finely Tuned)
2. The Solar System (Finely Tuned and Ordered)
3. The Earth (Created (Designed) to Be Inhabited)
4. Living Creatures on the Earth (Each with Design Features)
5. The Human Body (Amazingly Designed)
6. The Microscopic World (With Design Features though Very Small)
7. The Human Cell (Incredibly complex & designed)
8. DNA in the Nucleus of the Cell (Vast amounts of usable, ordered information)

Remember, these lessons are not designed to go into great detail but rather to introduce believers to these areas of evidence in a simple way that is easy to understand and remember. You are encouraged to read the book "Faith & Reason Made Simple" that goes along with these lessons and look into the additional resources listed in the appendix at the back of the book. This is a starting point!

As we look at the incredible levels of design at 8 different areas of creation we should remember that the Bible tells us in Romans 1:18-22 that God has revealed Himself to us through the things that He has made. God's invisible attributes, God's eternal **power**, and God's divine **nature** are all revealed to every human being through the created things around us that God has made. No one has an excuse to not believe in God. The revelation of His existence is easily seen by anyone who looks at the created world with an open mind and heart.

> Romans 1:20 NASB For since the creation of the world ①His invisible attributes, ②His eternal power and ③divine nature, have been clearly seen, being understood through what has been made, so that they are without excuse.

# #1 - The Finely Tuned Universe

At least 30 physical constants (or laws of physics) are set perfectly in order for the universe to exist and in order for stars and planets to exist.

Examples of the physical **constants**, or laws of **physics** that are precisely set are "The Law of Gravity", "The Speed of Light", "The Cosmological Constant" and "The Ratio of Electron to Protons."

The chart below shows how much precision is involved in the setting of these physical constants or laws of physics. The level of precision rules out chance as an explanation and confirms the designing work of a creator.

## FINE TUNING OF THE PHYSICAL CONSTANTS OF THE UNIVERSE

| PARAMETER | MAX. DEVIATION |
| --- | --- |
| Ratio of Electrons: Protons | $1:10^{37}$ |
| Ratio of Electromagnetic Force: Gravity | $1:10^{40}$ |
| Expansion Rate of Universe | $1:10^{55}$ |
| Mass Density of Universe | $1:10^{59}$ |
| Cosmological Constant | $1:10^{120}$ |

These numbers represent the maximum deviation from the accepted values, that would either prevent the universe from existing now, not having matter, or be unsuitable for any form of life.

Basically, all scientists have acknowledged the wonder of this fine-tuning. Many, even among those who hold to evolutionary views, have acknowledged that it creates the impression that the universe has a **designer**. For those who believe in a creator this evidence gives more than an impression of design, but rather, confirmation that God created the heavens and the earth. Note the following quotes:

"A commonsense interpretation of the facts suggests that a superintellect has monkeyed with physics, as well as with chemistry and biology, and that there are no blind forces worth speaking about in nature. The numbers one calculates from the facts seem to me so overwhelming as to put this conclusion almost beyond question."   Sir Fred Hoyle

"There is for me powerful evidence that there is something going on behind it all ... It seems as though somebody has fine tuned nature's numbers to make the Universe ... The impression of design is overwhelming."
Theoretical Physicist, Cosmologist, Astrobiologist - Dr. Paul Davies

"As we survey all the evidence, the thought insistently arises, that some supernatural agency must be involved. Is it possible that suddenly, without intending to, we have stumbled upon scientific proof of the existence of a Supreme Being? Was it God Who stepped in and so providentially crafted the cosmos for our benefit?"
Astronomer – Dr. George Greenstein

Evolutionists acknowledge that this amazing fine-tuning is seen within the universe. Their explanation is found in the "**Multiverse**" theory which states there may have been millions of **universes** produced and this one, out of the millions produced, is by chance, just right. Some have referred to this theory as "The Goldilocks Theory". Dr. Neil deGrasse Tyson has acknowledged that scientists have no **data** to support this theory, but only theoretical and philosophical reasons to believe that a Multiverse exists. It should be obvious to anyone looking at this truth about the universe with an open mind and heart that the universe has been created by an amazingly wise and powerful God!

PSALMS 19:1 – "THE HEAVENS ARE TELLING OF THE GLORY OF GOD, AND THEIR EXPANSE IS DECLARING THE WORK OF HIS HANDS."

## #2 - The Solar System (Wonderfully Ordered)

Note the following facts about our solar system that show evidence confirming design (creation).

1. Our solar system is perfectly ordered. We can know where each of the planets will be in their orbit around the sun, 100 years from now on this date, at this time. Nothing about the **orbit** of the planets around our sun gives the impression of randomness. It works like clockwork!
2. The makeup of the various planets is not at all the same. Some are gaseous, some are terrestrial, etc. This shows that they do not exist as the result of an explosion billions of years ago.
3. The Gas Giant planets within our solar system are critical for life to exist on the Earth. The gravitational pull of these huge planets protects us from incoming objects.
4. The planets do not all rotate in the same direction. **Venus**, Uranus and Pluto all rotate in different directions from the other planets. Again, this shows that the planets are not the result of an explosion of rotating matter.
5. Some of the moons within the solar system orbit their respective planets in the opposite direction as that of other moons. This again reveals design, not explosion!

The relationship of our **moon** to the earth also shows evidence of great design. It is just the right size and orbits at just the right distance from the earth so that it controls the tides of the oceans, which is critical for life, and so that it controls the tilt of the earth at 23 ½ degrees, allowing for the seasons we experience here on earth.

## #3 - The Earth

**The ability of a planet to sustain inhabited life forms involves over 75 different parameters. The Earth perfectly meets all of these parameters needed to support living creatures.**

The Bible says in Isaiah 45:18 that God created the Earth not to be a waste place, but to be **inhabited**.

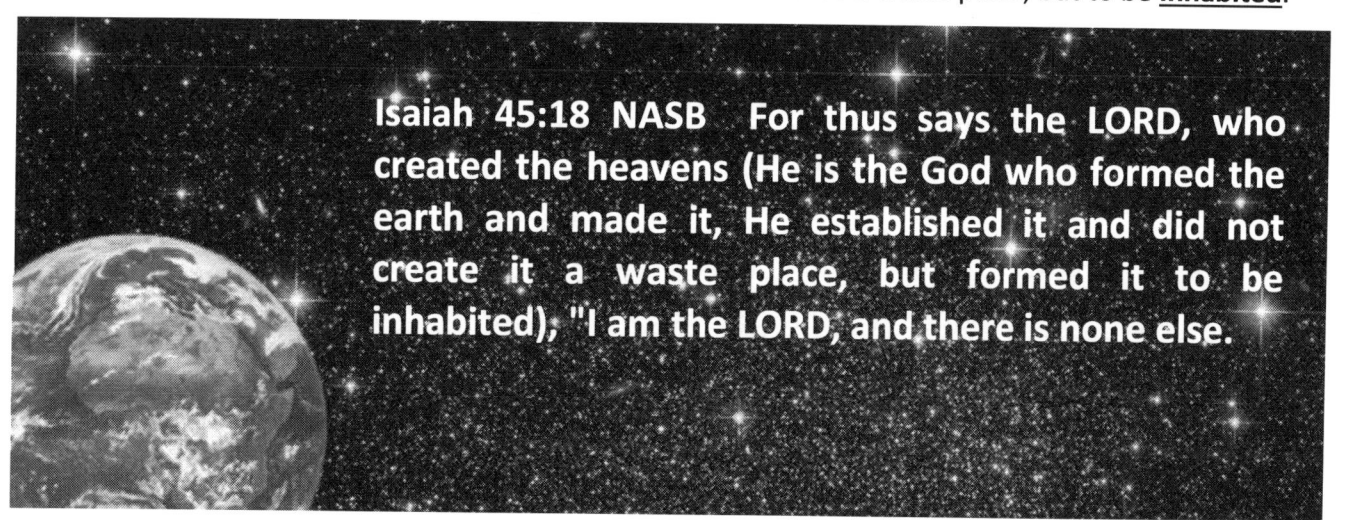

**Isaiah 45:18 NASB** For thus says the LORD, who created the heavens (He is the God who formed the earth and made it, He established it and did not create it a waste place, but formed it to be inhabited), "I am the LORD, and there is none else.

Scientists now understand that there are over 75 different parameters that a planet must have in place in order to be inhabited and sustain life. Some actually place the number at around **200**, so 75 is a very conservative number. These are very precise parameters that must be met. The earth meets every one of those parameters. There is no other planet known in the universe that meets these parameters. Everything about this gives the impression that the earth has been designed to be inhabited, just as the Bible says.

Examples of these are "being the right distance from the sun", "having the right **rotation** rate", "having the right atmosphere", "having the right amount of liquid water", "having a moon to control the tilt of the earth and the ocean tide", "having the right **electromagnetic** field", "having the right thickness of tectonic crust", "having the right amount of seismic and volcanic activity", "having the right amount of soil mineralization", "having the right amount of atmospheric pressure", "located in the right place within the galaxy", etc. The earth is perfectly designed with all of these characteristics to allow for life to inhabit the earth!

Some have estimated that the chances of any planet randomly having all of these qualities, so as to be able to sustain living creatures, would be 1 chance in a million, billion. That would be 1 chance in 1,000,000,000,000,000.

The earth also exhibits a number of amazing features in the way things function and fit together in the grand scheme of things. Consider just a few here.

### 1. – The Hydrological Cycle (The **Watering** System of the Earth)

We tend to take for granted the watering system here on earth that allows us to live and flourish. If we begin to think about how efficiently it works we will begin to marvel. The water evaporates from the oceans, seas and lakes into the atmosphere. The water condenses and forms clouds. The upper level winds push the clouds across the land. As the clouds mount higher in the atmosphere the water is eventually released in the form of rain, hail, snow or sleet. Crops and other plants are watered so that we can live. Water supplies are replenished. Then, excess water runs back into the rivers, lakes, seas and oceans. The entire process continues over and over, allowing for life.

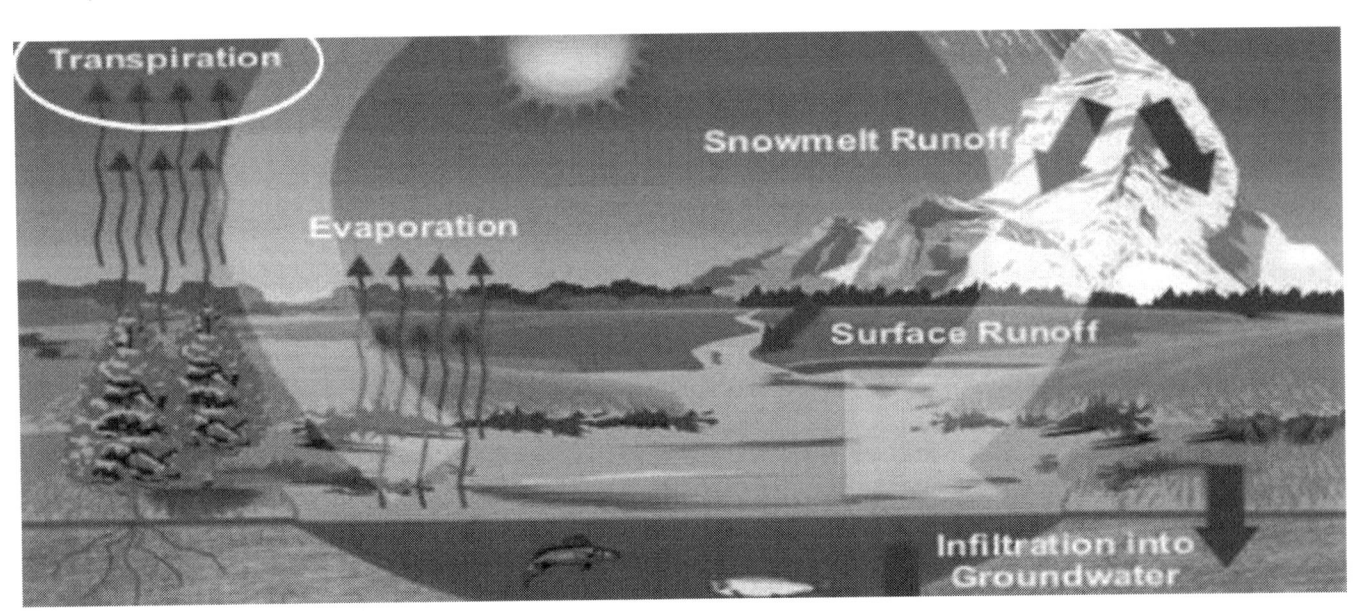

I did some calculations once to determine just how much water this system is moving in order for life to thrive here on earth. I calculated how much water would be released in one thunder storm that released an average of 2 inches of rain over an area 500 miles by 500 miles. That is a pretty good size storm but remember that some storms drop large amounts of rain across the U.S. from the west coast to the east coast, which is about 3,000 miles across. After doing the math I discovered that this storm would drop enough water to create a lake from where I live, just off the Mississippi River, to Chicago, 10 miles wide and 25 feet deep. This would be by far the largest lake in the state of Illinois! That's just one storm! Consider that every day this established watering system is dropping vast amounts of water all around the world, allowing life to flourish on the earth! It truly is amazing!

> One Rainstorm distributing an average of 2" of rain over an area 500 miles by 500 miles would drop enough water to create a lake from the Quad Cities to Chicago 10 miles wide and 25' Deep
>
> "LAKE RAINSTORM"

A major part of the hydrological cycle is something called "transpiration". This is what we call it when plants sweat. Just as we define our sweating as perspiration, so we define plants sweating as transpiration. I have come to understand that if this were not a reality we would all be dead. Trees of course are the biggest contributors to transpiration, although other plants transpire as well. On the underside of a tree's leaves there are tiny pours that open and close, depending on the weather conditions, allowing water vapor to exit the tree. The process itself is marvelous! The efficiency of the process is amazing! As an example of how efficient this process is consider that on a hot summer day a Maple Tree will transpire 50-60 gallons of water per hour!!! A Weeping Willow tree will transpire up to 80 gallons per hour!!! Now consider how many trees there are in the world, along with corn fields, flowers, grassy yards, etc. The plants use the moisture to live and then send it back to be recycled. What a design!!!

Example of "Transpiration"
Maple Tree
(50-60 Gallons Per Hour)

## Seeds & Soil

Consider the growth of seeds into plants of all types upon the earth. If we simply add soil, sunshine and water to a seed planted in the ground we will see life coming forth in amazing ways. One tiny seed can often times produce a huge tree or some other type of beneficial plant life.

Finally, consider the balance that is created in our atmosphere by living creatures and plants. Billions of people, along with billions of animals breathe in oxygen out of the atmosphere each second of the day, all around the world, and breathe out carbon dioxide. This would seem to be a problem since it would look as though the atmosphere would very quickly be filled with carbon dioxide and void of oxygen. This would be the case if it were not for the wonderful design of God here on earth! The fact is that trees and all other plant life around the world breathe in carbon dioxide to live and breathe out oxygen, creating a perfect balance and keeping the atmosphere filled with all that living creatures and living plants need to live.

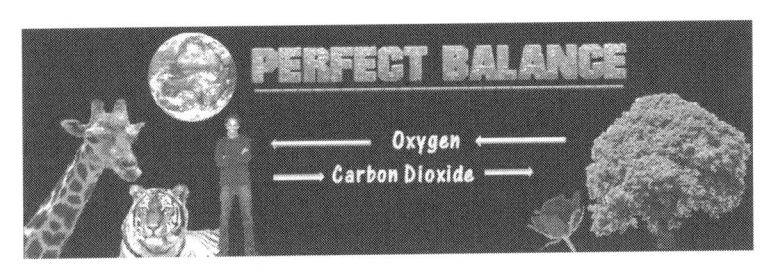

Truly the earth exhibits many characteristics that give us confirming evidence of a wonderful Creator!!!

# #4 - Living Creatures on the Earth
## (Each are uniquely and wonderfully designed)

The more that we learn about living creatures that inhabit the earth the more we come to understand that each of them exhibits tremendous design features, both in their structure and in their abilities. Nothing that we find in the living creatures here on earth gives the impression of random chance and unguided processes. They all look wonderfully designed. From insects, to large land animals, to sea creatures of all types we find evidence of design. We could look at the male Beetles that in their larvae form dig holes deeper than their female counterparts in order to allow for the formation of their large pinchers that will form. We could look at Ruminant Animals, such as Cows, Buffalo, and Rabbits with their intricate digestive systems, involving 4 separate stomachs. We could look at all of the remarkable features of the Camel which allow him to be the perfect choice for a travel companion in the dessert. We could look at the Bombardier Beetle, with its ability to shoot an exploding substance from its behind to ward off would be predators. We could look at the Squid's ability to quickly morph into a camouflaged state. We could look at the Salmon's ability to return to the very spot of her birth to lay her eggs after traveling hundreds, or even thousands of miles. We could consider the spider's abilities when it comes to creating a strong and artistic web for a home. There are almost unlimited numbers of creature to consider in which we could find great design features. Here a few examples that illustrate the point well!

### 1 – The Australian Brush Turkey
They make their nest on the ground, a mound 3-6 feet high and 10-15 feet wide. The female places the eggs inside the mound. The male keeps the nest within a degree or two of 91 degrees Fahrenheit, as well as the humidity levels at precise levels, for 7 weeks by placing and removing sticks, sand and leaves in various places. Without this ability by the father, the chicks would not hatch or live. The Brush Turkey's ability is evidence of design!

### 2 - Ear Mites
A certain type of Ear Mite only makes their home in the ear of a moth. These Ear Mites will sometimes make their home in the right ear of the moth and sometimes in the left ear. When the Ear Mites make their home in the ear of the moth the moth will go deaf in that ear. Amazingly, the Ear Mites will never make homes in both ears of the moth, allowing the moth to continue to hear and avoid predators.

### 3 - Monarch Butterflies

Monarch Butterflies primarily winter in mountainous trees found in southern Mexico. They only lay their eggs on Milkweed Plants. In the spring they begin to move north and lay eggs on Milkweed Plants now showing up in Mexico and the southern U.S. After laying her eggs the Monarch dies. The eggs hatch and the new caterpillars eat the Milkweed leaves. They then enter the Chrysalis stage and eventually emerge as beautiful new Monarchs. This generation will live for 6-8 weeks. This process continues throughout the spring, summer and early fall. Monarch will end up in the northern U.S. and in southern Canada by the end of summer. All of this, including what happens during the Chrysalis stage is truly remarkable when examined, but the most amazing fact is that the generation of Monarchs that are born in the northern parts of the U.S. and the southern parts of Canada will migrate back to the very trees that their great-great-great grandma and grandpa lived in last winter. Some will fly across the gulf of Mexico. This generation will live for about **8 months** instead of the normal 5-8 weeks!

### 4 – Beavers

Beavers are very well equipped for their lifestyle, with transparent eyelids so that they can see under water and a special flap in their mouth to allow them to carry sticks under water with their teeth without swallowing undue amounts of water. Their engineering abilities are remarkable allowing them to quickly build water dams that humans would struggle to build, even with special equipment.

### 5 - Honey Bees

Honey Bees are master engineers, utilizing the honeycomb shape to build their homes. They design each honeycomb chamber with the perfect amount of angle for holding honey and for housing their young. Scout bees communicate to the rest of hive after finding a food source through the use of a special **dance**. In this way they communicate the direction and distance of the food source as well as how good the food source is. Research has also shown that Honey Bees can figure out the best path to move from flower to flower in large fields to save energy and time. They do this is a very short time. The research revealed that it would take super computers great amounts of time to accomplish the same task.

### 6 – Giraffes

Giraffes are equipped by God with some special design features to accommodate their great height. First of all they have the largest heart of any creature, enabling them to pump blood against gravity all the way up their long neck. Secondly, they have special **valves** in their neck that no other creature has which open and close, depending on whether they have their head up or are lowering their head to get a drink of water. Without these valves they would certainly pass out, if not worse whenever they lowered their head and gravity began to work with their powerful heart, instead of against it. Finally, they have a sponge in the top of their head which fills when they have their head lowered so that they will have the proper amount of blood in their head when they stand upright after getting a drink, until the valves open and a new supply of blood reaches their head.

### 7 – Woodpeckers

Woodpeckers have a number of special design features which allow them to hunt for bugs inside of trees very effectively. They have special feet to allow them to cling to the side of a tree for long periods of time. They have special shock absorbers in their necks that no other bird has to protect them as they bang their head against a tree all day. They can open and close their eyelids with every strike to protect them from wood chips. They also have tongues that coil up in the back of their mouths and can be uncoiled to reach bugs within a tree. Their tongue also has a barbed end to stick the bug. Their tongue secretes a sticky substance to help them retrieve the bug. Once their tongue is back in their mouth they are able to secrete another substance to negate the sticky substance, allowing the bug to be swallowed and digested. Woodpeckers are pretty cool!

### 8 – Chickens

When we think about creatures with amazing, unique abilities we may not quickly think about common chickens as creatures with great skills or abilities. A few years ago I was thinking about how God has revealed Himself through the things that He has made and for some reason my thoughts went to chickens. I started thinking about how critical chickens are to our existence. What an amazing food source chickens and the eggs they lay are for each of us! I really think that chickens are a great gift that we should praise God for! We will look for a moment at how critical chickens are to our everyday lives and how uniquely equipped they are to play the role they play in life here on earth.

Consider these facts about birds and their egg-laying abilities and habits.

* Bald Eagle (typically will lay 1-3 eggs per year and approximately 40 in a lifetime)
* Cardinals (2-5 eggs in a clutch – Usually 2 times per year)
* Penguins (It varies among species but generally a maximum of **15 eggs** in a lifetime)
* Blue Jays (3-6 eggs each year in a clutch)
* Ringneck Doves (2 eggs per clutch)(a maximum of 16-18 per year)
* Turkeys (Another great food source!)(a maximum of 100 eggs per year)
* Chickens are egg-laying machines. A hen hits puberty only 18-24 weeks after hatching out of an egg herself. It only takes about 26 hours for a hen to make an egg, and she can start producing another one 40-60 minutes later. What's more, hens lay a lot of eggs--up to **300** a year.

Now consider these facts about our consumption of chickens and chicken eggs and you can see how important it is that these birds are uniquely adept at the production of eggs!

* 8 Billion Chickens Per Year are eaten by humans in the United States - Almost 26 per person each year or 1 per person every other week)
* In 2014 Americans consumed an average of 256 eggs per person - That's Over 81 Billion Eggs in just One Year!!!)
* Ask.com reports that Americans consume an average of 25 billion chicken wings each year, including 1.25 billion during Super Bowl weekend alone!)

If there were no chickens think of how it would affect our world! The stats above of just for the United States. It is hard to find stats for worldwide egg consumption. One stat I did see said that in 2002 it was estimated that there were over 53 million tons of eggs produced for consumption worldwide. The numbers truly are mindboggling. Of course chicken eggs are not just a part of our diet when eaten by themselves but are an ingredient in so many things that we cook each day. It is for this reason that I think it is safe to say that if there were no chickens the impact on our world would be catastrophic!

It should not be surprising, since God is a masterful designer, to discover that chicken eggs, which are produced so plentifully for us by these amazing birds, are very, very nutritious. Note the following information from an online article by Dr. Fred Kummerow.

"We've discussed how mother's milk is nature's most perfect food, and Figure 5 shows the egg to be in second place because its amino acid content mimics the levels in mother's milk. Moreover, the egg is also inexpensive and readily available. If you doubled the portion to two whole eggs, these would contain even more essential amino acids than one quart of human milk."

Later in the article he adds, "Although maligned in nutritional recommendations, eggs are the most nutritious and the least expensive protein source in the grocery store. At only 68 calories, one egg provides about 11 percent of your daily protein requirement. Eggs contain a variety of important nutrients including every vitamin, mineral and natural antioxidant that your body needs." He also dispels the myth that eggs are a source of high cholesterol. So the eggs of this bird that is so efficient in the production of eggs are arguably the most nutritious form of food available to us. I do not believe this is a coincidence! We should praise God for this!

There are multitudes of other examples of living creatures that have amazing abilities and features that cannot be explained by random evolution, but are examples of evidence that confirms creation!

Summary – In this session we looked at the first 4 of the 8 levels of evidence for creation.

**1 – The Finely Tuned Universe**
**2 – The Order of the Solar System**
**3 – The Earth (Designed to Be Inhabited)**
**4 – Living Creatures on the Earth (Each Showing Design Features)**

In the next session we will look at the remaining 4 levels of evidence for creation.

# FAITH & REASON MADE SIMPLE
## Part 4

## (Scientific Evidence That Confirms God Created Us (Cont.))

### #5 - The Human Body (Amazingly Designed)

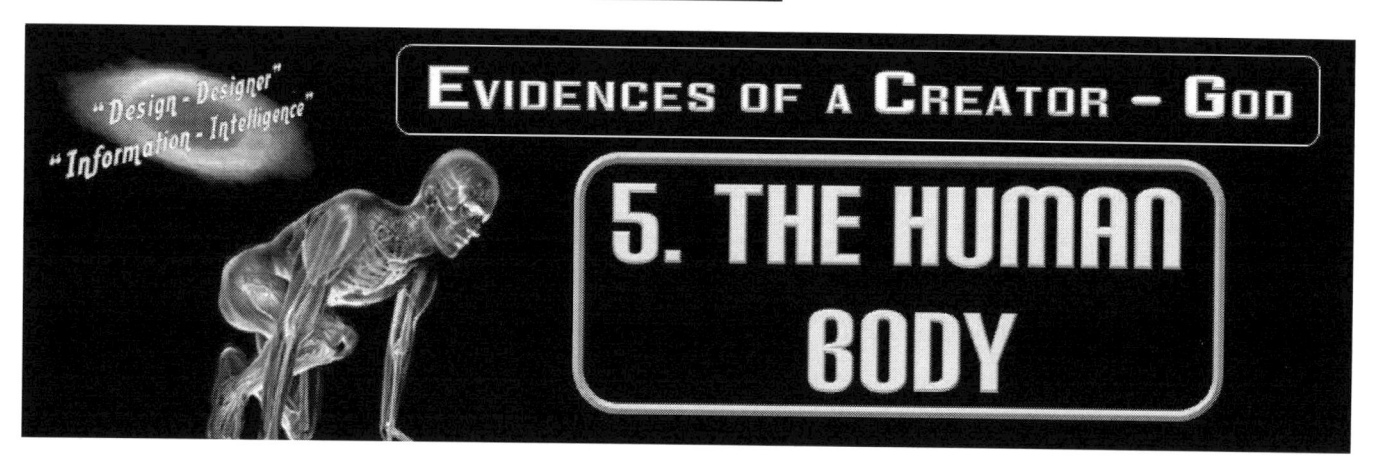

**EVIDENCES OF A CREATOR - GOD**
"Design - Designer"
"Information - Intelligence"
**5. THE HUMAN BODY**

> Psalms 139:13-17 NASB For You formed my inward parts; You wove me in my mother's womb. (14) I will give thanks to You, for I am fearfully and wonderfully made; Wonderful are Your works, And my soul knows it very well. (15) My frame was not hidden from You, When I was made in secret, And skillfully wrought in the depths of the earth; (16) Your eyes have seen my unformed substance; And in Your book were all written The days that were ordained for me, When as yet there was not one of them. (17) How precious also are Your thoughts to me, O God! How vast is the sum of them!

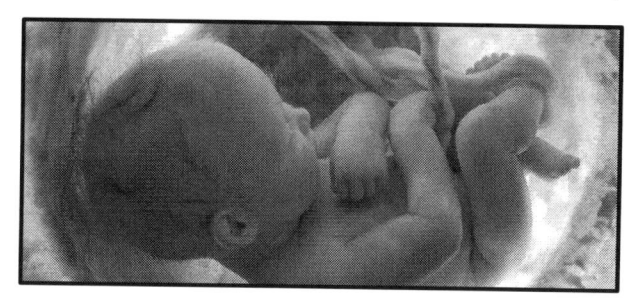

The Bible informs us that God formed each of us in our mother's womb. The descriptions of this found in Psalm 139 reveal an intimacy between God and each person He has created. He knows us and cares for us! A brief examination of the birth process and of the structures and functions of the human body will give us tremendous evidence to confirm that we are created by God, with purpose and value! Nothing about the human body looks like it is the result of random processes and chance. It clearly looks as though it is wonderfully designed!

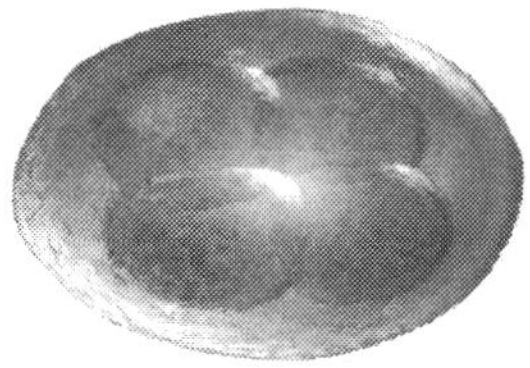

* Development of a human baby in the womb – Think about the miracle of one cell (called a zygote) multiplying into trillions of cells in just 9 months and also diversifying into hundreds of different types of cells which all find their place and begin working together as a unit. The whole process is very ordered and miraculous.

The human body is like an automobile with integrated systems and specialized parts all working together for a common purpose, enabling great function and ability. The 11 major systems of the body include: 1 – The Integumentary System, 2 – The Skeletal System, 3 – The Muscular System, 4 – The Nervous System, 5 – The Lymphatic System, 6 – The Cardiovascular System or The Circulatory System, 7 – The Respiratory System, 8 – The Digestive System, 9 – The Urinary System, 10 – The Reproductive System, and 11 – The Endocrine System.

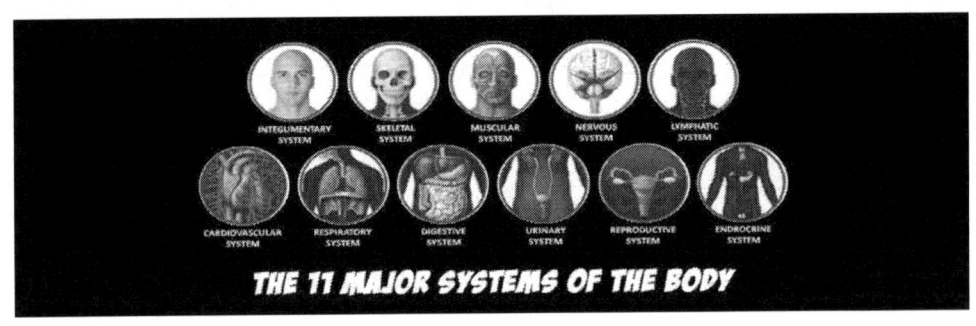

Consider these facts about various systems and parts within the human body. Note how each of these facts reveals evidence of design! None of it looks like it is the result of random processes and chance!

**Skeletal System** – _____ bones which vary greatly in size, shape and appearance all placed precisely in the body as needed and connected to each other and to the proper muscles by ligaments and tendons. Places where bones connect to other bones are covered with a padding material called cartilage. Connecting points within the skeletal system are called joints. We have various types of joints such as pivot joints, hinge joints, and ball and socket joints. Within the red bone marrow are red blood cell factories which produce 100 billion new red blood cells per day!

**Muscular System** – _____ skeletal muscles which are connected to our bones and give us tremendous structural stability, mobility and strength. We also have cardio muscles in our heart and smooth muscles in our organs which function involuntarily without conscious decisions on our part every moment of our lives.

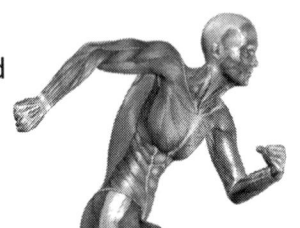

**Nervous System** – 7 trillion nerves which span 65,000 – 90,000 miles of sensation and carry messages at speeds up to 250 miles per hour. Our nervous system causes our heart to beat 35 million times per year, our eyes to blink 10 million times per year, the pupils of our eyes to dilate, our bladder to contract and relax. This system also signals for stomach secretions, saliva flow and much more. The control center for the nervous system is the human brain. Though our brain weighs only about 3 pounds it is considered to be the most sophisticated machine in the entire universe. Our brain contains 100 billion neurons and trillions of connecting points called synapses. Our brain processes 100,000 pieces of information per second, most of which are accomplished without us even being conscious of it! Some researchers have concluded that the human brain is more complex than an entire universe! Remember that this system is a communication system that is carrying coded messages and signals which control of our body's functions!

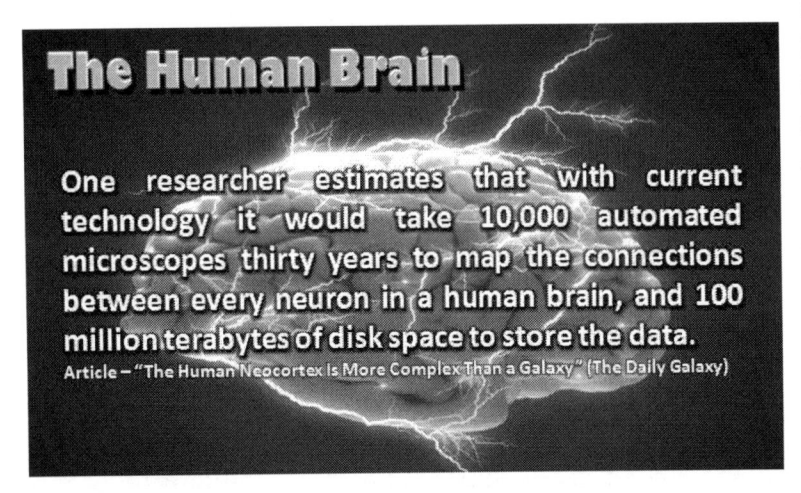

**The Human Brain**

One researcher estimates that with current technology it would take 10,000 automated microscopes thirty years to map the connections between every neuron in a human brain, and 100 million terabytes of disk space to store the data.
Article – "The Human Neocortex Is More Complex Than a Galaxy" (The Daily Galaxy)

**Cardiovascular (or Circulatory) System** - Our circulatory system involves enough blood vessels that if we could connect them all end to end they would be able to stretch 60,000 miles, which would wrap around the world 2 ½ times. Our heart will pump enough blood in an average lifetime to fill a train of tanker cars 25 miles long. The 4 valves in our heart are paper thin, yet strong enough to open and close successfully for 70 years or more, opening and closing about _____ _____ times. The greatest minds in the world have never been able to improve upon the design of the human heart!

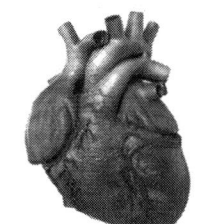

**Respiratory System** - Our respiratory system is designed to continually bring in needed oxygen from the outside world and filter the incoming air to protect us from harmful influences. One of the miraculous things about the respiratory system takes place within the walls of our lungs. With every breath that we take an amazing process must take place or we would die. Tiny sacs called "alveoli" in the walls of our lungs work with the tiny capillaries surrounding them to exchange oxygen molecules that are needed within the body and carbon dioxide molecules which are waste materials that need to be exhaled. Red blood cells in the tiny capillaries surrounding the alveoli release the carbon dioxide molecules through the membrane shared by the capillaries and the alveolus. At the same time oxygen molecules pass through the membrane and attach to hemoglobin proteins within the red blood cells as they pass by. It is like little rafts picking up needed cargo as they pass by and continue to the heart and on to other parts of the body. The average human lung has _____ _____ alveoli with a combined inner surface area that is about the same size as half of a full-size tennis court. That's 40 times the surface area of a person's skin! Amazing! This process occurs with every breath that we take throughout our lifetime without us even thinking about it.

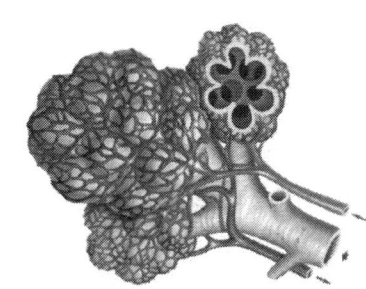

**Digestive System** – Our digestive system is so efficient that when we eat a meal the food is broken down into Amino Acids, Carbohydrates, Fatty Acids, Minerals and Vitamins that are absorbed into our blood stream for use throughout the body. Think about that! The details are amazing but just the basic process is marvelous to think about, a system that is so effective, it transforms food into molecular elements to nourish the body. All of this without us having to consciously do anything to accomplish it.

Consider this one design aspect of a part of the digestive system. it is within the small intestines that digested food is absorbed into the blood stream. For this to occur a lot of surface area is needed, covered with tiny blood capillaries. Our small intestine is about 23 feet long and based on its diameter should have an inner surface area of about 6 square feet. This would not be anywhere near enough to accomplish the task of absorbing food nutrients into the blood stream. So, God designed the inner wall of the small intestines in such a way so as to produce much more surface area. How much more? Instead of 6 square feet the surface area is about 2,700 square feet!!! How can this be you might ask? The inner wall of the small intestines is covered with finger like structures called "villi". These produce a lot more surface area. We have about _____ "villi" per square inch of the inner wall of our small intestines. This is still not enough to produce the surface area needed. So, on the entire surface of the "villi" we have hair like structures called "microvilli". It is estimated that we have about 130 billion "microvilli" per square inch of the inner wall of our small intestines. This produces the massive amount of surface area needed! Now there's some design work!!!

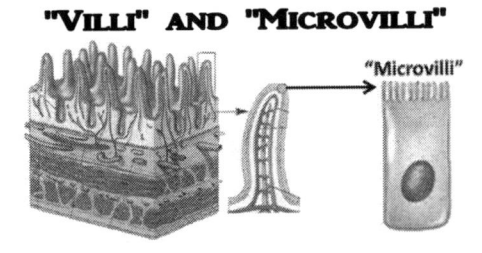

**Liver** – Some doctors think the liver may be the most amazing organ within the human body. The liver performs over _____ vital functions for the body. The liver is filled with thousands of processing plants called "Lobules" which process the food nutrients once they are absorbed into the blood.

**Kidneys** – Our kidneys filter our blood about _____ times per day, removing impurities and keeping our blood clean and healthy. This is accomplished by sophisticated filtering plants called "Nephrons". We have approximately 1 million Nephrons in each of our kidneys! Look at this picture here and ask yourself if this looks like something that has randomly come about or if it looks like something that is designed. The answer is easy isn't it? (* One million of these structures per kidney!!!)

**The Human Eye** – The human eyes has over 2 million working parts and over 10 million nerve cells which are continually interacting. One researcher has estimated that it would take super computers 100 years to simulate what takes place every second within the human eye. The efficiency of the eye is staggering. Consider this statement from a recent study on the human eye. "The basic building blocks of human eyesight turn out to be practically perfect. Scientists have learned that the fundamental units of vision, the photoreceptor cells that carpet the retinal tissue of the eye and respond to light, are not just good or great or fabulous at their job. They are not merely exceptionally impressive by the standards of biology, with whatever slop and wiggle room the animate category implies. Photoreceptors operate at the outermost boundary allowed by the laws of physics, which means they are as good as they can be, period."

**The Human Ear** – The human ear is so sophisticated that it is able to take sound waves, which are simply the movement of air molecules, and turn them into intelligible sounds. The moving air molecules hit the ear drum and cause a vibration. The vibration is amplified in the middle ear by 3 tiny bones working together. The amplified vibration is transferred into the liquid of the inner ear where multitudes of tiny hair like structures called cilia are found. These cilia vary in length to account for various frequencies. Movement in the liquid causes the cilia to move back and forth. For high frequencies cilia may move as much as 20,000 times per second. Each cilia has a trap door by it and a _____ attached to the cilia and the trap door. When the cilia moves the trap door is opened and closed allowing ions to enter. This creates electronic signals which are sent to the brain. The brain interprets the signals and allows us to not only hear noise, but to know what the noise is in minute detail. Wow! Think about that for a bit. You may want to experiment by closing your eyes and making note of how much detail you can discern just through hearing! We should give God praise for our abilities to see and hear!

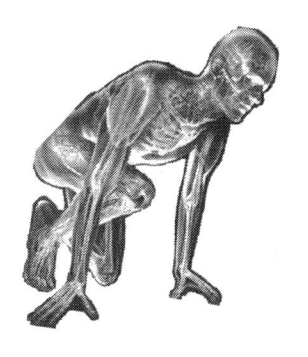

# The Human Body is The Most Amazing Machine in the Universe!!!

## #6 - The Microscopic World
### (Design Features in Extremely Tiny Creatures and Structures)

* The simplest life forms known are single celled bacteria. Amazingly, even here we find tremendous design features. Bacteria move about by a spinning tail called a "flagellum". The Bacterial Flagellum is like a rotary motor and has _____ different parts that are all necessary for the flagellum to work. This certainly shows evidence of design. Some scientists have pointed to this type of molecular machine with multiple parts that are all critical to the function of the machine as examples of "irreducible complexity". This means that if you remove any one of the parts (reducing the complexity) the machine could no longer work. This shows that it could not have evolved part by part. All the parts had to be there, functioning properly, at the same time for the machine to function and the creature to continue to live. If the complexity of the structure were less in the past the creature would have become extinct before the structure could evolve.

## #7 - The Human Cell
### (100 Trillion Cells within the Human Body)

* Cells are the structures upon which life is built.

* Each cell is like a miniature _____ with manufacturing plants, power plants, transportation systems, a postal service, quality control systems, security systems, communication systems, etc. (There are billions of parts functioning together for these tiny, living cells to function.

* Dr. Linus Pauling is widely considered the greatest chemist of the 20th Century. He made this amazing statement concerning the human cell. **"Just one living cell in the human body is more complex than _____ _____ _____."** This is truly remarkable!

* Dr. Michael Denton has made a similar observation concerning the complexity of the cell. "To grasp the reality of life as it has been revealed by molecular biology, we must magnify a cell a thousand million times until it is twenty kilometers in diameter and resembles a giant airship large enough to cover a great city like London or New York. What we would then see would be an object of unparalleled complexity and adaptive design ... we would find ourselves in a world of supreme technology and bewildering complexity." How could anyone look at this amount of complexity and technology and believe that it is the result of an explosion, followed by random, unguided processes?

*Even though living cells are extremely detailed and complicated, the human body produces billions of new cells every day.

* Human cells are examples of "Integrated Complexity", "_____ Complexity" or "_____ Complexity". This speaks of the fact that there are not just complex parts, but these parts must all be placed in the proper place and must be fulfilling their specific functions in order for the cell to function. Another example we view in life of "Integrated Complexity" is a jumbo jet. The jet contains millions of parts, none of which can fly. Yet when all the parts are integrated properly together, the entire jet can fly as it is designed to do.

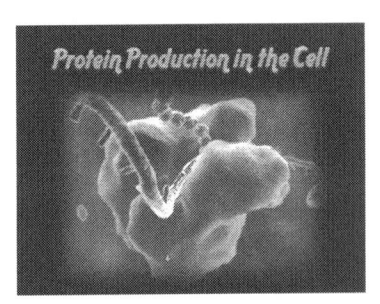

* Protein Production Within the Cell – On average, each of the 100 trillion cells of your body produce about _____ proteins per second. The process of is very complex and it involves the linking of hundreds of amino acids in the right order to produce one protein. The proteins that are produced have to be packaged, labeled and carried to the proper location for use. (Think for a while about the amazing process of the production of a protein that is directed by coded information in the DNA and carried out by specifically designed molecular machines. Any honest viewing of this leads to the conclusion that an intelligent designer has created these things.)

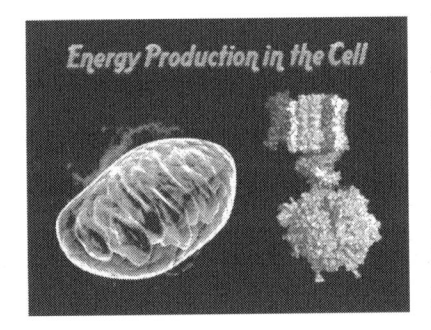

* Energy production in the cell – Approximately ___ _____ ATP molecules, which are like recharged batteries are produce on average in each of your cells per second. This process involves ATP Synthase Rotary Machines which are amazing nanoscale machines. These machines rotate at approximately _____ rpms and add a phosphate to ADP molecules to turn them into ATP molecules which are like recharged batteries. The machinery involved in this process has been called one of the wonders of the molecular world.

The human cell may very well be the greatest evidence of creation that we can view in the universe. Darwin thought that life at the cellular level was very simple. We now know that is not at all the case. The complexity and grandeur of the cell cannot be explained by random processes. The evidence for a designer is overwhelming!!!

## #8 - DNA within the Nucleus of the Human (or Living) Cell

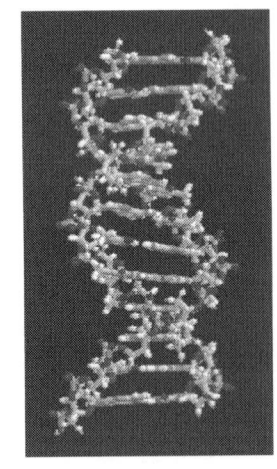

* DNA is the densest information storage system known in the universe! DNA is like a computer software program. Bill Gates has acknowledged this and stated that DNA is far more sophisticated than anything man has ever been able to design.

* All the development of life and functions of the human cell are directed by the usable, ordered information found within DNA.

**"Blueprint"**
(Instructions for Building)

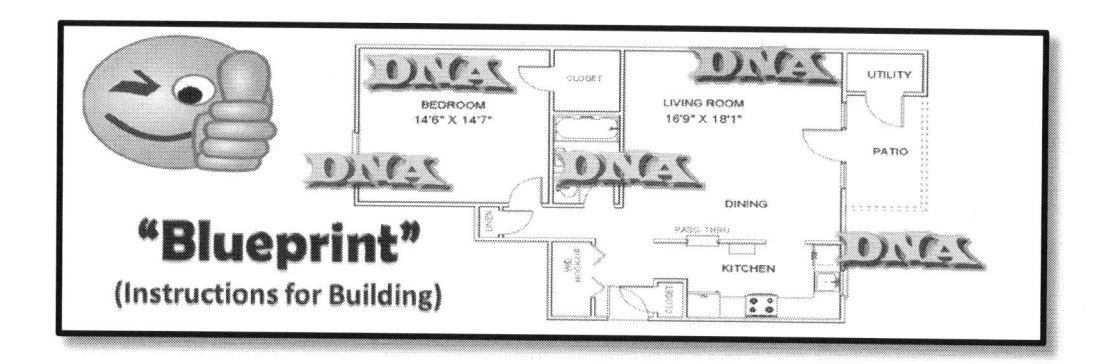

\* It is estimated that there is enough information in a pinhead of DNA to fill a stack of books _____ times higher that from the earth to the moon.

\* DNA clearly shows that all life is directed by coded _____ and is tremendous evidence that life has been designed by a tremendously wise and powerful person, God! Every book has an author and every computer software program has a programmer. Usable, coded information does not come from unintelligent matter. Usable, coded information comes from a source of intelligence!

\* Just as a simple message in the sand like "I love you" clearly indicates that a person with intelligence was present to write the message in the sand, DNA clearly indicates that God was present to give the blueprint information for life to exist and function.

**Summary of the 8 areas of Scientific Evidence that Confirms There is a Creator – God!**

## From Biggest to Smallest

1. The Universe (Finely Tuned)
2. The Solar System (Perfectly Ordered)
3. The Earth (Precisely Tuned to Be Inhabited)
4. Living Creatures (Design Features)
5. The Human Body (Design Features)
6. The Microscopic World (Irreducible Complexity)(Design Features)
7. The Human Cell (Amazing Design & Function)
8. DNA (Usable, Ordered (Coded) Information)

**Chance** – "The absence of any known reason why an event should turn out one way rather than another" – "fortune", "fate", "luck"   *(The American College Dictionary – Random House)*

**Design** – "To plan and fashion artistically or skillfully" 2. "To intend for a definite purpose" 3. "To form or conceive in the mind; Contrive; plan"   *(The American College Dictionary – Random House)*

*Note these definitions – Which describes what we see in living things & in the entire universe?*

55

# EVIDENCES OF A CREATOR - GOD

## Design & Information (From Biggest to Smallest)

(1) Finely Tuned Universe!
(2) Our Solar System!
(3) The Earth!
(4) The Earth!
(5) Living Creatures!
(6) The Human Body (1)
(7) The Human Body (2)
(8) Microscopic World!
(9) The Human Cell (1)
(10) The Human Cell (2)
(11) Information (DNA) (1)
(12) Information (DNA) (2)

* A Reminder – Free Memory Cards can be downloaded at localchurchapologetics.org

**The foundation of all Christian faith is the understanding that we are created by God in His image and likeness. (Genesis 1:26-28) He has given us much evidence to confirm this truth! We are called to be ready to give a defense to those who ask about the hope within us!**

* We need to strengthen our own faith by knowing the evidence that confirms our faith!

* We need to be ready to help other (especially young people) by knowing the evidence that confirms our Christian Faith!

# FAITH & REASON MADE SIMPLE — Part 4

## (Scientific Evidence That Confirms God Created Us (Cont.))

### #5 - The Human Body (Amazingly Designed)

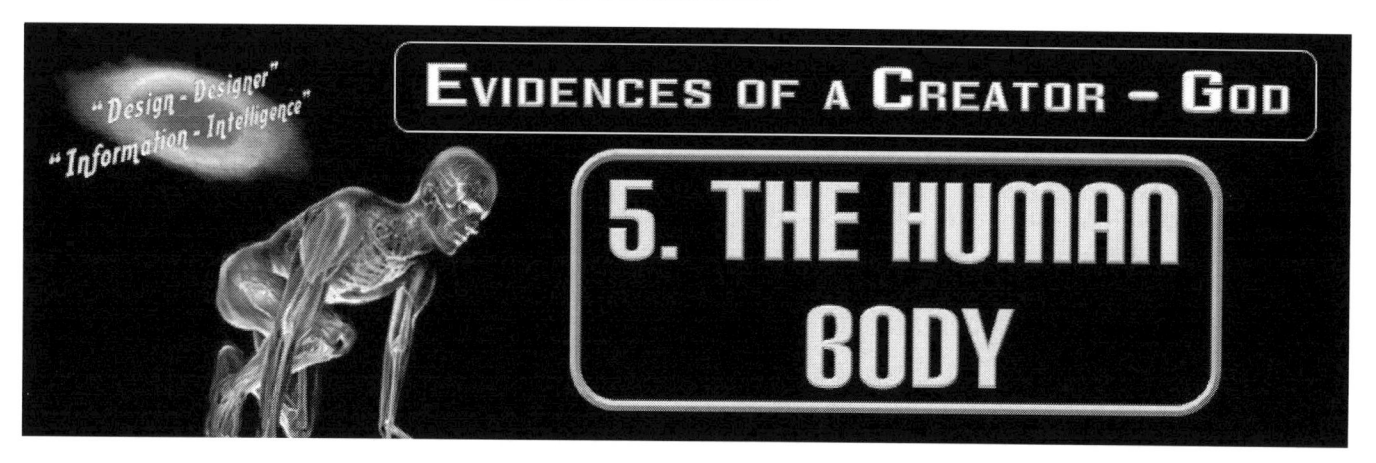

**EVIDENCES OF A CREATOR - GOD**
"Design - Designer" "Information - Intelligence"

**5. THE HUMAN BODY**

> Psalms 139:13-17 NASB  For You formed my inward parts; You wove me in my mother's womb. (14) I will give thanks to You, for I am fearfully and wonderfully made; Wonderful are Your works, And my soul knows it very well. (15) My frame was not hidden from You, When I was made in secret, And skillfully wrought in the depths of the earth; (16) Your eyes have seen my unformed substance; And in Your book were all written The days that were ordained for me, When as yet there was not one of them. (17) How precious also are Your thoughts to me, O God! How vast is the sum of them!

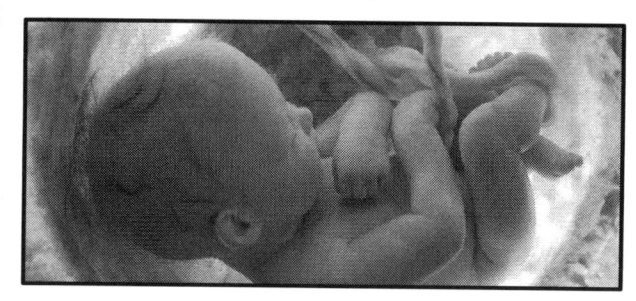

The Bible informs us that God formed each of us in our mother's womb. The descriptions of this found in Psalm 139 reveal an intimacy between God and each person He has created. He knows us and cares for us! A brief examination of the birth process and of the structures and functions of the human body will give us tremendous evidence to confirm that we are created by God, with purpose and value! Nothing about the human body looks like it is the result of random processes and chance. It clearly looks as though it is wonderfully designed!

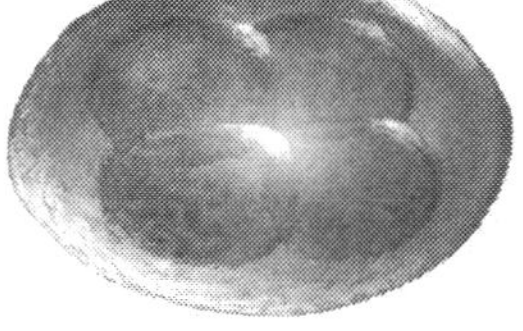

* Development of a human baby in the womb – Think about the miracle of one cell (called a zygote) multiplying into trillions of cells in just 9 months and also diversifying into hundreds of different types of cells which all find their place and begin working together as a unit. The whole process is very ordered and miraculous.

The human body is like an automobile with integrated systems and specialized parts all working together for a common purpose, enabling great function and ability. The 11 major systems of the body include: 1 – The Integumentary System, 2 – The Skeletal System, 3 – The Muscular System, 4 – The Nervous System, 5 – The Lymphatic System, 6 – The Cardiovascular System or The Circulatory System, 7 – The Respiratory System, 8 – The Digestive System, 9 – The Urinary System, 10 – The Reproductive System, and 11 – The Endocrine System.

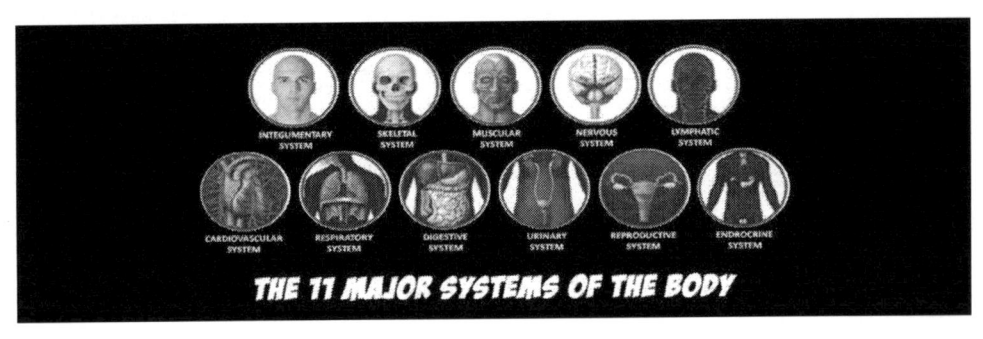

Consider these facts about various systems and parts within the human body. Note how each of these facts reveals evidence of design! None of it looks like it is the result of random processes and chance!

**Skeletal System** – **206** bones which vary greatly in size, shape and appearance all placed precisely in the body as needed and connected to each other and to the proper muscles by ligaments and tendons. Places where bones connect to other bones are covered with a padding material called cartilage. Connecting points within the skeletal system are called joints. We have various types of joints such as pivot joints, hinge joints, and ball and socket joints. Within the red bone marrow are red blood cell factories which produce 100 billion new red blood cells per day!

**Muscular System** – **650** skeletal muscles which are connected to our bones and give us tremendous structural stability, mobility and strength. We also have cardio muscles in our heart and smooth muscles in our organs which function involuntarily without conscious decisions on our part every moment of our lives.

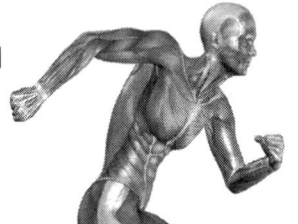

**Nervous System** – 7 trillion nerves which span 65,000 – 90,000 miles of sensation and carry messages at speeds up to 250 miles per hour. Our nervous system causes our heart to beat 35 million times per year, our eyes to blink 10 million times per year, the pupils of our eyes to dilate, our bladder to contract and relax. This system also signals for stomach secretions, saliva flow and much more. The control center for the nervous system is the human brain. Though our brain weighs only about 3 pounds it is considered to be the most sophisticated machine in the entire universe. Our brain contains 100 billion neurons and trillions of connecting points called synapses. Our brain processes 100,000 pieces of information per second, most of which are accomplished without us even being conscious of it! Some researchers have concluded that the human brain is more complex than an entire universe! Remember that this system is a communication system that is carrying coded messages and signals which control of our body's functions!

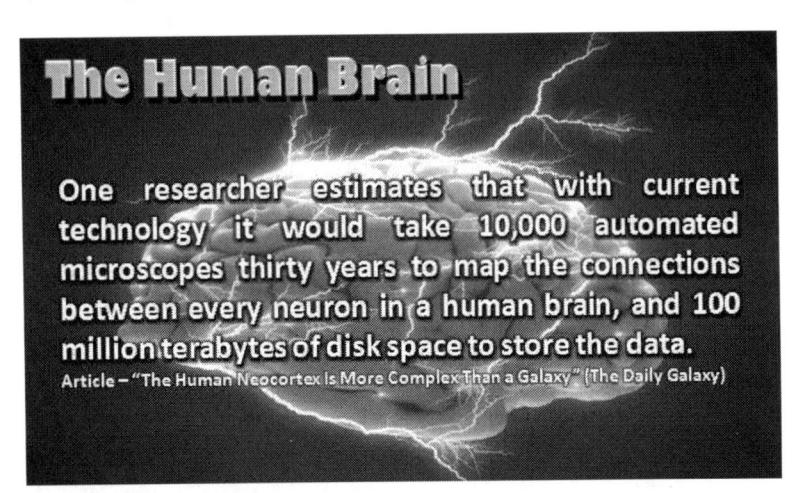

**Cardiovascular (or Circulatory) System** - Our circulatory system involves enough blood vessels that if we could connect them all end to end they would be able to stretch 60,000 miles, which would wrap around the world 2 ½ times. Our heart will pump enough blood in an average lifetime to fill a train of tanker cars 25 miles long. The 4 valves in our heart are paper thin, yet strong enough to open and close successfully for 70 years or more, opening and closing about **2.5 billion** times. The greatest minds in the world have never been able to improve upon the design of the human heart!

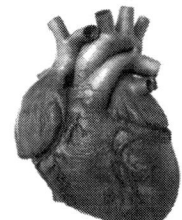

**Respiratory System** - Our respiratory system is designed to continually bring in needed oxygen from the outside world and filter the incoming air to protect us from harmful influences. One of the miraculous things about the respiratory system takes place within the walls of our lungs. With every breath that we take an amazing process must take place or we would die. Tiny sacs called "alveoli" in the walls of our lungs work with the tiny capillaries surrounding them to exchange oxygen molecules that are needed within the body and carbon dioxide molecules which are waste materials that need to be exhaled. Red blood cells in the tiny capillaries surrounding the alveoli release the carbon dioxide molecules through the membrane shared by the capillaries and the alveolus. At the same time oxygen molecules pass through the membrane and attach to hemoglobin proteins within the red blood cells as they pass by. It is like little rafts picking up needed cargo as they pass by and continue to the heart and on to other parts of the body. The average human lung has **300-500 million** alveoli with a combined inner surface area that is about the same size as half of a full-size tennis court. That's 40 times the surface area of a person's skin! Amazing! This process occurs with every breath that we take throughout our lifetime without us even thinking about it.

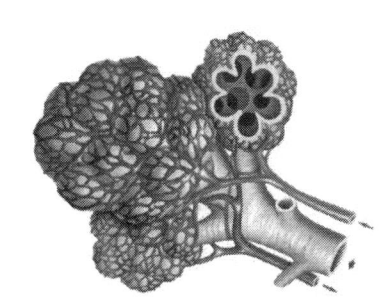

**Digestive System** – Our digestive system is so efficient that when we eat a meal the food is broken down into Amino Acids, Carbohydrates, Fatty Acids, Minerals and Vitamins that are absorbed into our blood stream for use throughout the body. Think about that! The details are amazing but just the basic process is marvelous to think about, a system that is so effective, it transforms food into molecular elements to nourish the body. All of this without us having to consciously do anything to accomplish it.

Consider this one design aspect of a part of the digestive system. it is within the small intestines that digested food is absorbed into the blood stream. For this to occur a lot of surface area is needed, covered with tiny blood capillaries. Our small intestine is about 23 feet long and based on its diameter should have an inner surface area of about 6 square feet. This would not be anywhere near enough to accomplish the task of absorbing food nutrients into the blood stream. So, God designed the inner wall of the small intestines in such a way so as to produce much more surface area. How much more? Instead of 6 square feet the surface area is about 2,700 square feet!!! How can this be you might ask? The inner wall of the small intestines is covered with finger like structures called "villi". These produce a lot more surface area. We have about **20,000** "villi" per square inch of the inner wall of our small intestines. This is still not enough to produce the surface area needed. So, on the entire surface of the "villi" we have hair like structures called "microvilli". It is estimated that we have about 130 billion "microvilli" per square inch of the inner wall of our small intestines. This produces the massive amount of surface area needed! Now there's some design work!!!

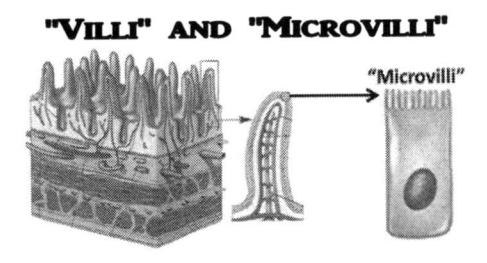

**"VILLI" AND "MICROVILLI"**

**Liver** – Some doctors think the liver may be the most amazing organ within the human body. The liver performs over **500** vital functions for the body. The liver is filled with thousands of processing plants called "Lobules" which process the food nutrients once they are absorbed into the blood.

**Kidneys** – Our kidneys filter our blood about **400** times per day, removing impurities and keeping our blood clean and healthy. This is accomplished by sophisticated filtering plants called "Nephrons". We have approximately 1 million Nephrons in each of our kidneys! Look at this picture here and ask yourself if this looks like something that has randomly come about or if it looks like something that is designed. The answer is easy isn't it? (* One million of these structures per kidney!!!)

**The Human Eye** – The human eyes has over 2 million working parts and over 10 million nerve cells which are continually interacting. One researcher has estimated that it would take super computers 100 years to simulate what takes place every second within the human eye. The efficiency of the eye is staggering. Consider this statement from a recent study on the human eye. "The basic building blocks of human eyesight turn out to be practically perfect. Scientists have learned that the fundamental units of vision, the photoreceptor cells that carpet the retinal tissue of the eye and respond to light, are not just good or great or fabulous at their job. They are not merely exceptionally impressive by the standards of biology, with whatever slop and wiggle room the animate category implies. Photoreceptors operate at the outermost boundary allowed by the laws of physics, which means they are as good as they can be, period."

**The Human Ear** – The human ear is so sophisticated that it is able to take sound waves, which are simply the movement of air molecules, and turn them into intelligible sounds. The moving air molecules hit the ear drum and cause a vibration. The vibration is amplified in the middle ear by 3 tiny bones working together. The amplified vibration is transferred into the liquid of the inner ear where multitudes of tiny hair like structures called cilia are found. These cilia vary in length to account for various frequencies. Movement in the liquid causes the cilia to move back and forth. For high frequencies cilia may move as much as 20,000 times per second. Each cilia has a trap door by it and a **spring** attached to the cilia and the trap door. When the cilia moves the trap door is opened and closed allowing ions to enter. This creates electronic signals which are sent to the brain. The brain interprets the signals and allows us to not only hear noise, but to know what the noise is in minute detail. Wow! Think about that for a bit. You may want to experiment by closing your eyes and making note of how much detail you can discern just through hearing! We should give God praise for our abilities to see and hear!

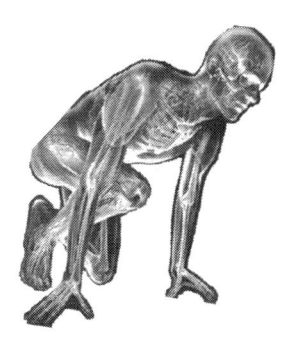

# The Human Body is The Most Amazing Machine in the Universe!!!

## #6 - The Microscopic World
### (Design Features in Extremely Tiny Creatures and Structures)

* The simplest life forms known are single celled bacteria. Amazingly, even here we find tremendous design features. Bacteria move about by a spinning tail called a "flagellum". The Bacterial Flagellum is like a rotary motor and has **40** different parts that are all necessary for the flagellum to work. This certainly shows evidence of design. Some scientists have pointed to this type of molecular machine with multiple parts that are all critical to the function of the machine as examples of "irreducible complexity". This means that if you remove any one of the parts (reducing the complexity) the machine could no longer work. This shows that it could not have evolved part by part. All the parts had to be there, functioning properly, at the same time for the machine to function and the creature to continue to live. If the complexity of the structure were less in the past the creature would have become extinct before the structure could evolve.

## #7 - The Human Cell
### (100 Trillion Cells within the Human Body)

* Cells are the structures upon which life is built.

* Each cell is like a miniature **city** with manufacturing plants, power plants, transportation systems, a postal service, quality control systems, security systems, communication systems, etc. (There are billions of parts functioning together for these tiny, living cells to function.

* Dr. Linus Pauling is widely considered the greatest chemist of the 20th Century. He made this amazing statement concerning the human cell. **"Just one living cell in the human body is more complex than New York City."** This is truly remarkable!

* Dr. Michael Denton has made a similar observation concerning the complexity of the cell. "To grasp the reality of life as it has been revealed by molecular biology, we must magnify a cell a thousand million times until it is twenty kilometers in diameter and resembles a giant airship large enough to cover a great city like London or New York. What we would then see would be an object of unparalleled complexity and adaptive design ... we would find ourselves in a world of supreme technology and bewildering complexity." How could anyone look at this amount of complexity and technology and believe that it is the result of an explosion, followed by random, unguided processes?

*Even though living cells are extremely detailed and complicated, the human body produces billions of new cells every day.

* Human cells are examples of "Integrated Complexity", "**Specified** Complexity" or "**Ordered** Complexity". This speaks of the fact that there are not just complex parts, but these parts must all be placed in the proper place and must be fulfilling their specific functions in order for the cell to function. Another example we view in life of "Integrated Complexity" is a jumbo jet. The jet contains millions of parts, none of which can fly. Yet when all the parts are integrated properly together, the entire jet can fly as it is designed to do.

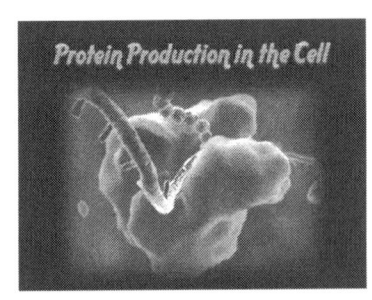

* Protein Production Within the Cell – On average, each of the 100 trillion cells of your body produce about **2,000** proteins per second. The process of is very complex and it involves the linking of hundreds of amino acids in the right order to produce one protein. The proteins that are produced have to be packaged, labeled and carried to the proper location for use. (Think for a while about the amazing process of the production of a protein that is directed by coded information in the DNA and carried out by specifically designed molecular machines. Any honest viewing of this leads to the conclusion that an intelligent designer has created these things.)

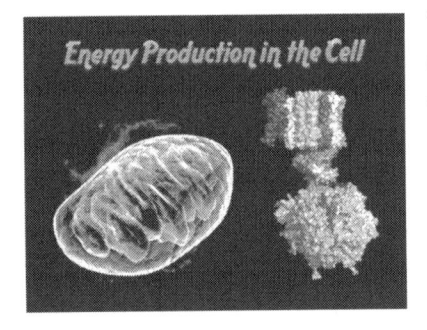

* Energy production in the cell – Approximately **10 million** ATP molecules, which are like recharged batteries are produce on average in each of your cells per second. This process involves ATP Synthase Rotary Machines which are amazing nanoscale machines. These machines rotate at approximately **1,000** rpms and add a phosphate to ADP molecules to turn them into ATP molecules which are like recharged batteries. The machinery involved in this process has been called one of the wonders of the molecular world.

The human cell may very well be the greatest evidence of creation that we can view in the universe. Darwin thought that life at the cellular level was very simple. We now know that is not at all the case. The complexity and grandeur of the cell cannot be explained by random processes. The evidence for a designer is overwhelming!!!

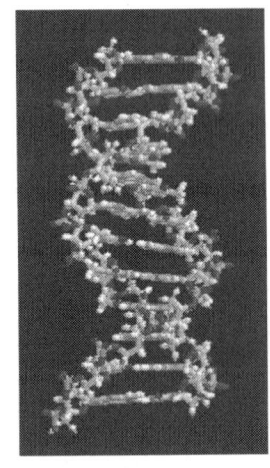

## #8 - DNA within the Nucleus of the Human (or Living) Cell

* DNA is the densest information storage system known in the universe! DNA is like a computer software program. Bill Gates has acknowledged this and stated that DNA is far more sophisticated than anything man has ever been able to design.

* All the development of life and functions of the human cell are directed by the usable, ordered information found within DNA.

**"Blueprint"**
(Instructions for Building)

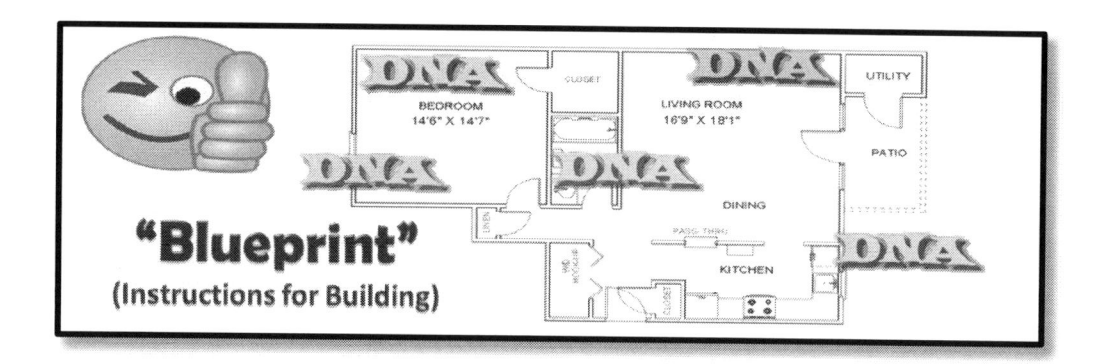

* It is estimated that there is enough information in a pinhead of DNA to fill a stack of books **500** times higher that from the earth to the moon.

* DNA clearly shows that all life is directed by coded **information** and is tremendous evidence that life has been designed by a tremendously wise and powerful person, God! Every book has an author and every computer software program has a programmer. Usable, coded information does not come from unintelligent matter. Usable, coded information comes from a source of intelligence!

* Just as a simple message in the sand like "I love you" clearly indicates that a person with intelligence was present to write the message in the sand, DNA clearly indicates that God was present to give the blueprint information for life to exist and function.

Summary of the 8 areas of Scientific Evidence that Confirms There is a Creator – God!

## From Biggest to Smallest

1. The Universe (Finely Tuned)
2. The Solar System (Perfectly Ordered)
3. The Earth (Precisely Tuned to Be Inhabited)
4. Living Creatures (Design Features)
5. The Human Body (Design Features)
6. The Microscopic World (Irreducible Complexity)(Design Features)
7. The Human Cell (Amazing Design & Function)
8. DNA (Usable, Ordered (Coded) Information)

**Chance** – "The absence of any known reason why an event should turn out one way rather than another" – "fortune", "fate", "luck"   (The American College Dictionary – Random House)

**Design** – "To plan and fashion artistically or skillfully" 2. "To intend for a definite purpose" 3. "To form or conceive in the mind; Contrive; plan"   (The American College Dictionary – Random House)

*Note these definitions – Which describes what we see in living things & in the entire universe?*

# Evidences of a Creator - God

## Design & Information (From Biggest to Smallest)

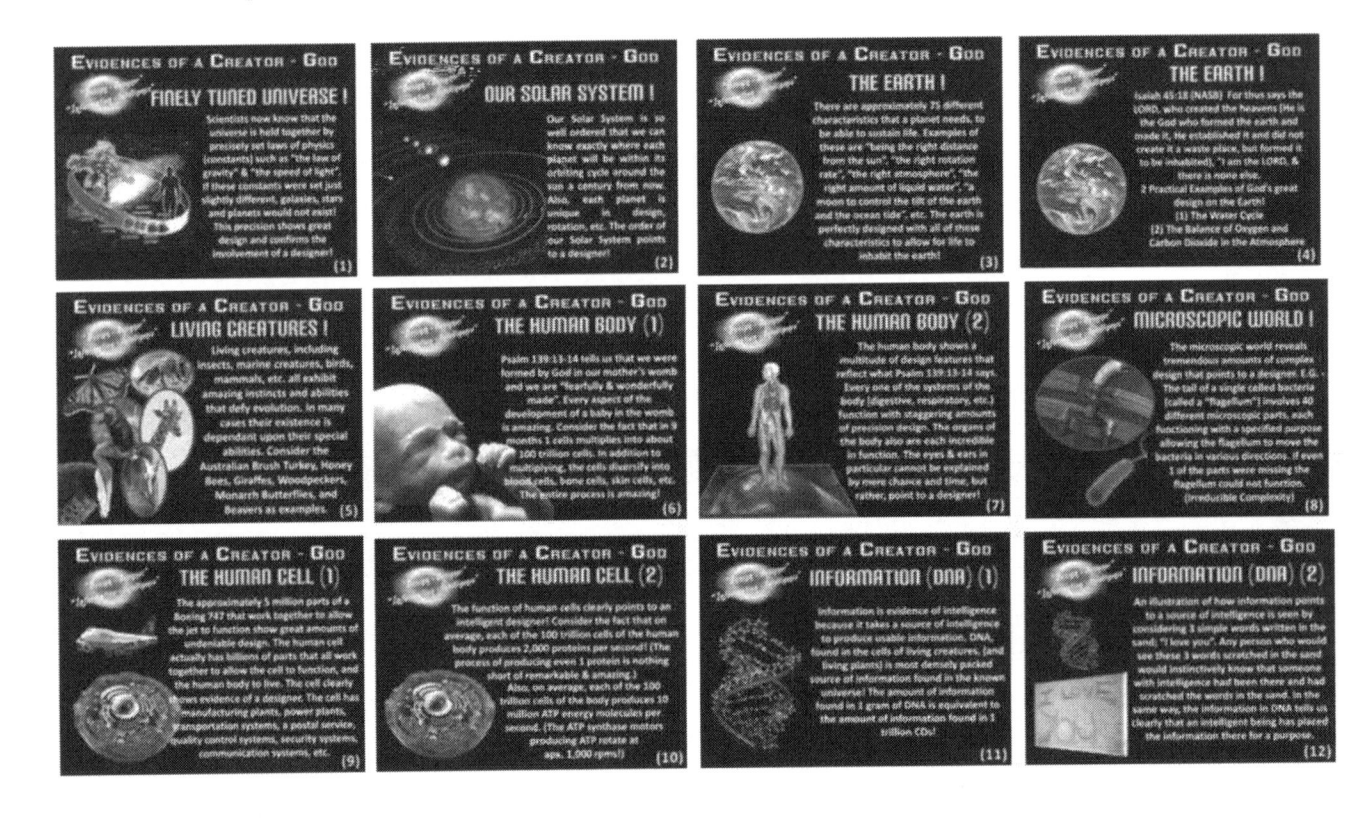

|  |  |  |  |
|---|---|---|---|
| (1) Finely Tuned Universe! | (2) Our Solar System! | (3) The Earth! | (4) The Earth! |
| (5) Living Creatures! | (6) The Human Body (1) | (7) The Human Body (2) | (8) Microscopic World! |
| (9) The Human Cell (1) | (10) The Human Cell (2) | (11) Information (DNA) (1) | (12) Information (DNA) (2) |

\* A Reminder – Free Memory Cards can be downloaded at localchurchapologetics.org

**The foundation of all Christian faith is the understanding that we are created by God in His image and likeness. (Genesis 1:26-28) He has given us much evidence to confirm this truth! We are called to be ready to give a defense to those who ask about the hope within us!**

   \* We need to strengthen our own faith by knowing the evidence that confirms our faith!

   \* We need to be ready to help other (especially young people) by knowing the evidence that confirms our Christian Faith!

# FAITH & REASON MADE SIMPLE — Part 5

## (Confirming Evidence That The Bible is The Word of God)

* When looking at the evidence that confirms the Bible is God's Word it is good to do so after looking at the evidence that confirms that God created us! Apologetics should be approached systematically starting with the issue of _____. Once we see the clear evidence that we are created by a wise, powerful and personal God, we would assume that He has spoken to us. Therefore we can begin our search for evidence that confirms the Bible to be God's Word with the expectation that God has given His Word to us so that we can know Him.

* As we have seen in previous sessions, God has revealed Himself through the things He has made (Romans 1:20). This type of revelation is called "_____ Revelation" or "Natural Revelation". In this type of revelation God reveals His existence and characteristics about Himself. To reveal specific things about His plan for mankind God has given us "_____ Revelation" in two aspects. The Bible and the person of Jesus Christ (God come in the flesh) are the two aspects of _____ revelation.

> **2 Timothy 3:16 NASB** All Scripture is inspired by God and profitable for teaching, for reproof, for correction, for training in righteousness;

> **John 17:17 KJV** Sanctify them through thy truth: thy word is truth.

## Introduction

* Attacks on the Bible today! (Calling it Fiction) (Denying that it is God's Word) (Etc.)
   (Attacks upon the Bible are especially found in _____ across America)

> According to a 2006 study by sociologists Neil Gross (Harvard University) & Solon Simmons (George Mason University) *Only 6 percent of college professors said the Bible is —the actual word of God while 51 percent described it as —an ancient book of fables, legends, history and moral precepts.*

## Why Do You Believe the Bible is the Word of God?

It is important to take a moment to think about how you would answer this question if it were asked of you. Remember that 1 Peter 3:15 says that we are to always be ready to give and answer, or make a defense to those who ask about the hope that is in us.

Dr. Voddie Baucham was asked to consider this question while he attended Oxford University. Here is the answer he gave a professor there – "I choose to believe the Bible because it is a _____ collection of historical documents written down by _____ _____ during the lifetime of other eye witnesses. They report to us supernatural events that took place in fulfillment of specific prophecies and claim to be divine rather than human in origin."

Dr. Baucham's answer reveals an apologetic understanding of the issue behind the question. After my studies of these issues I would add this to Dr. Baucham's answer. "These events are confirmed by, and give us understanding of, other historical events and the _____ of the world today."

## Confirming Evidences – The Bible Is God's Word!

In this session and the next we will examine 8 areas of evidence that confirm to us that the Bible truly is the Word of God. The 8 areas of evidence are listed in the picture below. We will look at the first 4 areas in this session and the final four areas in session 6.

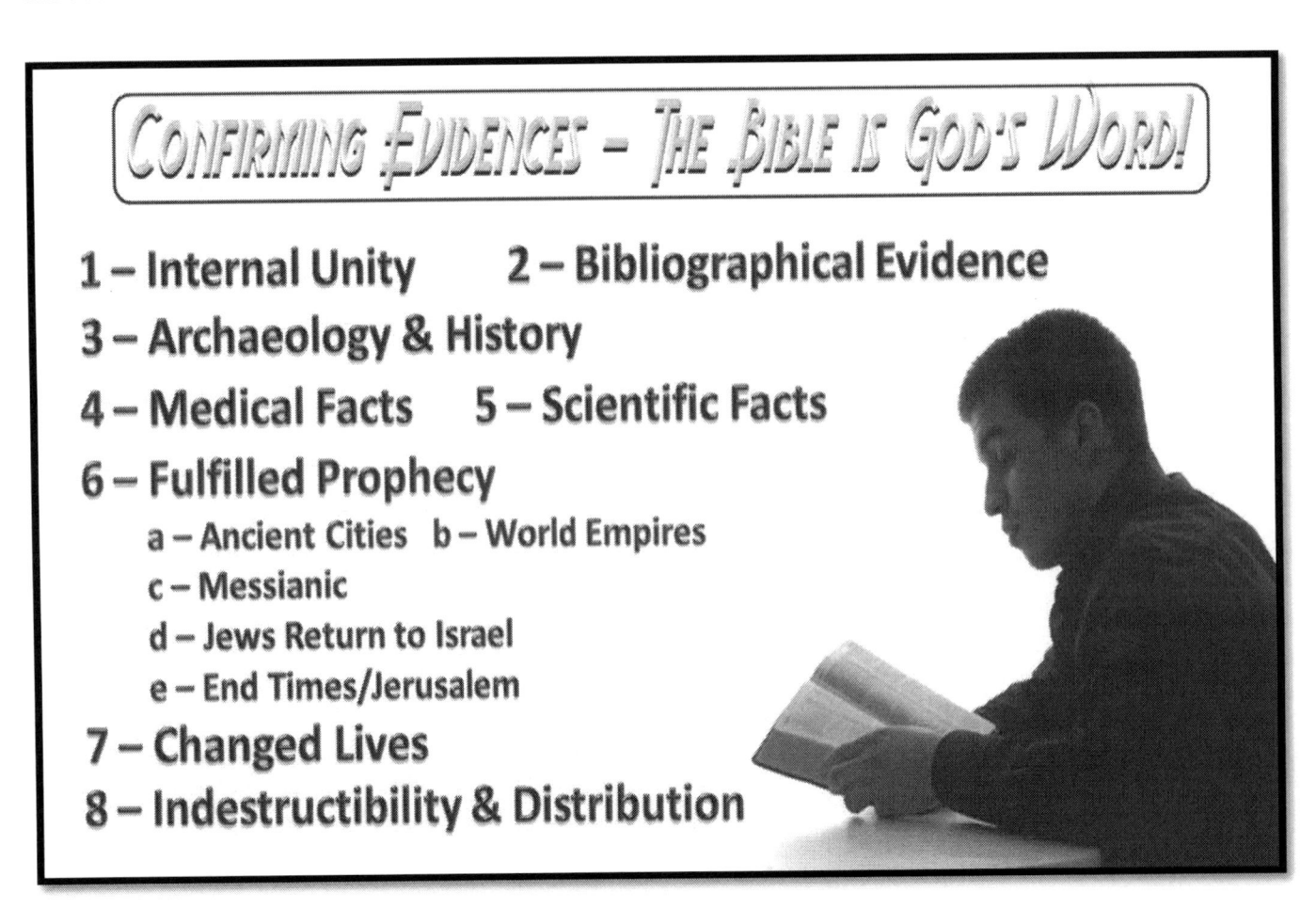

**Confirming Evidences – The Bible is God's Word!**

1 – Internal Unity
2 – Bibliographical Evidence
3 – Archaeology & History
4 – Medical Facts
5 – Scientific Facts
6 – Fulfilled Prophecy
   a – Ancient Cities   b – World Empires
   c – Messianic
   d – Jews Return to Israel
   e – End Times/Jerusalem
7 – Changed Lives
8 – Indestructibility & Distribution

## #1 – Internal Unity

### * Simple outline of the Bible's Message
A – God Created Mankind to Be His Sons and Daughters (Genesis 1-2)
B – Mankind Sinned and Was Separated From God (Results – Death & Corruption) (Gen. 3)
C – God Fulfilled His Plan to Redeem Mankind in Christ (Genesis 3 – Revelation 20)
D – All God Planned in Creation Is Eternally Restored in Christ (Revelation 21-22)

### * The Bible <u>Claims</u> to Be the Word of God!
* (2 Timothy 3:16) (John 17:17) (1 Peter 1:21)
* Over 2,600 times the phrase "God said" or its equivalent is found in the Bible

### * 40 Different Authors Over a 1,500 Year Period
* 40 different authors wrote from 3 different continents over a _____ year period of time in 3 different languages. Shepherds, kings, scholars, fishermen, prophets, a military general, a cupbearer, and a priest all penned portions of Scripture. From just this information we would expect the Bible to be a tangled mess, but it certainly is not. The message of the Bible is a clear, continual unfolding message of _____.
The more that this internal unity is examined the more remarkable it appears.

### * 400 Year Gap Between the Old & New Testaments
* Though there was an approximate 400 year gap between the Old & New Testaments, yet the connection between the two can be easily seen in many ways.
#### Examples include –
* Old Testament – The Law is Given and Emphasized
New Testament – The Law is Seen not as a Way to Salvation but as a Tutor to lead people to Christ Jesus for Salvation. (The Law shows us our need!)
* _____ (Genesis 14) (Hebrews 5-7 – The Priesthood of Jesus Christ)
* Abraham's _____ (Genesis 12-22) (Romans 4) (Galatians 3)
* Abraham Sacrifices Isaac (On Mt. Calvary) – (Genesis 22) (22:18) (Galatians 3:16)
* Prophecies of the coming of Elijah (Malachi 4) – John the Baptist (N. T. Beginnings)

## Claims of Sincerity & Truthfulness
In numerous places the authors of Scripture specifically indicate that they are sincerely and truthfully relating accurate historic information. Here a couple of examples.

Luke 1:1-4 NASB  Inasmuch as many have undertaken to compile an account of the things accomplished among us, (2) just as they were handed down to us by those who from the beginning were eyewitnesses and servants of the word, (3) it seemed fitting for me as well, having _____ everything _____ from the beginning, to write it out for you in consecutive order, most excellent Theophilus; (4) so that you may know the exact truth about the things you have been taught.

1 Thessalonians 2:3-5 NASB  (3)  For our exhortation does not come from _____ or _____ or by way of deceit; (4) but just as we have been approved by God to be entrusted with the gospel, so we speak, not as pleasing men, but God who examines our hearts.  (5)  For we never came with flattering speech, as you know, nor with a pretext for greed--God is witness--

## * Many <u>Types & Shadows</u> in the Old Testament point to Jesus Christ of the N.T.
* Passover Lamb    * Ark    * Scapegoat    * Rahab's Scarlet Cord    * Brazen _____
* Melchizedek    * Sin & Guilt Offerings    * Moses/Joshua – The Promise Land
* Manna (Bread from Heaven) (John 6)    * Water from the Rock  (1 Corinthians 10:4)

**REPHIDIM (In Modern Saudi Arabia)**
Smite the Rock – Ex. 17:6
Speak to the Rock – Num. 20:8
*Water From The Rock*

## * Over 300 Old Testament Prophecies Fulfilled by Jesus in the New Testament
This point will be covered in more detail in a later session but with relationship to the internal unity of the Bible it is important to note that over 300 prophecies that were written in the Old Testament about the coming Messiah were fulfilled hundreds of years later in the person of Jesus Christ. These fulfillments are recorded in the New Testament.

## * <u>Embarrassing</u> Testimony
The significance of this is that anyone attempting to make up a religion would not record embarrassing events and actions in the lives of the stars of the documents being written. The Bible is filled with true life events that show the worst moments in the lives of its star characters. This reveals that the Bible is not a manmade document but a true, historic record given to us by God.

**Embarrassing Testimony**

| | | |
|---|---|---|
| Adam & Eve (Sin) | Joseph's Brothers | Birth of Jesus (Humble) |
| Cain & Abel (Murder) | Judah (Prostitution) | Disciples (Greatest?) |
| Noah (Drunk) | Israel (Murmers) | Disciples (Afraid at Sea) |
| Abraham (Lying) | Moses (Angry) | Peter (Rebuked 2x) |
| Jacob (Deception) | Israel (Rebellion) | Peter (Denied Jesus) |
| | Samson (Lust) | Disciples (Sleeping) |
| | Eli's & Samuel's Sons | Disciples (Fleeing) |
| | David (Adultery/Murder) | Crucifixion |
| | Jesus' Genealogy | Women Witnesses |

# #2 – Bibliographical Evidence

* Many critics claim that the Bibles we read today do not communicate the same message as the original writings did. They say that the Bible has been corrupted through the centuries. Bibliographical evidence deals with this issue. Bibliographical evidence examines the number of manuscript copies that are available and looks at the amount of time between the original writings and the oldest known manuscript copies available. The more manuscript copies and the closer they are in time to the originals, the more trustworthy the documents are that come from them.

* Note the comparison between the New Testament manuscript copies compared to other famous writings of _____. Other ancient writings are trusted.

| Author | Written | Earliest Copies | Time Span | # of copies |
|---|---|---|---|---|
| Caesar | 100-44 B.C. | A.D. 900 | 1,000 yrs. | 10 |
| Plato (Tetralogies) | 427-347 B.C. | A.D. 900 | 1,200 yrs. | 7 |
| Thucydides | 460-400 B.C. | A.D. 900 | 1,300 yrs. | 8 |
| Sophocles | 496-406 B.C. | A.D. 1,000 | 1,400 yrs. | 100 |
| Catullus | 54 B.C. | A.D. 1,550 | 1,600 yrs. | 3 |
| Euripides | 480-406 B.C. | A.D. 1,100 | 1,500 yrs. | 9 |
| Aristotle | 384-322 B.C. | A.D. 1,100 | 1,400 yrs. | 5 |
| THE SECOND RUNNER UP..... ||||
| Homer (Iliad) | 750-700 B.C. | 200 B.C. | 500 yrs. | 643 |
| AND THE WINNER IS...... ||||
| God (The N.T.) | A.D. 40-100 | A.D. 125 | 25 yrs. | 24,000+ |

Their trustworthiness is rarely questioned, yet there is far more bibliographical evidence for the Bible!

## * Old Testament Torah (Genesis – Deuteronomy) Scrolls

There exists today, Torah Scrolls that date back as far 1450 A.D. and can be seen up close today. For example Josh McDowell has such a scroll that He displays during Apologetics Conferences. The precision and meticulous attention to detail that was used by copying scribes is easy to see. Scribes observed about _____ scribal laws when copying Scripture!!! They even had to know exactly how many words and letters were in the entire text and use this knowledge to make sure they had copied the text correctly. Mistakes often meant scrapping a copy and starting over! It took about 2 years for a scribe to produce a copy of a Torah Scroll (which is the first 5 books of the Bible).

* The care which has been taken over the centuries to preserve the text of Scripture is unparalleled!

## * Numerous Variants Found In Manuscripts?

In his book "Misquoting Jesus", Dr. Bart Ehrman questions the validity of the Bibles that we read today and states there are between 200,000 and 400,000 differences found in the New Testament manuscripts. He compares this number to the 138,162 words in a complete Greek New Testament. He attempts to show that this reveals the unreliability of the New Testament we read today. The wide range in the number of differences mentioned should immediately be a cause for questioning. There is quite a difference between 200,000 and 400,000. A closer look reveals a number of facts that Dr. Ehrman does not reveal. First of all, of the differences found in manuscripts about _____ of them are simple spelling issues. Secondly, about 19% are cases where different synonyms or sentence structures are used leaving the meaning unchanged. That leaves only about 1% that have any chance of affecting the meaning of the text. Of these there are no variations that affect the core teachings of the Scriptures or the basic doctrines of the Christian faith! Finally, it should be noted that the reason for as many variations as are found is the fact that there are so many manuscripts to compare. For example, there are _____ Greek manuscripts, 60 of those are complete copies of the New Testament.

* **The Dead Sea Scrolls,** found in 1947 have shown just how accurate that the copying of the Old Testament has been over the centuries.

* A copy of Isaiah 53 in the Dead Sea Scrolls which is believed to be 1,000 years older than the next oldest copy known, showed just _____ word of _____ letters difference than the other copy that was made 1,000 years later. This minor difference did not change the meaning of the text at all. Amazing! After 1,000 years of copying there was almost no differences found! Again, we should note that the care taken to preserve the Bible, both Old Testament and New Testament is unparalleled in history!

## #3 – Archaeology & History

* Archaeological finds continue to confirm _____, places & events found in the Bible!

Famous Archaeologist Nelson Glueck said, "As a matter of fact, however, it may be stated categorically that no archaeological discovery has ever _____ a Biblical reference."

James Mann wrote in the August 24, 1981 edition of U.S. News and World Report - "A wave of archaeological discoveries is altering old ideas about the roots of Christianity and Judaism – and affirming the Bible is more historically _____ than many scholars thought."

* Note the examples below of archaeological finds confirming both Old & New Testament details.

**The Bible – God's Word** — OLD TESTAMENT
Written Tablets (2000 B.C.) - Billions of Fossils in Sedimentary Rock
Numerous Ancient Writings about a Flood - Collapsed Walls of the City of Jericho
Inscription "David, the King of Israel" (1993) - Capital City of the Hittites
Ancient City of Nineveh - Hezekiah's Tunnel (2 Kings 20:20)
Babylon (Bricks w/inscription "Nebuchadnezzar, King of Babylon"
Babylonian Chronicle Tablets – (Speak of Siege of Jerusalem)
Babylonian Chronicle Tablets – ("Belshazzar") (Daniel 5)

**The Bible – God's Word** — NEW TESTAMENT
Herod the Great (Pottery, Coins, Palaces)
John the Baptist (Josephus) (Palace Dungeon)
The Pool of Bethesda (5 Covered Porches) - Caiaphas (Bone Ossuary)
Pontius Pilate ("Prefect of Judea") (Limestone Block)
Jesus (Mosaic Floor – "In Memory of the God, Jesus Christ")
Jesus (Ossuary of James, "Brother of Jesus") - Lysanias, Tetrarch of Abilene (Luke 3:1)

\* Luke includes many historical details in his writings in the books of Luke and Acts that have now been confirmed through archaeology and other historical documents. As he records the events that occurred in his ordered account he mentions countries, cities, islands, names and titles of priests and political leaders, deities that certain cities worshipped, shipping ports, weather patterns, particular shipping lanes, and laws and customs in the places the events occurred. All of these types of details give opportunity for checking the historical accuracy of his account. Archaeological research continues to confirm the details that Luke spoke of in his writings. Consider this, Consider this, over \_\_\_\_ details found in the book of Acts alone have been confirmed by archaeological and historical research.

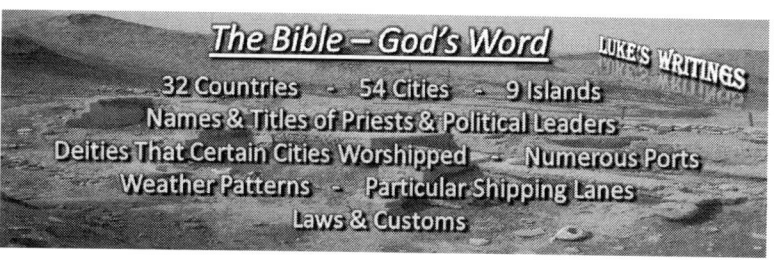

\* Other Historical Documents and writings also confirm the history of the Bible!

## #4 – Medical Facts in the Bible

\* There are medical facts that were written in the Bible 2,500 to 3,500 years ago that have now been discovered to be true by modern medicine in the past 250 years. If the Bible were just the writings of men it would be very difficult to explain how these medical facts could have been known by the writers at that time, centuries before these things were discovered by those in modern medical fields.

(Here are 3 examples)

### 1. - The danger of germs
Throughout the book of Leviticus the Bible gives very details regulation to help prevent the spreading of germs. Beyond the Bible, this knowledge was not known until last couple of centuries. Before relatively recent discoveries a physician might have worked on a dead body and then delivered a baby without even washing his hands because the dangers of germs were not understood.

### 2. - Life is in the blood  (Leviticus 17:14)

> Leviticus 17:14 NASB "For as for the life of all flesh, its blood is identified with its life. Therefore I said to the sons of Israel, 'You are not to eat the blood of any flesh, for the life of all flesh is its blood; whoever eats it shall be cut off.'

As recent as the 1700s doctors did not understand this principle. As a result, the practice of "_____" a patient was used at times to attempt to heal them. This was done to try to rid the body of disease, not realizing that the life of the body is in the blood, just as the Bible says. The account of George Washington's death reveals that this practice of "bleeding" was used a number of times in the last days of George Washington's life, as an attempt to rid him of infection. The practice contributed to his death.

# 3. - Circumcision on the 8th Day (Leviticus 12:3)

> Leviticus 12:3 NASB 'On the eighth day the flesh of his foreskin shall be circumcised.

In the law, God gave commandment that every male child that was born among the Jewish people should be circumcised on the 8th day of his life. That is pretty specific instruction. Why the 8th day? No one could have answered that question until research in the 1930s revealed some very telling facts about blood clotting. Blood clotting is a very complicated process and involves a number of factors. Critical to this process are Prothrombin and Vitamin K. Research has now revealed that humans are born with a deficiency of Vitamin K. The body begins to produce Vitamin K in good quantities and reaches a peak amount of Vitamin K production on the 8th day of a person's life. After that the amount levels off. For this reason it is now known that the 8th day of a baby boys life is the best day of his life for blood clotting! Wow! The Bible wrote about circumcising a male child on the 8th day of their life _____ years ago!

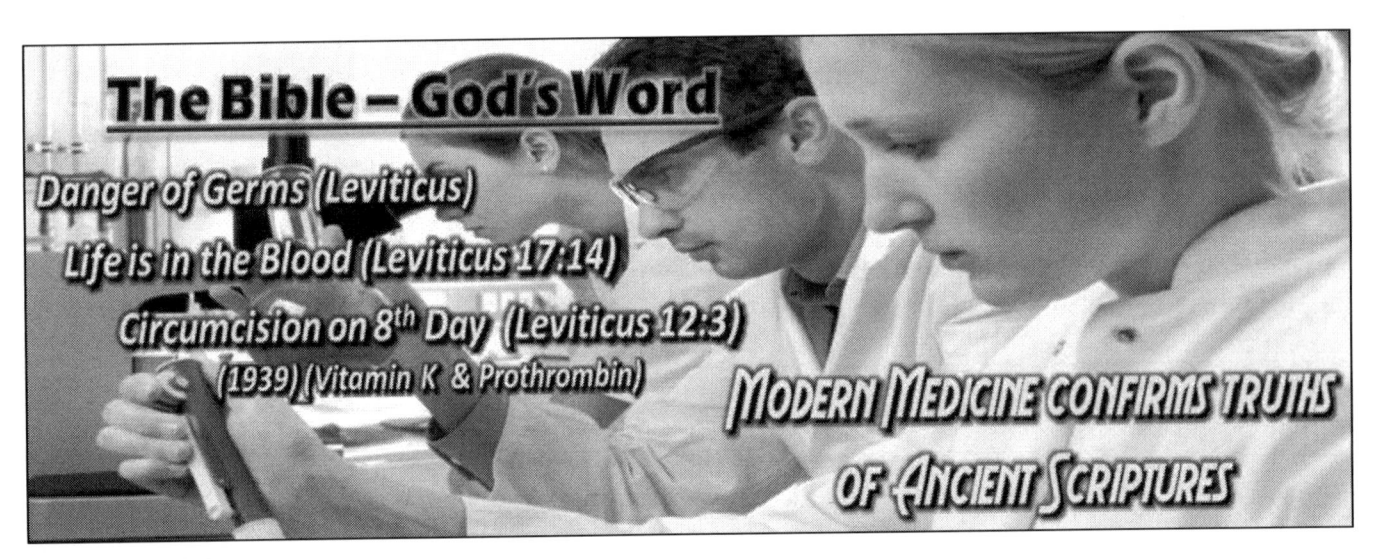

**The Bible – God's Word**
Danger of Germs (Leviticus)
Life is in the Blood (Leviticus 17:14)
Circumcision on 8th Day (Leviticus 12:3)
(1939) (Vitamin K & Prothrombin)

**MODERN MEDICINE CONFIRMS TRUTHS OF ANCIENT SCRIPTURES**

**Summary of this Session** – We have looked at the first 4 areas of evidence that confirm to us that the Bible is the Word of God. These 4 areas are –

1 – The Internal Unity of the Bible
2 – The Bibliographical Evidence
3 – Archaeological & Historical Evidence
4 – Medical Facts Found In the Bible

# FAITH & REASON MADE SIMPLE — Part 5

## (Confirming Evidence That The Bible is The Word of God)

* When looking at the evidence that confirms the Bible is God's Word it is good to do so after looking at the evidence that confirms that God created us! Apologetics should be approached systematically starting with the issue of **creation**. Once we see the clear evidence that we are created by a wise, powerful and personal God, we would assume that He has spoken to us. Therefore we can begin our search for evidence that confirms the Bible to be God's Word with the expectation that God has given His Word to us so that we can know Him.

* As we have seen in previous sessions, God has revealed Himself through the things He has made (Romans 1:20). This type of revelation is called "**General** Revelation" or "Natural Revelation". In this type of revelation God reveals His existence and characteristics about Himself. To reveal specific things about His plan for mankind God has given us "**Special** Revelation" in two aspects. The Bible and the person of Jesus Christ (God come in the flesh) are the two aspects of **special** revelation.

> 2 Timothy 3:16 NASB  All Scripture is inspired by God and profitable for teaching, for reproof, for correction, for training in righteousness;

> John 17:17 KJV  Sanctify them through thy truth: thy word is truth.

## Introduction

* Attacks on the Bible today! (Calling it Fiction) (Denying that it is God's Word) (Etc.)
  (Attacks upon the Bible are especially found in **universities** across America)

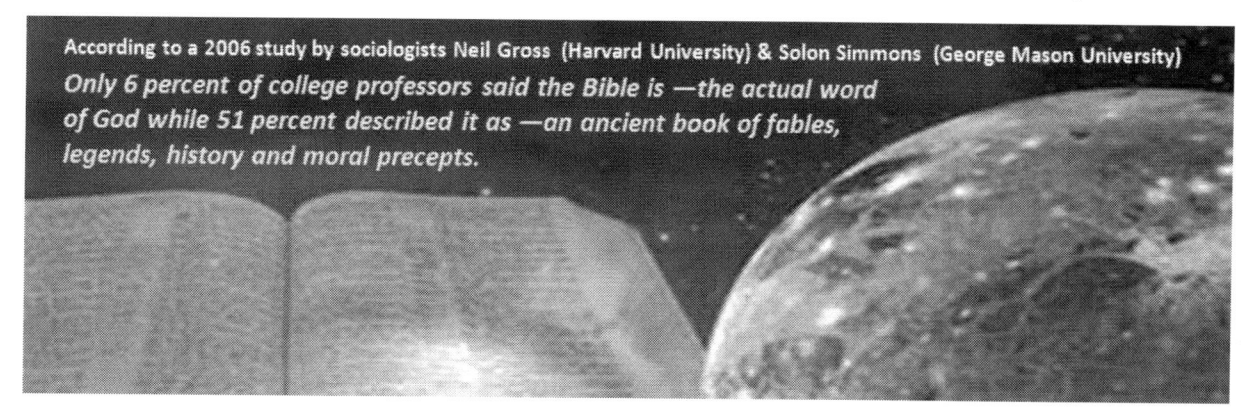

> According to a 2006 study by sociologists Neil Gross (Harvard University) & Solon Simmons (George Mason University) Only 6 percent of college professors said the Bible is —the actual word of God while 51 percent described it as —an ancient book of fables, legends, history and moral precepts.

## Why Do You Believe the Bible is the Word of God?

It is important to take a moment to think about how you would answer this question if it were asked of you. Remember that 1 Peter 3:15 says that we are to always be ready to give and answer, or make a defense to those who ask about the hope that is in us.

Dr. Voddie Baucham was asked to consider this question while he attended Oxford University. Here is the answer he gave a professor there – "I choose to believe the Bible because it is a **reliable** collection of historical documents written down by **eye witnesses** during the lifetime of other eye witnesses. They report to us supernatural events that took place in fulfillment of specific prophecies and claim to be divine rather than human in origin."

Dr. Baucham's answer reveals an apologetic understanding of the issue behind the question. After my studies of these issues I would add this to Dr. Baucham's answer. "These events are confirmed by, and give us understanding of, other historical events and the **realities** of the world today."

## Confirming Evidences – The Bible Is God's Word!

In this session and the next we will examine 8 areas of evidence that confirm to us that the Bible truly is the Word of God. The 8 areas of evidence are listed in the picture below. We will look at the first 4 areas in this session and the final four areas in session 6.

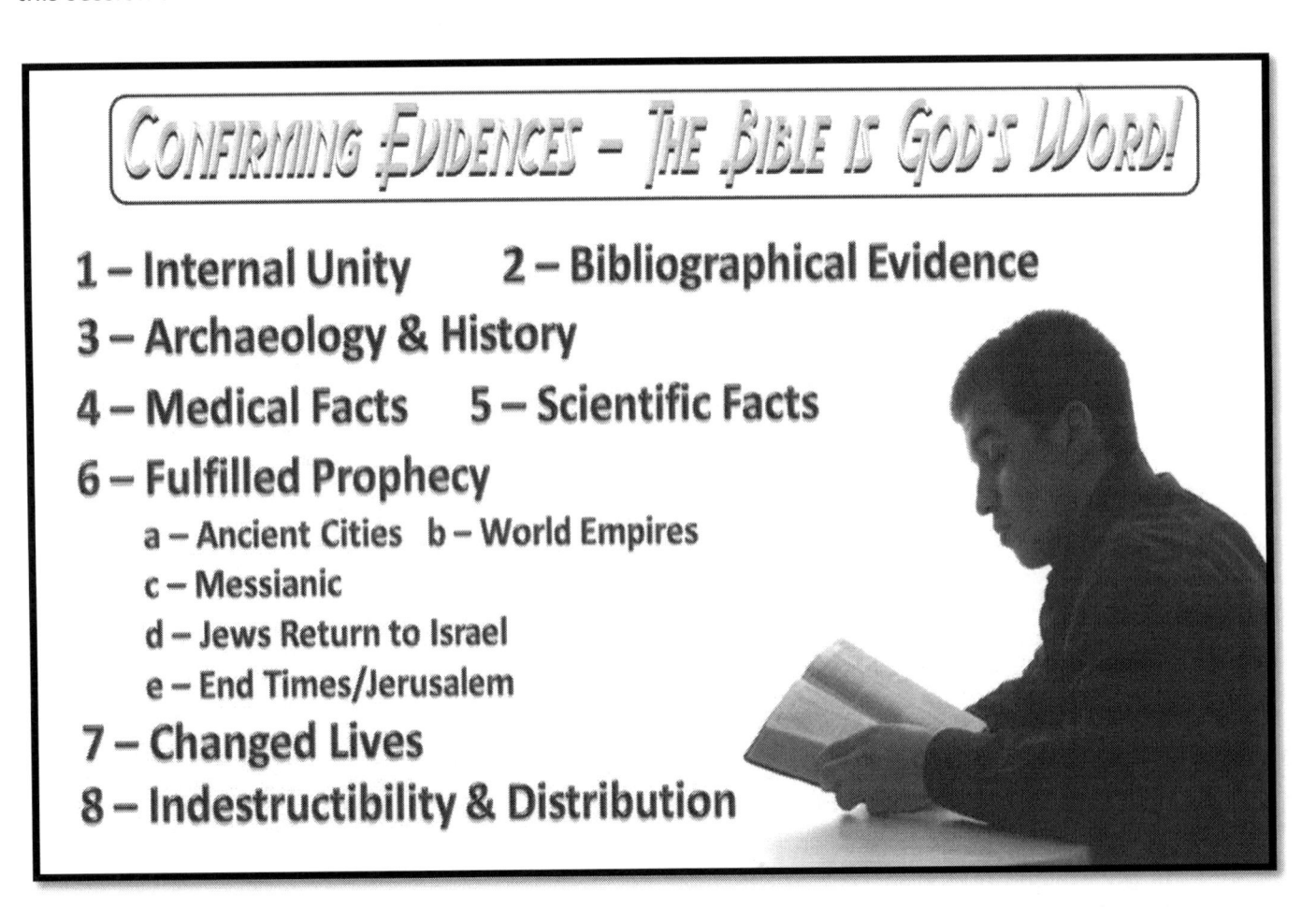

### Confirming Evidences – The Bible is God's Word!

1 – Internal Unity
2 – Bibliographical Evidence
3 – Archaeology & History
4 – Medical Facts
5 – Scientific Facts
6 – Fulfilled Prophecy
   a – Ancient Cities   b – World Empires
   c – Messianic
   d – Jews Return to Israel
   e – End Times/Jerusalem
7 – Changed Lives
8 – Indestructibility & Distribution

## #1 – Internal Unity

### * Simple outline of the Bible's Message
- A – God Created Mankind to Be His Sons and Daughters (Genesis 1-2)
- B – Mankind Sinned and Was Separated From God (Results – Death & Corruption) (Gen. 3)
- C – God Fulfilled His Plan to Redeem Mankind in Christ (Genesis 3 – Revelation 20)
- D – All God Planned in Creation Is Eternally Restored in Christ (Revelation 21-22)

### * The Bible <u>Claims</u> to Be the Word of God!
- * (2 Timothy 3:16) (John 17:17) (1 Peter 1:21)
- * Over 2,600 times the phrase "God said" or its equivalent is found in the Bible

### * 40 Different Authors Over a 1,500 Year Period
* 40 different authors wrote from 3 different continents over a <u>**1,500**</u> year period of time in 3 different languages. Shepherds, kings, scholars, fishermen, prophets, a military general, a cupbearer, and a priest all penned portions of Scripture. From just this information we would expect the Bible to be a tangled mess, but it certainly is not. The message of the Bible is a clear, continual unfolding message of <u>**redemption**</u>. The more that this internal unity is examined the more remarkable it appears.

### * 400 Year Gap Between the Old & New Testaments
* Though there was an approximate 400 year gap between the Old & New Testaments, yet the connection between the two can be easily seen in many ways.

**Examples include –**
- * Old Testament – The Law is Given and Emphasized
  New Testament – The Law is Seen not as a Way to Salvation but as a Tutor to lead people to Christ Jesus for Salvation. (The Law shows us our need!)
- * <u>Melchizedek</u> (Genesis 14) (Hebrews 5-7 – The Priesthood of Jesus Christ)
- * Abraham's <u>**Faith**</u>   (Genesis 12-22) (Romans 4) (Galatians 3)
- * Abraham Sacrifices Isaac (On Mt. Calvary) – (Genesis 22) (22:18) (Galatians 3:16)
- * Prophecies of the coming of Elijah (Malachi 4) – John the Baptist (N. T. Beginnings)

## Claims of Sincerity & Truthfulness
In numerous places the authors of Scripture specifically indicate that they are sincerely and truthfully relating accurate historic information. Here a couple of examples.

Luke 1:1-4 NASB  Inasmuch as many have undertaken to compile an account of the things accomplished among us, (2) just as they were handed down to us by those who from the beginning were eyewitnesses and servants of the word, (3) it seemed fitting for me as well, having <u>**investigated**</u> everything <u>**carefully**</u> from the beginning, to write it out for you in consecutive order, most excellent Theophilus; (4) so that you may know the exact truth about the things you have been taught.

1 Thessalonians 2:3-5 NASB  (3)  For our exhortation does not come from **error** or **impurity** or by way of deceit;  (4)  but just as we have been approved by God to be entrusted with the gospel, so we speak, not as pleasing men, but God who examines our hearts.  (5)  For we never came with flattering speech, as you know, nor with a pretext for greed--God is witness--

## * Many Types & Shadows in the Old Testament point to Jesus Christ of the N.T.

* Passover Lamb   * Ark   * Scapegoat   * Rahab's Scarlet Cord   * Brazen **Serpent**
* Melchizedek   * Sin & Guilt Offerings   * Moses/Joshua – The Promise Land
* Manna (Bread from Heaven) (John 6)   * Water from the Rock  (1 Corinthians 10:4)

**REPHIDIM** (In Modern Saudi Arabia)
Smite the Rock – Ex. 17:6
Speak to the Rock – Num. 20:8
*Water From The Rock*

## * Over 300 Old Testament Prophecies Fulfilled by Jesus in the New Testament

This point will be covered in more detail in a later session but with relationship to the internal unity of the Bible it is important to note that over 300 prophecies that were written in the Old Testament about the coming Messiah were fulfilled hundreds of years later in the person of Jesus Christ. These fulfillments are recorded in the New Testament.

## * Embarrassing Testimony

The significance of this is that anyone attempting to make up a religion would not record embarrassing events and actions in the lives of the stars of the documents being written. The Bible is filled with true life events that show the worst moments in the lives of its star characters. This reveals that the Bible is not a manmade document but a true, historic record given to us by God.

**Embarrassing Testimony**

| | | |
|---|---|---|
| Adam & Eve (Sin) | Joseph's Brothers | Birth of Jesus (Humble) |
| Cain & Abel (Murder) | Judah (Prostitution) | Disciples (Greatest?) |
| Noah (Drunk) | Israel (Murmers) | Disciples (Afraid at Sea) |
| Abraham (Lying) | Moses (Angry) | Peter (Rebuked 2x) |
| Jacob (Deception) | Israel (Rebellion) | Peter (Denied Jesus) |
| | Samson (Lust) | Disciples (Sleeping) |
| | Eli's & Samuel's Sons | Disciples (Fleeing) |
| | David (Adultery/Murder) | Crucifixion |
| | Jesus' Genealogy | Women Witnesses |

## #2 – Bibliographical Evidence

* Many critics claim that the Bibles we read today do not communicate the same message as the original writings did. They say that the Bible has been corrupted through the centuries. Bibliographical evidence deals with this issue. Bibliographical evidence examines the number of manuscript copies that are available and looks at the amount of time between the original writings and the oldest known manuscript copies available. The more manuscript copies and the closer they are in time to the originals, the more trustworthy the documents are that come from them.

* Note the comparison between the New Testament manuscript copies compared to other famous writings of **antiquity**. Other ancient writings are trusted.

| Author | Written | Earliest Copies | Time Span | # of copies |
|---|---|---|---|---|
| Caesar | 100-44 B.C. | A.D. 900 | 1,000 yrs. | 10 |
| Plato (Tetralogies) | 427-347 B.C. | A.D. 900 | 1,200 yrs. | 7 |
| Thucydides | 460-400 B.C. | A.D. 900 | 1,300 yrs. | 8 |
| Sophocles | 496-406 B.C. | A.D. 1,000 | 1,400 yrs. | 100 |
| Catullus | 54 B.C. | A.D. 1,550 | 1,600 yrs. | 3 |
| Euripides | 480-406 B.C. | A.D. 1,100 | 1,500 yrs. | 9 |
| Aristotle | 384-322 B.C. | A.D. 1,100 | 1,400 yrs. | 5 |
| **THE SECOND RUNNER UP.....** | | | | |
| Homer (Iliad) | 750-700 B.C. | 200 B.C. | 500 yrs. | 643 |
| **AND THE WINNER IS......** | | | | |
| God (The N.T.) | A.D. 40-100 | A.D. 125 | 25 yrs. | 24,000+ |

Their trustworthiness is rarely questioned, yet there is far more bibliographical evidence for the Bible!

### * Old Testament Torah (Genesis – Deuteronomy) Scrolls

There exists today, Torah Scrolls that date back as far 1450 A.D. and can be seen up close today. For example Josh McDowell has such a scroll that He displays during Apologetics Conferences. The precision and meticulous attention to detail that was used by copying scribes is easy to see. Scribes observed about **4,000** scribal laws when copying Scripture!!! They even had to know exactly how many words and letters were in the entire text and use this knowledge to make sure they had copied the text correctly. Mistakes often meant scrapping a copy and starting over! It took about 2 years for a scribe to produce a copy of a Torah Scroll (which is the first 5 books of the Bible).

* The care which has been taken over the centuries to preserve the text of Scripture is unparalleled!

### * Numerous Variants Found In Manuscripts?

In his book "Misquoting Jesus", Dr. Bart Ehrman questions the validity of the Bibles that we read today and states there are between 200,000 and 400,000 differences found in the New Testament manuscripts. He compares this number to the 138,162 words in a complete Greek New Testament. He attempts to show that this reveals the unreliability of the New Testament we read today. The wide range in the number of differences mentioned should immediately be a cause for questioning. There is quite a difference between 200,000 and 400,000. A closer look reveals a number of facts that Dr. Ehrman does not reveal. First of all, of the differences found in manuscripts about **80%** of them are simple spelling issues. Secondly, about 19% are cases where different synonyms or sentence structures are used leaving the meaning unchanged. That leaves only about 1% that have any chance of affecting the meaning of the text. Of these there are no variations that affect the core teachings of the Scriptures or the basic doctrines of the Christian faith! Finally, it should be noted that the reason for as many variations as are found is the fact that there are so many manuscripts to compare. For example, there are **5700** Greek manuscripts, 60 of those are complete copies of the New Testament.

* **The Dead Sea Scrolls,** found in 1947 have shown just how accurate that the copying of the Old Testament has been over the centuries.
    * A copy of Isaiah 53 in the Dead Sea Scrolls which is believed to be 1,000 years older than the next oldest copy known, showed just **one** word of **three** letters difference than the other copy that was made 1,000 years later. This minor difference did not change the meaning of the text at all. Amazing! After 1,000 years of copying there was almost no differences found! Again, we should note that the care taken to preserve the Bible, both Old Testament and New Testament is unparalleled in history!

## #3 – Archaeology & History

* Archaeological finds continue to confirm **people**, places & events found in the Bible!

Famous Archaeologist Nelson Glueck said, "As a matter of fact, however, it may be stated categorically that no archaeological discovery has ever **controverted** a Biblical reference."

James Mann wrote in the August 24, 1981 edition of U.S. News and World Report - "A wave of archaeological discoveries is altering old ideas about the roots of Christianity and Judaism – and affirming the Bible is more historically **accurate** than many scholars thought."

* Note the examples below of archaeological finds confirming both Old & New Testament details.

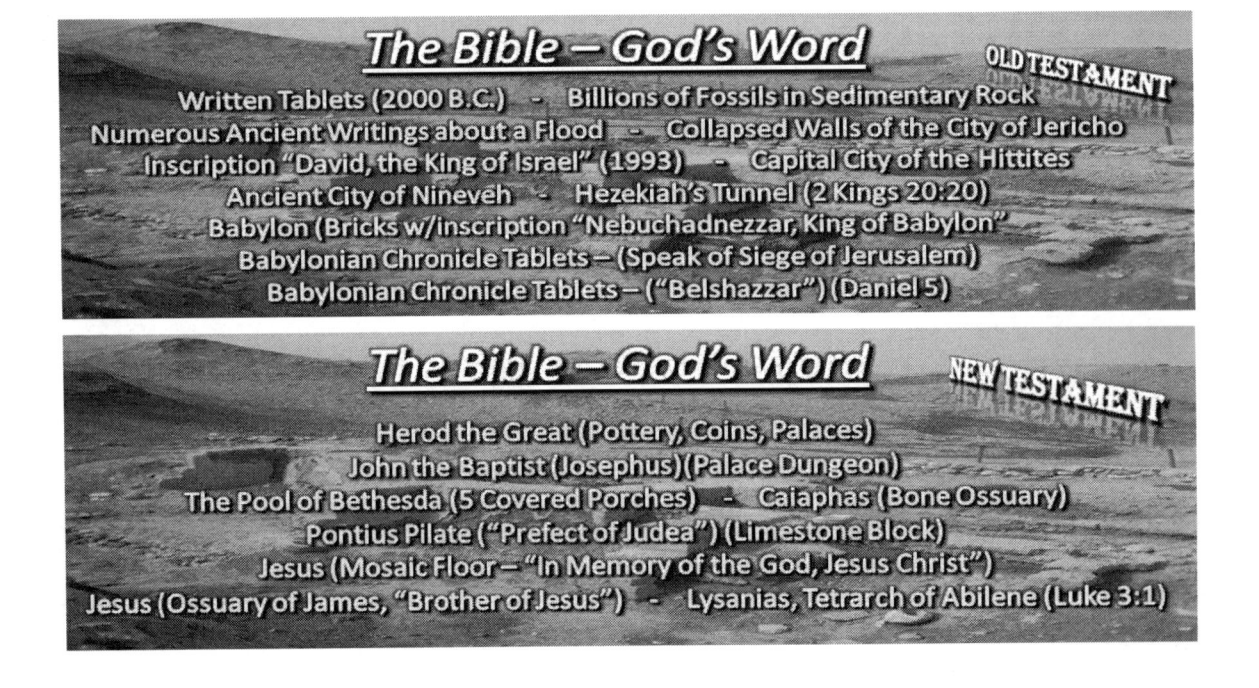

### The Bible – God's Word — OLD TESTAMENT
Written Tablets (2000 B.C.) - Billions of Fossils in Sedimentary Rock
Numerous Ancient Writings about a Flood - Collapsed Walls of the City of Jericho
Inscription "David, the King of Israel" (1993) - Capital City of the Hittites
Ancient City of Nineveh - Hezekiah's Tunnel (2 Kings 20:20)
Babylon (Bricks w/Inscription "Nebuchadnezzar, King of Babylon"
Babylonian Chronicle Tablets – (Speak of Siege of Jerusalem)
Babylonian Chronicle Tablets – ("Belshazzar") (Daniel 5)

### The Bible – God's Word — NEW TESTAMENT
Herod the Great (Pottery, Coins, Palaces)
John the Baptist (Josephus) (Palace Dungeon)
The Pool of Bethesda (5 Covered Porches) - Caiaphas (Bone Ossuary)
Pontius Pilate ("Prefect of Judea") (Limestone Block)
Jesus (Mosaic Floor – "In Memory of the God, Jesus Christ")
Jesus (Ossuary of James, "Brother of Jesus") - Lysanias, Tetrarch of Abilene (Luke 3:1)

* Luke includes many historical details in his writings in the books of Luke and Acts that have now been confirmed through archaeology and other historical documents. As he records the events that occurred in his ordered account he mentions countries, cities, islands, names and titles of priests and political leaders, deities that certain cities worshipped, shipping ports, weather patterns, particular shipping lanes, and laws and customs in the places the events occurred. All of these types of details give opportunity for checking the historical accuracy of his account. Archaeological research continues to confirm the details that Luke spoke of in his writings. Consider this, Consider this, over **80** details found in the book of Acts alone have been confirmed by archaeological and historical research.

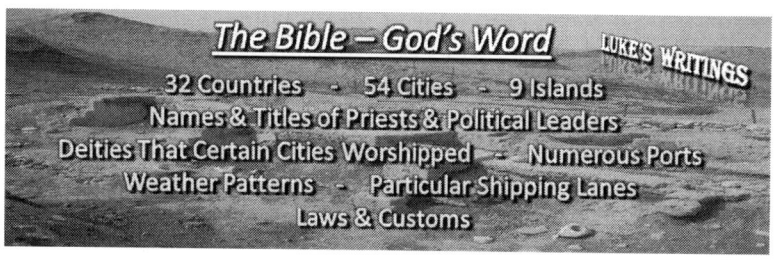

*The Bible – God's Word — LUKE'S WRITINGS*
*32 Countries - 54 Cities - 9 Islands*
*Names & Titles of Priests & Political Leaders*
*Deities That Certain Cities Worshipped - Numerous Ports*
*Weather Patterns - Particular Shipping Lanes*
*Laws & Customs*

* Other Historical Documents and writings also confirm the history of the Bible!

## #4 – Medical Facts in the Bible

* There are medical facts that were written in the Bible 2,500 to 3,500 years ago that have now been discovered to be true by modern medicine in the past 250 years. If the Bible were just the writings of men it would be very difficult to explain how these medical facts could have been known by the writers at that time, centuries before these things were discovered by those in modern medical fields.

(Here are 3 examples)

### 1. - The danger of germs
Throughout the book of Leviticus the Bible gives very details regulation to help prevent the spreading of germs. Beyond the Bible, this knowledge was not known until last couple of centuries. Before relatively recent discoveries a physician might have worked on a dead body and then delivered a baby without even washing his hands because the dangers of germs were not understood.

### 2. - Life is in the blood  (Leviticus 17:14)

> Leviticus 17:14 NASB "For as for the life of all flesh, its blood is identified with its life. Therefore I said to the sons of Israel, 'You are not to eat the blood of any flesh, for the life of all flesh is its blood; whoever eats it shall be cut off.'

As recent as the 1700s doctors did not understand this principle. As a result, the practice of "**bleeding**" a patient was used at times to attempt to heal them. This was done to try to rid the body of disease, not realizing that the life of the body is in the blood, just as the Bible says. The account of George Washington's death reveals that this practice of "bleeding" was used a number of times in the last days of George Washington's life, as an attempt to rid him of infection. The practice contributed to his death.

## 3. - Circumcision on the 8th Day (Leviticus 12:3)

> Leviticus 12:3 NASB 'On the eighth day the flesh of his foreskin shall be circumcised.

In the law, God gave commandment that every male child that was born among the Jewish people should be circumcised on the 8th day of his life. That is pretty specific instruction. Why the 8th day? No one could have answered that question until research in the 1930s revealed some very telling facts about blood clotting. Blood clotting is a very complicated process and involves a number of factors. Critical to this process are Prothrombin and Vitamin K. Research has now revealed that humans are born with a deficiency of Vitamin K. The body begins to produce Vitamin K in good quantities and reaches a peak amount of Vitamin K production on the 8th day of a person's life. After that the amount levels off. For this reason it is now known that the 8th day of a baby boys life is the best day of his life for blood clotting! Wow! The Bible wrote about circumcising a male child on the 8th day of their life **3,500** years ago!

**Summary of this Session** – We have looked at the first 4 areas of evidence that confirm to us that the Bible is the Word of God. These 4 areas are –

1 – The Internal Unity of the Bible
2 – The Bibliographical Evidence
3 – Archaeological & Historical Evidence
4 – Medical Facts Found In the Bible

# FAITH & REASON MADE SIMPLE — Part 6

## (Confirming Evidence That The Bible is The Word of God – Cont.)

In our last session we viewed the first 4 of our 8 areas of evidence that confirm to us that the Bible is the Word of God. In this session we will look into the final 4 areas of evidence.

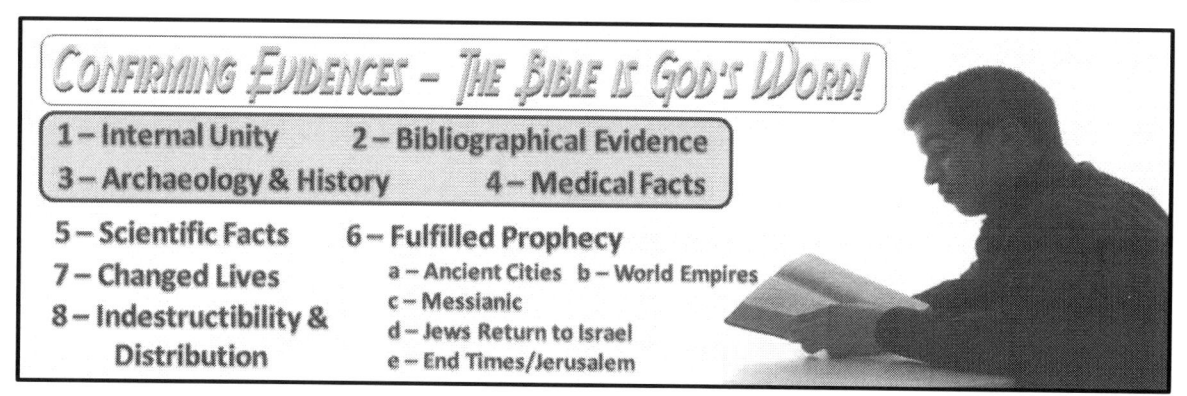

**Confirming Evidences – The Bible is God's Word!**

1 – Internal Unity
2 – Bibliographical Evidence
3 – Archaeology & History
4 – Medical Facts
5 – Scientific Facts
6 – Fulfilled Prophecy
  a – Ancient Cities  b – World Empires
  c – Messianic
  d – Jews Return to Israel
  e – End Times/Jerusalem
7 – Changed Lives
8 – Indestructibility & Distribution

## #5 – Scientific Facts in the Bible

* There are numerous scientific facts that were written in the Bible 2,500 to 3,500 years ago that have now been confirmed by modern scientific study. The fact that the Bible spoke of these things hundreds of years before mankind came to understand them shows that the Bible is given to us by God Himself, the Creator! Examples –
    * The Earth is a _____ – Isaiah 40:22
    * The Universe is _____ (Stretched Out by God) – Psalm 104:2, Psalm 144:5, Job 9:8, Isaiah 40:22, Isaiah 42:5, Isaiah 44:24, Isaiah 45:12, Isaiah 48:13, Jeremiah 10:12, Zech. 12:1
    * The stars of the Pleiades constellation are gravitationally bound together while the stars of the Orion constellation are not - Job 38:31
    * Innumerable Amount of Stars – Genesis 15:5, Jeremiah 33:22
    * Mountains on the Ocean Floor – Jonah 2:5-6
    * Currents (or Paths) in the _____ & _____ - Psalm 8:8, Isaiah 43:16
    * Hydrological Cycle – Job 36:27-28, Psalm 135:6-7, Ecclesiastes 1:7, Amos 9:6
    * The Existence of Dinosaurs – Job 40 & 41, Psalm 74:14 (note – the word "dinosaur" was invented in the mid 1800s so the Bible does not use that word)
    * There Are Springs in the Seas – Job 38:16
    * The Earth is Hung on Nothing – Job 26:7

# #6 – Fulfilled Prophecies In The Bible

There are many prophecies written in the Bible which have come to pass just at the Bible indicated they would or are coming to pass even now. Most of these were written in the Old Testament, 3500 – 2500 years ago. These fulfilled prophecies that can be seen to have been fulfilled by world history or by the news of our time give wonderful evidence that the Bible is the Word of God!

An example of these fulfilled prophecies is seen in Isaiah's prophecies about Cyrus the Great, who became a ruler of the _____ a couple of hundred years after Isaiah wrote the prophetic words. The prophecy indicated that it would be Cyrus who God would use to allow the Jews to return to the land of Israel after decades of captivity, and to begin the rebuilding of the Temple. History reveals that Cyrus did just as the Bible predicted he would.

**\* Cyrus the Great**
(Isaiah 44:28) (Isaiah 45:1) (200 Years Before His Birth)

Isaiah 44:28 NASB "It is I who says of Cyrus, 'He is My shepherd! And he will perform all My desire.' And he declares of Jerusalem, 'She will be built,' And of the temple, 'Your foundation will be laid.'"

## A – Destruction of Powerful Ancient Cities

\* The Bible gives detailed prophecies concerning the destruction of some of the most powerful ancient cities that existed in the times the Old Testament was written.

> \* Petra – (Obadiah 1) (Isaiah 34:5-15) Petra (Referred to as the house of Esau dwelling in the clefts of the rocks or as Edom) was especially strong because it was built within rocky cliffs and could not be reached by enemies without approaching it from underneath which left soldiers venerable.
> \* _____ – (Jeremiah 50 & 51) The city of Babylon was the strongest city of its day but the Bible prophesied it would become a desolate, habitat for wild animals. The prophesy was fulfilled.
> \* _____ – (Ezekiel 26 & 27) The city of Tyre was on the coast of the Mediterranean Sea. It consisted of a mainland city and an island fortress about ½ mile off the coast. Ezekiel prophesied of the destruction of Tyre in great detail including destruction by Nebuchadnezzar and the scraping of the debris from the mainland into the sea which was fulfilled by Alexander the Great in \_\_\_\_\_ BC. Alexander commanded his soldiers to use the debris from the previous destruction of the mainland city in order to create a causeway from the mainland to the island fortress of Tyre. They scrapped it bare like a rock. An aerial view of Tyre today shows that the causeway they created is still there today!

## B- World Empires to Rise & Fall

* In the book of _____ there are detailed prophecies concerning the rising and falling of world empires through a dream Nebuchadnezzar had in Daniel 2 and through visions that Daniel had in Daniel 7 & 8. The Bible predicts that the Babylonian Empire would be followed by the Medo-Persian Empire and that the Medo-Persian Empire would be followed by the Greek Empire. It names these 3 empires. It indicates that the first ruler of the Greek Empire would die at an early age and that the empire would then be divided into 4 parts. It then predicts that the Greek Empire will be conquered and followed by a 4th world empire that would stronger than the first 3. Finally, it predicts that there will be another world empire that will emerge from among the nations in the last days.

* World history shows us that the Bible was accurate in foretelling all of these things. The Babylonian Empire was conquered and followed by the Medo-Persian Empire. The Medo-Persian Empire was conquered and followed by the Greek Empire. The first ruler of the Greek Empire was _____ who died in his 30s. After his death the Greek Empire was divided into 4 parts. The Greek Empire was conquered and followed by the _____ Empire which was more powerful than any previous world empire. It stood for hundreds of years. Today there is movement toward a New World Order which is emerging from among the nations. The Bible has accurately foretold world history!

## C – Messianic Prophecies

The Old Testament contains over _____ Messianic prophecies that were all fulfilled in the New Testament by Jesus Christ. This fact speaks to the internal unity of the Bible and the identity of Jesus as the Christ, as well as the Bible's ability to proclaim future events prior to them coming to pass. Here is a list of some of the Messianic prophecies fulfilled by Jesus Christ.

* Would be born in _____ – (Micah 5:2)
* Would be born of a virgin – (Isaiah 7:14)
* Would be betrayed for ____ pieces of silver – (Zechariah 11:12-13) (The price of a slave)
* Would ride into Jerusalem on a donkey – (Zechariah 9:9)
* Soldiers would gamble for His outer garment – (Psalm 22:18)
* Would be pierced in His side – (Isaiah 53:5) (Zechariah 12:10)
* Not a _____ of His body would be _____ – (Exodus 12:46) (Psalm 34:20)
* He would speak in parables – (Psalm 78:2)
* He would live and minister in Galilee – (Isaiah 9:1-2)
* He would be the Savior of the Jews & a Light to the Nations – (Isaiah 49:5-6)
* Would have nails driven through His hands and feet – (Psalm 22:16)
* Buried in the grave of a rich man – (Isaiah 53:9)

* In his book "Science Speaks", Dr. Peter Stoner explains a research project that he and students at Pasadena City College, where he was a professor, did to estimate the probability of one person fulfilling various Old Testament Messianic prophecies. Here are the conservative estimates their research revealed concerning just 8 of the Old Testament messianic prophecies.

"When multiplied together it was found that even using these very conservative estimates, there would be a **1 in 10$^{28}$** chance of someone fulfilling just __ of these Messianic prophecies."
"That number looks like this when written out - 10,000,000,000,000,000,000,000,000,000."

## D – The Scattering & Regathering of the Jewish People

Maybe the most startling example of fulfilled Bible prophecy that confirms the fact that the Bible is the Word of God are the prophecies concerning the scattering of the _____ _____ and the regathering of the Jewish people to the land of Israel from the nations of world. We have been witnessing the fulfillment of these prophecies throughout our lifetime. In addition to the regathering of the Jewish people the Bible also prophecies that the land of Israel will blossom and become fruitful, and the cities will be renewed. All of these things are being fulfilled in the world today and much of world history over the past 100 years can be seen to be related to these fulfillments.

> *\* The scattering of the Jewish people to the Nations*
> **Deuteronomy 28:64 NASB** "Moreover, the LORD will scatter you among all peoples, from one end of the earth to the other end of the earth; and there you shall serve other gods, wood and stone, which you or your fathers have not known.
>
> *\* The regathering of the Jewish people to the land of Israel*
> **Ezekiel 36:24 NASB** "For I will take you from the nations, gather you from all the lands and bring you into your own land.
> **Isaiah 11:11-12 NASB** Then it will happen on that day that the Lord Will again recover the second time with His hand The remnant of His people, who will remain, From Assyria, Egypt, Pathros, Cush, Elam, Shinar, Hamath, And from the islands of the sea. (12) And He will lift up a standard for the nations And assemble the banished ones of Israel, And will gather the dispersed of Judah From the four corners of the earth.
> **Ezekiel 38:8 NASB** "After many days you will be summoned; in the latter years you will come into the land that is restored from the sword, whose inhabitants have been gathered from many nations to the mountains of Israel which had been a continual waste; but its people were brought out from the nations, and they are living securely, all of them.
> **Ezekiel 28:25-26 NASB** 'Thus says the Lord GOD, "When I gather the house of Israel from the peoples among whom they are scattered, and will manifest My holiness in them in the sight of the nations, then they will live in their land which I gave to My servant Jacob. (26) "They will live in it securely; and they will build houses, plant vineyards and live securely when I execute judgments upon all who scorn them round about them. Then they will know that I am the LORD their God."''

**Jeremiah 29:11-14 NASB** 'For I know the plans that I have for you,' declares the LORD, 'plans for welfare and not for calamity to give you a future and a hope. (12) 'Then you will call upon Me and come and pray to Me, and I will listen to you. (13) 'You will seek Me and find Me when you search for Me with all your heart. (14) 'I will be found by you,' declares the LORD, 'and I will restore your fortunes and will gather you from all the nations and from all the places where I have driven you,' declares the LORD, 'and I will bring you back to the place from where I sent you into exile.'

   *** *The Land of Israel & the Cities of Israel Will Become Fruitful Again***
   **Ezekiel 36:30-35 NASB** "I will multiply the fruit of the tree and the produce of the field, so that you will not receive again the disgrace of famine among the nations. ... (34) "The desolate land will be cultivated instead of being a desolation in the sight of everyone who passes by. (35) "They will say, 'This desolate land has become like the garden of Eden; and the waste, desolate and ruined cities are fortified and inhabited.'
   **Ezekiel 36:8-11 NASB** 'But you, O mountains of Israel, you will put forth your branches and bear your fruit for My people Israel; for they will soon come. (9) 'For, behold, I am for you, and I will turn to you, and you will be cultivated and sown. (10) 'I will multiply men on you, all the house of Israel, all of it; and the cities will be inhabited and the waste places will be rebuilt. (11) 'I will multiply on you man and beast; and they will increase and be fruitful; and I will cause you to be inhabited as you were formerly and will treat you better than at the first. Thus you will know that I am the LORD.

* **The Jews have been returning to Israel for the last 120 years from the nations of the world!**
   * Jewish population in Israel (1948 – About ¼ million)(Today – Over 6 million)
   * 1917 (World War 1) (Jerusalem rescued from 400 years of Muslim control)
   * 1917 (_____ Declaration)
   * 1945 – 1947 (Holocaust)(Homeland for the Jews in Israel laid out)
   * May 14, _____ (Israel becomes a nation)
   * 1989 (Iron curtain falls) (Over 1 million Jews return to Israel)
   * Jewish immigration from all over the world to Israel continues today

* **The Land of Israel has been restored and it has become very fruitful!**
   * Mid 1800s – _____ _____ declared the land of Israel as the most desolate place on earth. He wrote "It is a hopeless, dreary, heart-broken land.". He also said that the land was "… a silent, mournful expanse "
   * Since that time the land has blossomed, just as the Bible said it would!
   * More than _____ _____ trees have been planted
   * Rains have returned
   * World class modern irrigation systems have been installed
   * Israel now is a fruit exporting nation
   * The cities have been inhabited and become productive
      (Tel Aviv – World Class Technology)
   * Natural Gas & _____ Reserves have been found in Israel

* **Also worth noting -**
   * Israel has been supernaturally protected through _____ _____!

* The _____ _____ has been restored! (Zephaniah 3:9)
* The Golden (Eastern) Gate remains closed up as the Bible foretold! (Ezekiel 44:1-3)
* The Jewish people have blessed the nations (Genesis 12:2-3)(22:18)(26:4)(28:14)
(201 of the 892 Nobel Prize winners are Jewish!)

## E – The City of Jerusalem & End Time Prophecies

* The Bible prophecies in Zechariah 12 & 14 that _____ will be the focus of international attention in the last days and eventually will be surrounded by the nations of the world, just before Jesus returns!

* **Zechariah 12:1-3 NASB** The burden of the word of the LORD concerning Israel. Thus declares the LORD who stretches out the heavens, lays the foundation of the earth, and forms the spirit of man within him, (2) "Behold, I am going to make Jerusalem a cup that causes reeling to all the peoples around; and when the siege is against Jerusalem, it will also be against Judah. (3) "It will come about in that day that I will make Jerusalem a heavy stone for all the peoples; all who lift it will be severely injured. And all the nations of the earth will be gathered against it.

* **Zechariah 14:1-4 NASB** Behold, a day is coming for the LORD when the spoil taken from you will be divided among you. (2) For I will gather all the nations against Jerusalem to battle, and the city will be captured, the houses plundered, the women ravished and half of the city exiled, but the rest of the people will not be cut off from the city. (3) Then the LORD will go forth and fight against those nations, as when He fights on a day of battle. (4) In that day His feet will stand on the Mount of Olives, which is in front of Jerusalem on the east; and the Mount of Olives will be split in its middle from east to west by a very large valley, so that half of the mountain will move toward the north and the other half toward the south.

* There is no question that _____ is the most contention place on the face of the earth today. Conflicts between Palestinians & Jews over the city of Jerusalem are very much at the center of international attention.
* The contention over the city of Jerusalem was increased in 2018 when the United States moved its _____ to Jerusalem and acknowledged it as Israel's capital city.
* In 2015 the United Nations began flying the Palestinian flag at the United Nations Headquarters in New York. It appears that they are very close to declaring Palestinian statehood. The Palestinians have said that when this happens Jerusalem will be their capital. The Israeli leaders have said that this will not happen.
* In 2012 during the revolution in Egypt as the new leader Mohamed Morsi was being inaugurated, Islamic Cleric Safwat Higazi spoke to a massive crowd in Cairo, Egypt. He stated "We can see how the dream of the Islamic Caliphate is being realized ... _____ _____ shall not be Cairo, Mecca, or Medina. It shall be Jerusalem! ... Yes, Jerusalem is our goal. We shall pray in Jerusalem, or else we shall die as martyrs on its threshold" He then led the massive crowd in a repeated emotional chat, "Millions of martyrs march toward Jerusalem
* Chinese believers have been organizing for some time the "Back to Jerusalem" movement. Their goal is to enlist 100 thousand believers who are willing to become martyrs for the gospel of

Jesus Christ. They are being sent from China to take the gospel of Jesus to all the nations and people between China and Jerusalem. They plan to end up sharing the gospel of Jesus Christ to the people of the city of Jerusalem.

* The United Nations approves more resolutions against Israel than against all other nations combined. Many of them have to do with the city of Jerusalem.
* 2500 years ago the Bible foretold that this particular city would be the focus of the nations of the world in the last days. Jerusalem was destroyed in 70 A.D. (C.E.). It lay barren for many years and was insignificant. What are the chances of this one medium size city would emerge from oblivion to be the focal point of _____ _____ just as the Bible had foretold? The chances would be almost zero if the Bible were just a book written by men!

## * The Increase of <u>Travel</u> & <u>Knowledge</u> In the Last Days

Daniel 12:4 makes an astounding statement about the last days when we consider what has transpired over the past 100 years in the world we live in. It is easy to see that the 2 most notable developments in the past 100 years are the increase of travel and the increase of knowledge. 2500 years ago the Bible foretold

Daniel 12:4 NASB "But as for you, Daniel, conceal these words and seal up the book until the end of time; many will go back and forth, and knowledge will increase."

this very thing concerning the last days. This is another indicator that the Bible is the Word of God!

## * The Eastern (or <u>Golden</u>) Gate

Ezekiel 44:1-3 NASB Then He brought me back by the way of the outer gate of the sanctuary, which faces the east; and it was shut. (2) The LORD said to me, "This gate shall be shut; it shall not be opened, and no one shall enter by it, for the LORD God of Israel has entered by it; therefore it shall be shut. (3) "As for the prince, he shall sit in it as prince to eat bread before the LORD; he shall enter by way of the porch of the gate and shall go out by the same way."

About _____ years ago this Biblical prophecy was written, indicating a specific gate in the old city walls of the city of Jerusalem would be shut and not opened until the Messiah (the Prince) comes again and travels through this gate. The Eastern Gate is the closest gate to the Temple Mount. Remarkably it is shut today, just as the Bible said it would be. It is the only gate in the old city walls that is shut. Coincidence? I think not!

## * The mark of the beast (666) – Revelation 13:16-18

* The Bible foretold 1,900 years ago that in the last days there would be a worldwide economic system involving the number 666 that would enable a world leader to prevent anyone not taking the number mark from being able to buy or sell. Today, every product we buy is marked with the number 666 through the universal product code. This obviously is not a coincidence, but rather is

another indicator that the Bible is the Word of God! Examine numerous products and notice the first two lines, the middle two lines, and the last two lines of the code marked on the products. You will find them to be the same on all products (at least on those using this form of the UPC). These 3 sets of lines each represent a 6. The number 666 is already marked on our products. This is not the mark of the beast at this time. It is just the overarching number of the Universal Product Code. It is not hard to image though that this number will be a part of the worldwide economic system that is developing. The technology has now been developed to place a computer chip under the skin in the back of the hand or in the forehead of people around the world. The Bible says that a day will come that a person will not be able to buy or sell without a number assigned to them that will include the number 666. It is easy to see today that the world is moving toward that time.

## #7 – Changed Lives

* Millions (or Billions) of lives have been radically changed in a positive way by the message of hope, love and salvation found in the Bible! This is true throughout the centuries since Christ came, but is especially true of the past 100+ years. Note the examples in the picture below.

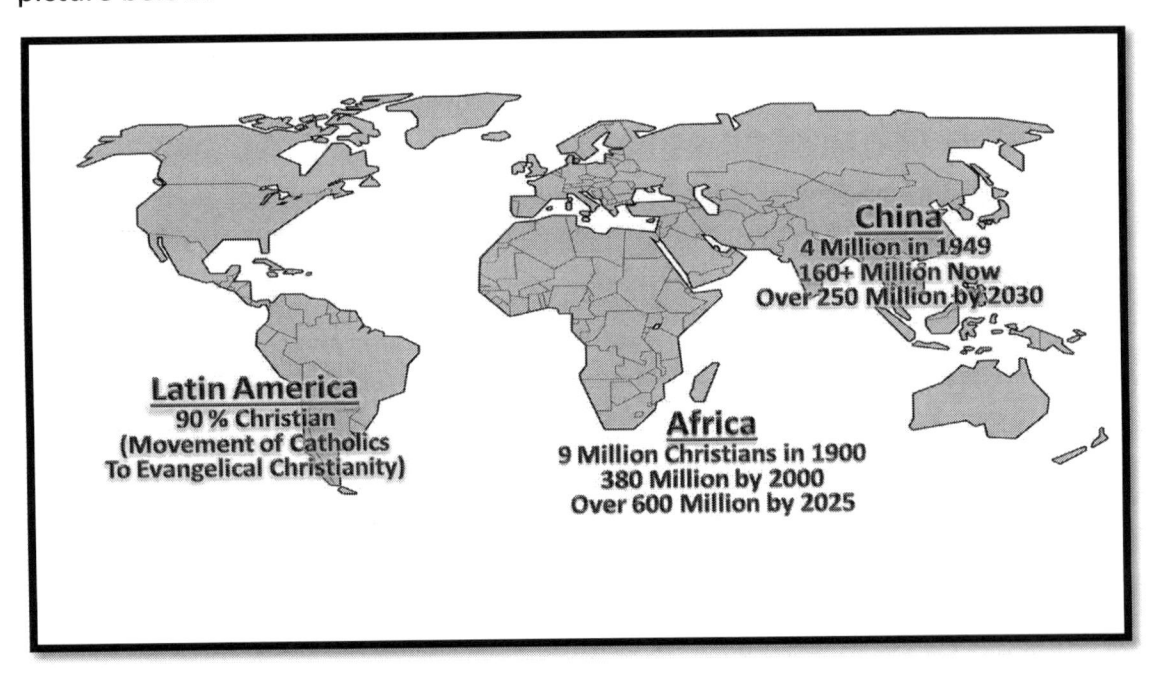

**Latin America**
90 % Christian
(Movement of Catholics
To Evangelical Christianity)

**China**
4 Million in 1949
160+ Million Now
Over 250 Million by 2030

**Africa**
9 Million Christians in 1900
380 Million by 2000
Over 600 Million by 2025

* Many _____ are now coming to know Christ as Savior!
  (More than any other time in history) (Maybe over a million in Iran)
  (God is giving dreams and visions to many Muslims to bring them to Christ)

Acts 2:17 NASB 'AND IT SHALL BE IN THE LAST DAYS,' God says, 'THAT I WILL POUR FORTH OF MY SPIRIT ON ALL MANKIND; AND YOUR SONS AND YOUR DAUGHTERS SHALL PROPHESY, AND YOUR YOUNG MEN SHALL SEE VISIONS, AND YOUR OLD MEN SHALL DREAM DREAMS;

* Many _____ are turning to Christ now, especially in the last 5 years!
* The changed lives of millions (or billions) of people testifies to the truth of the Bible's message!

## #8 – Indestructibility & Distribution

* The Bible has been _____ and _____ for centuries by nations, leaders and antagonists, yet it has withstood every attack. Despite so much opposition the Bible continues to be the most published and distributed book in the world every year!

* Example 1 - In an article entitled "The Indestructibility of the Bible" on the web site entitled Truth Magazine, Cecil Willis explains, "Many of their efforts were directed toward destroying the Bible. Of Diocletian (284-316), the ruler immediately preceding Constantine, Eusebius, the historian said, "royal edicts were published everywhere, commanding that the churches be leveled to the ground and the Scriptures destroyed by fire" (Church History, Book VIII, Ch. 1). Diocletian went on to say that if one had a copy of the Scriptures and did not surrender it to be burned, if it were discovered, he would be killed. During this time many, many copies of the Bible were burned, copies laboriously written in longhand. After this edict had been in force for two years, Diocletian boasted, "I have completely exterminated the _____ _____ from the face of the earth!" (Rimmer, Seven Wonders of the Wonderful Word, p. 15). But had he completely destroyed it? History tells us that the next ruler, Constantine, became a Christian. He requested that copies of the Scriptures be made for all the churches."

* Example 2 - "Voltaire, the noted French infidel, who died in 1778, made his attempt to destroy the Bible. He boldly made the prediction that within one hundred years the Bible and Christianity would have been swept from existence into oblivion. But Voltaire's efforts and his bold prophecy failed as miserably as did those of his unbelieving predecessors. In fact, within 100 years, the very printing press upon whicli Voltaire had printed his infidel literature, was being used to print copies of the Bible. And afterward, the very house in which the boasting Voltaire had lived, was literally stacked with Bibles prepared by the Geneva _____ _____.

Though attacked in so many ways over the centuries and still today, the Bible has been, and is the most widely distributed and translated book of all time by far!

* **The Bible's Vast Distribution** - Guiness World Records says that the Bible is clearly the most widely read and sold book of all times. Note the following from their web site: "Although it is impossible to obtain exact figures, there is little doubt that the Bible is the worlds best-selling and most widely distributed book. A survey by the Bible Society concluded that around 2.5 billion copies were printed between 1815 and 1975, but more recent estimates put the number at more than 5 billion."

**Bible Distribution**
* **Gideons**
Distributed 1 Billion Bibles & N.T. – (1908 - 2001)
Distributed a 2nd Billion – (2002 – 2015)
Averaging over 1 Million Every 4 Days
* Many Other Organizations Involved As Well

They go on to say "the whole Bible had been translated into 349 languages; 2123 languages have at least one book of the Bible in that language." Wycliff Bible Translators say that the number *of* languages that have complete Bibles is now up to 550! As a part of their "_____ _____" Wycliffe Bible Translators have said "We embrace the vision that by the year 2025 a Bible translation project will be in progress for every people group that needs it."

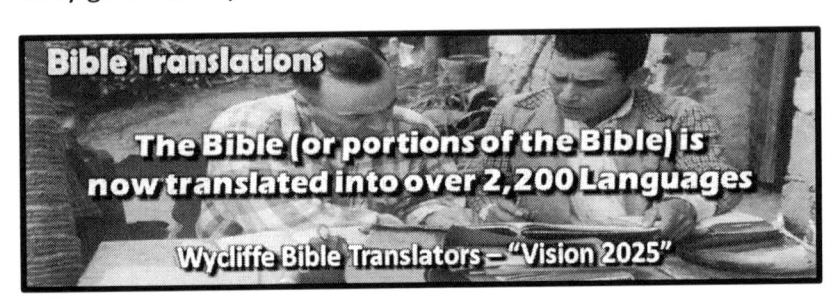

**Bible Translations**
The Bible (or portions of the Bible) is now translated into over 2,200 Languages
Wycliffe Bible Translators – "Vision 2025"

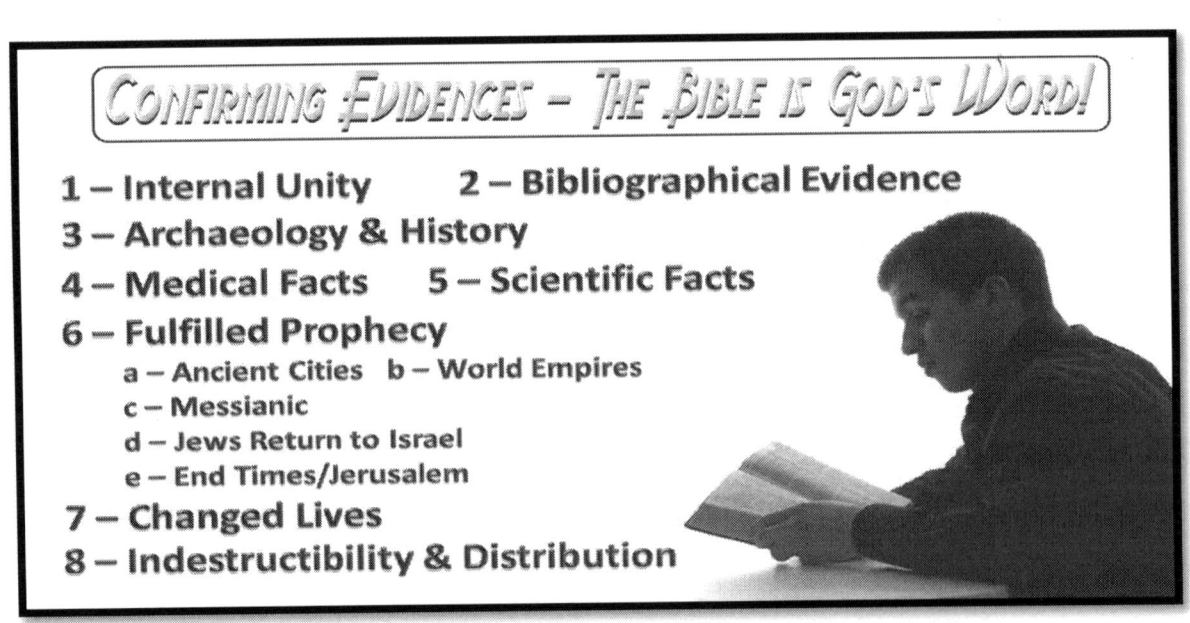

---

### CONFIRMING EVIDENCES – THE BIBLE IS GOD'S WORD!

1 – Internal Unity     2 – Bibliographical Evidence
3 – Archaeology & History
4 – Medical Facts     5 – Scientific Facts
6 – Fulfilled Prophecy
   a – Ancient Cities   b – World Empires
   c – Messianic
   d – Jews Return to Israel
   e – End Times/Jerusalem
7 – Changed Lives
8 – Indestructibility & Distribution

---

**Conclusion - Confirming Evidences Show That the Bible is the Word of God!**

(Remember that free Memory Cards to assist you in remembering these main points of evidence are available for download at localchurchapologetics.org)

# FAITH & REASON MADE SIMPLE — Part 6

## (Confirming Evidence That The Bible is The Word of God – Cont.)

In our last session we viewed the first 4 of our 8 areas of evidence that confirm to us that the Bible is the Word of God. In this session we will look into the final 4 areas of evidence.

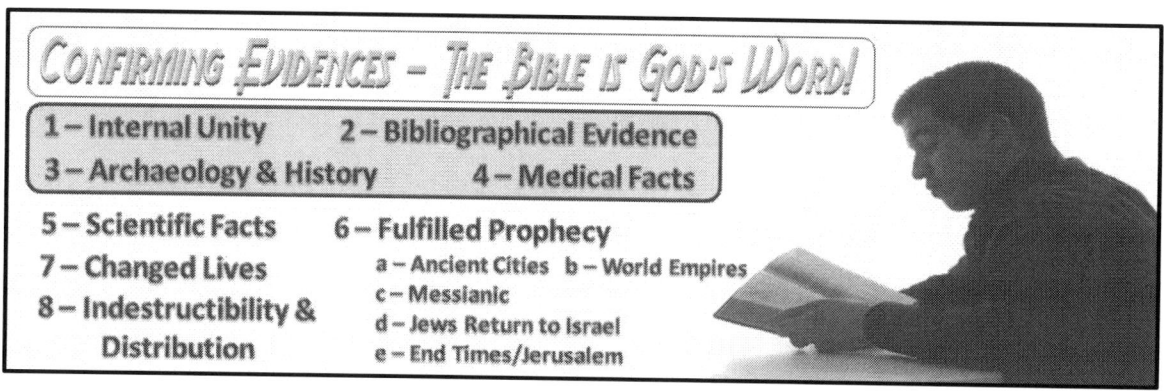

**Confirming Evidences – The Bible is God's Word!**

1 – Internal Unity    2 – Bibliographical Evidence
3 – Archaeology & History    4 – Medical Facts
5 – Scientific Facts    6 – Fulfilled Prophecy
7 – Changed Lives
    a – Ancient Cities    b – World Empires
    c – Messianic
8 – Indestructibility & Distribution
    d – Jews Return to Israel
    e – End Times/Jerusalem

## #5 – Scientific Facts in the Bible

\* There are numerous scientific facts that were written in the Bible 2,500 to 3,500 years ago that have now been confirmed by modern scientific study. The fact that the Bible spoke of these things hundreds of years before mankind came to understand them shows that the Bible is given to us by God Himself, the Creator! Examples –

* \* The Earth is a **sphere** – Isaiah 40:22
* \* The Universe is **expanding** (Stretched Out by God) – Psalm 104:2, Psalm 144:5, Job 9:8, Isaiah 40:22, Isaiah 42:5, Isaiah 44:24, Isaiah 45:12, Isaiah 48:13, Jeremiah 10:12, Zech. 12:1
* \* The stars of the Pleiades constellation are gravitationally bound together while the stars of the Orion constellation are not - Job 38:31
* \* Innumerable Amount of Stars – Genesis 15:5, Jeremiah 33:22
* \* Mountains on the Ocean Floor – Jonah 2:5-6
* \* Currents (or Paths) in the **Oceans** & **Seas** - Psalm 8:8, Isaiah 43:16
* \* Hydrological Cycle – Job 36:27-28, Psalm 135:6-7, Ecclesiastes 1:7, Amos 9:6
* \* The Existence of Dinosaurs – Job 40 & 41, Psalm 74:14 (note – the word "dinosaur" was invented in the mid 1800s so the Bible does not use that word)
* \* There Are Springs in the Seas – Job 38:16
* \* The Earth is Hung on Nothing – Job 26:7

# #6 – Fulfilled Prophecies In The Bible

There are many prophecies written in the Bible which have come to pass just at the Bible indicated they would or are coming to pass even now. Most of these were written in the Old Testament, 3500 – 2500 years ago. These fulfilled prophecies that can be seen to have been fulfilled by world history or by the news of our time give wonderful evidence that the Bible is the Word of God!

An example of these fulfilled prophecies is seen in Isaiah's prophecies about Cyrus the Great, who became a ruler of the **Medo-Persian Empire** a couple of hundred years after Isaiah wrote the prophetic words. The prophecy indicated that it would be Cyrus who God would use to allow the Jews to return to the land of Israel after decades of captivity, and to begin the rebuilding of the Temple. History reveals that Cyrus did just as the Bible predicted he would.

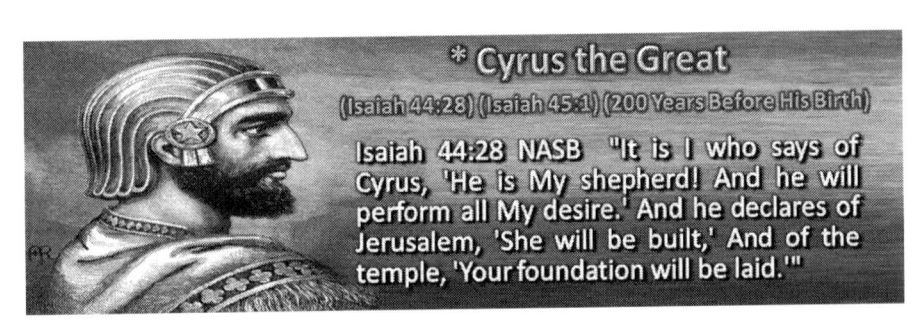

**Cyrus the Great**
(Isaiah 44:28) (Isaiah 45:1) (200 Years Before His Birth)
Isaiah 44:28 NASB "It is I who says of Cyrus, 'He is My shepherd! And he will perform all My desire.' And he declares of Jerusalem, 'She will be built,' And of the temple, 'Your foundation will be laid.'"

## A – Destruction of Powerful Ancient Cities

\* The Bible gives detailed prophecies concerning the destruction of some of the most powerful ancient cities that existed in the times the Old Testament was written.

* **Petra** – (Obadiah 1) (Isaiah 34:5-15) Petra (Referred to as the house of Esau dwelling in the clefts of the rocks or as Edom) was especially strong because it was built within rocky cliffs and could not be reached by enemies without approaching it from underneath which left soldiers venerable.
* **Babylon** – (Jeremiah 50 & 51) The city of Babylon was the strongest city of its day but the Bible prophesied it would become a desolate, habitat for wild animals. The prophesy was fulfilled.
* **Tyre** – (Ezekiel 26 & 27) The city of Tyre was on the coast of the Mediterranean Sea. It consisted of a mainland city and an island fortress about ½ mile off the coast. Ezekiel prophesied of the destruction of Tyre in great detail including destruction by Nebuchadnezzar and the scraping of the debris from the mainland into the sea which was fulfilled by Alexander the Great in **332** BC. Alexander commanded his soldiers to use the debris from the previous destruction of the mainland city in order to create a causeway from the mainland to the island fortress of Tyre. They scrapped it bare like a rock. An aerial view of Tyre today shows that the causeway they created is still there today!

**Arial View of Tyre from 1934**

## B- World Empires to Rise & Fall

* In the book of **Daniel** there are detailed prophecies concerning the rising and falling of world empires through a dream Nebuchadnezzar had in Daniel 2 and through visions that Daniel had in Daniel 7 & 8. The Bible predicts that the Babylonian Empire would be followed by the Medo-Persian Empire and that the Medo-Persian Empire would be followed by the Greek Empire. It names these 3 empires. It indicates that the first ruler of the Greek Empire would die at an early age and that the empire would then be divided into 4 parts. It then predicts that the Greek Empire will be conquered and followed by a 4th world empire that would stronger than the first 3. Finally, it predicts that there will be another world empire that will emerge from among the nations in the last days.

* World history shows us that the Bible was accurate in foretelling all of these things. The Babylonian Empire was conquered and followed by the Medo-Persian Empire. The Medo-Persian Empire was conquered and followed by the Greek Empire. The first ruler of the Greek Empire was **Alexander the Great** who died in his 30s. After his death the Greek Empire was divided into 4 parts. The Greek Empire was conquered and followed by the **Roman** Empire which was more powerful than any previous world empire. It stood for hundreds of years. Today there is movement toward a New World Order which is emerging from among the nations. The Bible has accurately foretold world history!

## C – Messianic Prophecies

The Old Testament contains over **300** Messianic prophecies that were all fulfilled in the New Testament by Jesus Christ. This fact speaks to the internal unity of the Bible and the identity of Jesus as the Christ, as well as the Bible's ability to proclaim future events prior to them coming to pass. Here is a list of some of the Messianic prophecies fulfilled by Jesus Christ.

* Would be born in **Bethlehem** – (Micah 5:2)
* Would be born of a virgin – (Isaiah 7:14)
* Would be betrayed for **30** pieces of silver – (Zechariah 11:12-13) (The price of a slave)
* Would ride into Jerusalem on a donkey – (Zechariah 9:9)
* Soldiers would gamble for His outer garment – (Psalm 22:18)
* Would be pierced in His side – (Isaiah 53:5) (Zechariah 12:10)
* Not a **bone** of His body would be **broken** – (Exodus 12:46) (Psalm 34:20)
* He would speak in parables – (Psalm 78:2)
* He would live and minister in Galilee – (Isaiah 9:1-2)
* He would be the Savior of the Jews & a Light to the Nations – (Isaiah 49:5-6)
* Would have nails driven through His hands and feet – (Psalm 22:16)
* Buried in the grave of a rich man – (Isaiah 53:9)

* In his book "Science Speaks", Dr. Peter Stoner explains a research project that he and students at Pasadena City College, where he was a professor, did to estimate the probability of one person fulfilling various Old Testament Messianic prophecies. Here are the conservative estimates their research revealed concerning just 8 of the Old Testament messianic prophecies.

"When multiplied together it was found that even using these very conservative estimates, there would be a **1 in 10$^{28}$** chance of someone fulfilling just **8** of these Messianic prophecies."
"That number looks like this when written out - 10,000,000,000,000,000,000,000,000,000."

## D – The Scattering & Regathering of the Jewish People

Maybe the most startling example of fulfilled Bible prophecy that confirms the fact that the Bible is the Word of God are the prophecies concerning the scattering of the **Jewish people** and the regathering of the Jewish people to the land of Israel from the nations of world. We have been witnessing the fulfillment of these prophecies throughout our lifetime. In addition to the regathering of the Jewish people the Bible also prophecies that the land of Israel will blossom and become fruitful, and the cities will be renewed. All of these things are being fulfilled in the world today and much of world history over the past 100 years can be seen to be related to these fulfillments.

* ***The scattering of the Jewish people to the Nations***
**Deuteronomy 28:64 NASB** "Moreover, the LORD will scatter you among all peoples, from one end of the earth to the other end of the earth; and there you shall serve other gods, wood and stone, which you or your fathers have not known.

* ***The regathering of the Jewish people to the land of Israel***
**Ezekiel 36:24 NASB** "For I will take you from the nations, gather you from all the lands and bring you into your own land.
**Isaiah 11:11-12 NASB** Then it will happen on that day that the Lord Will again recover the second time with His hand The remnant of His people, who will remain, From Assyria, Egypt, Pathros, Cush, Elam, Shinar, Hamath, And from the islands of the sea. (12) And He will lift up a standard for the nations And assemble the banished ones of Israel, And will gather the dispersed of Judah From the four corners of the earth.
**Ezekiel 38:8 NASB** "After many days you will be summoned; in the latter years you will come into the land that is restored from the sword, whose inhabitants have been gathered from many nations to the mountains of Israel which had been a continual waste; but its people were brought out from the nations, and they are living securely, all of them.
**Ezekiel 28:25-26 NASB** 'Thus says the Lord GOD, "When I gather the house of Israel from the peoples among whom they are scattered, and will manifest My holiness in them in the sight of the nations, then they will live in their land which I gave to My servant Jacob. (26) "They will live in it securely; and they will build houses, plant vineyards and live securely when I execute judgments upon all who scorn them round about them. Then they will know that I am the LORD their God."'"

**Jeremiah 29:11-14 NASB** 'For I know the plans that I have for you,' declares the LORD, 'plans for welfare and not for calamity to give you a future and a hope. (12) 'Then you will call upon Me and come and pray to Me, and I will listen to you. (13) 'You will seek Me and find Me when you search for Me with all your heart. (14) 'I will be found by you,' declares the LORD, 'and I will restore your fortunes and will gather you from all the nations and from all the places where I have driven you,' declares the LORD, 'and I will bring you back to the place from where I sent you into exile.'

* *The Land of Israel & the Cities of Israel Will Become Fruitful Again*
**Ezekiel 36:30-35 NASB** "I will multiply the fruit of the tree and the produce of the field, so that you will not receive again the disgrace of famine among the nations. ... (34) "The desolate land will be cultivated instead of being a desolation in the sight of everyone who passes by. (35) "They will say, 'This desolate land has become like the garden of Eden; and the waste, desolate and ruined cities are fortified and inhabited.'
**Ezekiel 36:8-11 NASB** 'But you, O mountains of Israel, you will put forth your branches and bear your fruit for My people Israel; for they will soon come. (9) 'For, behold, I am for you, and I will turn to you, and you will be cultivated and sown. (10) 'I will multiply men on you, all the house of Israel, all of it; and the cities will be inhabited and the waste places will be rebuilt. (11) 'I will multiply on you man and beast; and they will increase and be fruitful; and I will cause you to be inhabited as you were formerly and will treat you better than at the first. Thus you will know that I am the LORD.

* **The Jews have been returning to Israel for the last 120 years from the nations of the world!**
    * Jewish population in Israel  (1948 – About ¼ million)(Today – Over 6 million)
    * 1917 (World War 1) (Jerusalem rescued from 400 years of Muslim control)
    * 1917 (**Balfour** Declaration)
    * 1945 – 1947  (Holocaust)(Homeland for the Jews in Israel laid out)
    * May 14, **1948** (Israel becomes a nation)
    * 1989 (Iron curtain falls) (Over 1 million Jews return to Israel)
    * Jewish immigration from all over the world to Israel continues today

* **The Land of Israel has been restored and it has become very fruitful!**
    * Mid 1800s – **Mark Twain** declared the land of Israel as the most desolate place on earth. He wrote "It is a hopeless, dreary, heart-broken land.". He also said that the land was "... a silent, mournful expanse "
    * Since that time the land has blossomed, just as the Bible said it would!
    * More than **400 million** trees have been planted
    * Rains have returned
    * World class modern irrigation systems have been installed
    * Israel now is a fruit exporting nation
    * The cities have been inhabited and become productive
        (Tel Aviv – World Class Technology)
    * Natural Gas & **Oil** Reserves have been found in Israel

* **Also worth noting -**
    * Israel has been supernaturally protected through **numerous wars**!

* The **Hebrew language** has been restored! (Zephaniah 3:9)
* The Golden (Eastern) Gate remains closed up as the Bible foretold! (Ezekiel 44:1-3)
* The Jewish people have blessed the nations (Genesis 12:2-3)(22:18)(26:4)(28:14)
(201 of the 892 Nobel Prize winners are Jewish!)

## E – The City of Jerusalem & End Time Prophecies

* The Bible prophecies in Zechariah 12 & 14 that **Jerusalem** will be the focus of international attention in the last days and eventually will be surrounded by the nations of the world, just before Jesus returns!

* **Zechariah 12:1-3 NASB** The burden of the word of the LORD concerning Israel. Thus declares the LORD who stretches out the heavens, lays the foundation of the earth, and forms the spirit of man within him, (2) "Behold, I am going to make Jerusalem a cup that causes reeling to all the peoples around; and when the siege is against Jerusalem, it will also be against Judah. (3) "It will come about in that day that I will make Jerusalem a heavy stone for all the peoples; all who lift it will be severely injured. And all the nations of the earth will be gathered against it.

* **Zechariah 14:1-4 NASB** Behold, a day is coming for the LORD when the spoil taken from you will be divided among you. (2) For I will gather all the nations against Jerusalem to battle, and the city will be captured, the houses plundered, the women ravished and half of the city exiled, but the rest of the people will not be cut off from the city. (3) Then the LORD will go forth and fight against those nations, as when He fights on a day of battle. (4) In that day His feet will stand on the Mount of Olives, which is in front of Jerusalem on the east; and the Mount of Olives will be split in its middle from east to west by a very large valley, so that half of the mountain will move toward the north and the other half toward the south.

   * There is no question that **Jerusalem** is the most contention place on the face of the earth today. Conflicts between Palestinians & Jews over the city of Jerusalem are very much at the center of international attention.
   * The contention over the city of Jerusalem was increased in 2018 when the United States moved its **Embassy** to Jerusalem and acknowledged it as Israel's capital city.
   * In 2015 the United Nations began flying the Palestinian flag at the United Nations Headquarters in New York. It appears that they are very close to declaring Palestinian statehood. The Palestinians have said that when this happens Jerusalem will be their capital. The Israeli leaders have said that this will not happen.
   * In 2012 during the revolution in Egypt as the new leader Mohamed Morsi was being inaugurated, Islamic Cleric Safwat Higazi spoke to a massive crowd in Cairo, Egypt. He stated "We can see how the dream of the Islamic Caliphate is being realized … **Our capital** shall not be Cairo, Mecca, or Medina. It shall be Jerusalem! … Yes, Jerusalem is our goal. We shall pray in Jerusalem, or else we shall die as martyrs on its threshold" He then led the massive crowd in a repeated emotional chat, "Millions of martyrs march toward Jerusalem
   * Chinese believers have been organizing for some time the "Back to Jerusalem" movement. Their goal is to enlist 100 thousand believers who are willing to become martyrs for the gospel of

Jesus Christ. They are being sent from China to take the gospel of Jesus to all the nations and people between China and Jerusalem. They plan to end up sharing the gospel of Jesus Christ to the people of the city of Jerusalem.

* The United Nations approves more resolutions against Israel than against all other nations combined. Many of them have to do with the city of Jerusalem.
* 2500 years ago the Bible foretold that this particular city would be the focus of the nations of the world in the last days. Jerusalem was destroyed in 70 A.D. (C.E.). It lay barren for many years and was insignificant. What are the chances of this one medium size city would emerge from oblivion to be the focal point of **world** **attention** just as the Bible had foretold? The chances would be almost zero if the Bible were just a book written by men!

## * The Increase of Travel & Knowledge In the Last Days

Daniel 12:4 makes an astounding statement about the last days when we consider what has transpired over the past 100 years in the world we live in. It is easy to see that the 2 most notable developments in the past 100 years are the increase of travel and the increase of knowledge. 2500 years ago the Bible foretold

Daniel 12:4   NASB   "But as for you, Daniel, conceal these words and seal up the book until the end of time; many will go back and forth, and knowledge will increase."

this very thing concerning the last days. This is another indicator that the Bible is the Word of God!

## * The Eastern (or Golden) Gate

Ezekiel 44:1-3 NASB  Then He brought me back by the way of the outer gate of the sanctuary, which faces the east; and it was shut. (2) The LORD said to me, "This gate shall be shut; it shall not be opened, and no one shall enter by it, for the LORD God of Israel has entered by it; therefore it shall be shut. (3) "As for the prince, he shall sit in it as prince to eat bread before the LORD; he shall enter by way of the porch of the gate and shall go out by the same way."

About **2600** years ago this Biblical prophecy was written, indicating a specific gate in the old city walls of the city of Jerusalem would be shut and not opened until the Messiah (the Prince) comes again and travels through this gate. The Eastern Gate is the closest gate to the Temple Mount. Remarkably it is shut today, just as the Bible said it would be. It is the only gate in the old city walls that is shut. Coincidence? I think not!

## * The mark of the beast (666) – Revelation 13:16-18

* The Bible foretold 1,900 years ago that in the last days there would be a worldwide economic system involving the number 666 that would enable a world leader to prevent anyone not taking the number mark from being able to buy or sell. Today, every product we buy is marked with the number 666 through the universal product code. This obviously is not a coincidence, but rather is

another indicator that the Bible is the Word of God! Examine numerous products and notice the first two lines, the middle two lines, and the last two lines of the code marked on the products. You will find them to be the same on all products (at least on those using this form of the UPC). These 3 sets of lines each represent a 6. The number 666 is already marked on our products. This is not the mark of the beast at this time. It is just the overarching number of the Universal Product Code. It is not hard to image though that this number will be a part of the worldwide economic system that is developing. The technology has now been developed to place a computer chip under the skin in the back of the hand or in the forehead of people around the world. The Bible says that a day will come that a person will not be able to buy or sell without a number assigned to them that will include the number 666. It is easy to see today that the world is moving toward that time.

## #7 – Changed Lives

* Millions (or Billions) of lives have been radically changed in a positive way by the message of hope, love and salvation found in the Bible! This is true throughout the centuries since Christ came, but is especially true of the past 100+ years. Note the examples in the picture below.

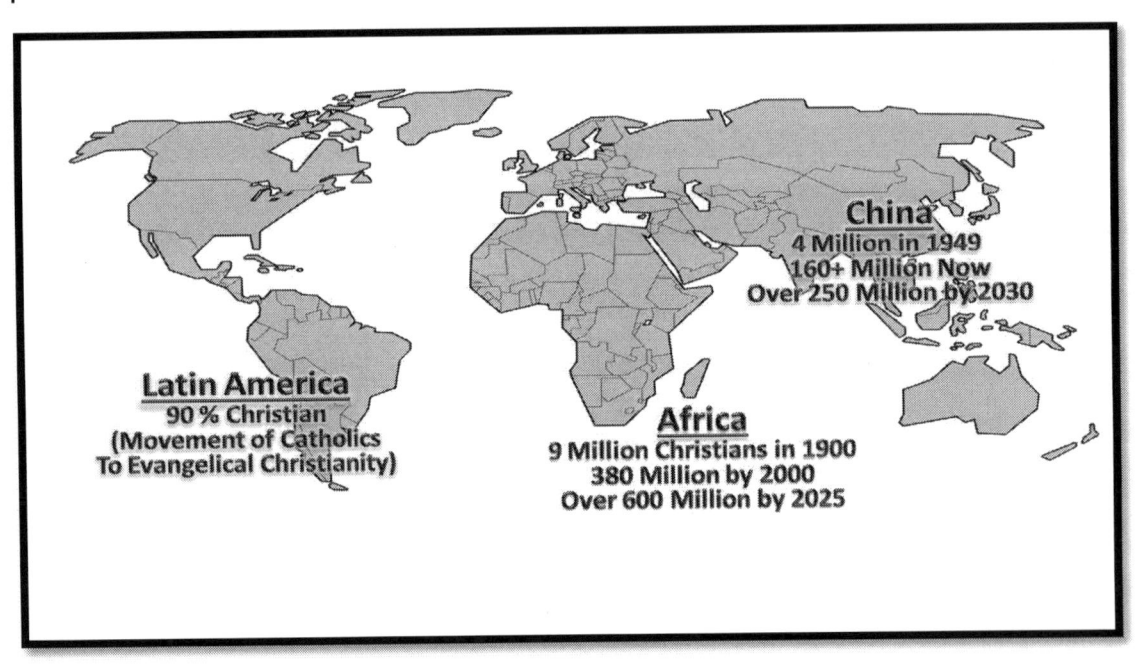

**China**
4 Million in 1949
160+ Million Now
Over 250 Million by 2030

**Latin America**
90 % Christian
(Movement of Catholics
To Evangelical Christianity)

**Africa**
9 Million Christians in 1900
380 Million by 2000
Over 600 Million by 2025

* Many **Muslims** are now coming to know Christ as Savior!
    (More than any other time in history) (Maybe over a million in Iran)
    (God is giving dreams and visions to many Muslims to bring them to Christ)

Acts 2:17 NASB 'AND IT SHALL BE IN THE LAST DAYS,' God says, 'THAT I WILL POUR FORTH OF MY SPIRIT ON ALL MANKIND; AND YOUR SONS AND YOUR DAUGHTERS SHALL PROPHESY, AND YOUR YOUNG MEN SHALL SEE VISIONS, AND YOUR OLD MEN SHALL DREAM DREAMS;

* Many **Jews** are turning to Christ now, especially in the last 5 years!
* The changed lives of millions (or billions) of people testifies to the truth of the Bible's message!

## #8 – Indestructibility & Distribution

* The Bible has been **opposed** and **attacked** for centuries by nations, leaders and antagonists, yet it has withstood every attack. Despite so much opposition the Bible continues to be the most published and distributed book in the world every year!

* Example 1 - In an article entitled "The Indestructibility of the Bible" on the web site entitled Truth Magazine, Cecil Willis explains, "Many of their efforts were directed toward destroying the Bible. Of Diocletian (284-316), the ruler immediately preceding Constantine, Eusebius, the historian said, "royal edicts were published everywhere, commanding that the churches be leveled to the ground and the Scriptures destroyed by fire" (Church History, Book VIII, Ch. 1). Diocletian went on to say that if one had a copy of the Scriptures and did not surrender it to be burned, if it were discovered, he would be killed. During this time many, many copies of the Bible were burned, copies laboriously written in longhand. After this edict had been in force for two years, Diocletian boasted, "I have completely exterminated the **Christian** **writings** from the face of the earth!" (Rimmer, Seven Wonders of the Wonderful Word, p. 15). But had he completely destroyed it? History tells us that the next ruler, Constantine, became a Christian. He requested that copies of the Scriptures be made for all the churches."

* Example 2 - "Voltaire, the noted French infidel, who died in 1778, made his attempt to destroy the Bible. He boldly made the prediction that within one hundred years the Bible and Christianity would have been swept from existence into oblivion. But Voltaire's efforts and his bold prophecy failed as miserably as did those of his unbelieving predecessors. In fact, within 100 years, the very printing press upon whicli Voltaire had printed his infidel literature, was being used to print copies of the Bible. And afterward, the very house in which the boasting Voltaire had lived, was literally stacked with Bibles prepared by the Geneva **Bible** **Society**.

Though attacked in so many ways over the centuries and still today, the Bible has been, and is the most widely distributed and translated book of all time by far!

* **The Bible's Vast Distribution** - Guiness World Records says that the Bible is clearly the most widely read and sold book of all times. Note the following from their web site: "Although it is impossible to obtain exact figures, there is little doubt that the Bible is the worlds best-selling and most widely distributed book. A survey by the Bible Society concluded that around 2.5 billion copies were printed between 1815 and 1975, but more recent estimates put the number at more than 5 billion."

**Bible Distribution**
* **Gideons**
Distributed 1 Billion Bibles & N.T. – (1908 - 2001)
Distributed a 2nd Billion – (2002 – 2015)
Averaging over 1 Million Every 4 Days
* Many Other Organizations Involved As Well

They go on to say "the whole Bible had been translated into 349 languages; 2123 languages have at least one book of the Bible in that language." Wycliff Bible Translators say that the number of languages that have complete Bibles is now up to 550! As a part of their "**Vision 2025**" Wycliffe Bible Translators have said "We embrace the vision that by the year 2025 a Bible translation project will be in progress for every people group that needs it."

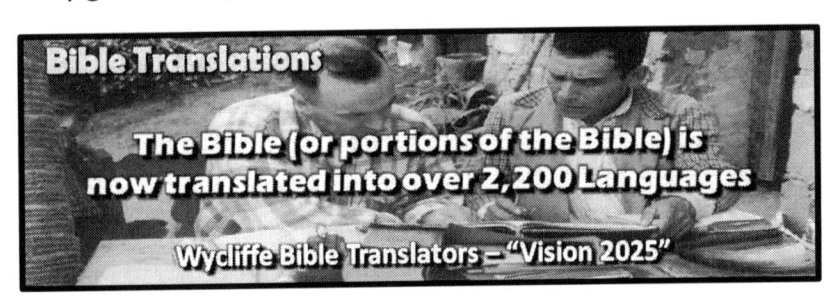

**Bible Translations**
The Bible (or portions of the Bible) is now translated into over 2,200 Languages
Wycliffe Bible Translators – "Vision 2025"

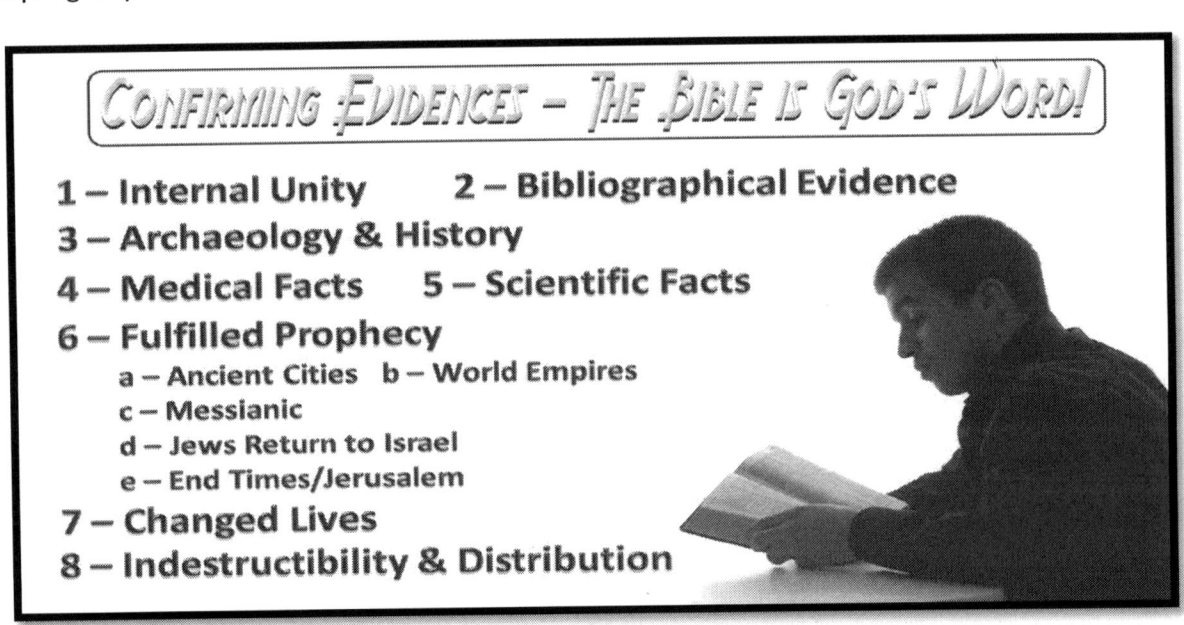

---

**Confirming Evidences – The Bible is God's Word!**

1 – Internal Unity     2 – Bibliographical Evidence
3 – Archaeology & History
4 – Medical Facts     5 – Scientific Facts
6 – Fulfilled Prophecy
    a – Ancient Cities   b – World Empires
    c – Messianic
    d – Jews Return to Israel
    e – End Times/Jerusalem
7 – Changed Lives
8 – Indestructibility & Distribution

---

**Conclusion - Confirming Evidences Show That the Bible is the Word of God!**

(Remember that free Memory Cards to assist you in remembering these main points of evidence are available for download at localchurchapologetics.org)

# FAITH & REASON MADE SIMPLE — Part 7

## (The Person of Jesus Christ)

### Introduction – Review

We have looked at evidences which confirm that God created the heavens, the earth, and each of us!
We have looked at evidences which confirm that the Bible is the Word of God!
We will now approach the questions surrounding who Jesus Christ is with these issues in mind! Though we will look at external evidences beyond the Bible it is important to understand that the Bible is the Word of God and to look at what the Bible has to say about who Jesus Christ is! Note the progression of thought and inquiry listed here –

1. – Did God Create the Heavens & the Earth? - Yes
2. – Is God a Personal God Who Created Us in His Image? – Yes
3. – Is the Bible God's Word Given to Us to Reveal His Plans to Us? – Yes
4. – Is Jesus God, the Messiah (Christ), and the Savior of the World?
   (We look at this question after answering the first 3 as a basis.)

## The Identity of Jesus Christ is Attacked Today

### THE ATTACKS UPON THE IDENTITY OF JESUS CHRIST

**Challenge #1:** Scholars Are Uncovering a Radically Different Jesus through Ancient Documents (Gnostic Gospels) Just as Credible as the Four Gospels
**Challenge #2:** The Bible's Portrait of Jesus Can't Be Trusted Because the Church Tampered with the Text
**Challenge #3:** New Explanations Have Disproved Jesus' _____
**Challenge #4:** Christianity's Beliefs about Jesus Were Copied from Pagan Religions
**Challenge #5:** Jesus Was an Impostor Who Failed to Fulfill the _____ about the Messiah
**Challenge #6:** People Should Be Free to Pick and Choose What to Believe about Jesus
(Note – These 6 challenges are addressed in Lee Stobel's book "The Case For the Real Jesus"

*The DaVinci Code by Dan Brown (Over 80 Million Copies Sold Worldwide) (Plus 2006 Blockbuster Movie)
Portrays Jesus Christ as a mortal prophet who was _____ to Mary Magdalene. Claims that Jesus and Mary had children together and that their descendants are alive today. Also claims that the church has altered the story of Jesus to make him appear divine.

* **"Religulous" by Bill Maher** – (Documentary Movie – 2008)
    Among other things claims that the Christian narrative of Jesus in the Bible is a retelling of ancient deity myths from Persia, Egypt, etc., such as myths about "Mithras", "Horus" and others.

* **The Jesus Seminar** (Research Seminar by So-Called Scholars) (1985-1991)
    In 1985 numerous liberal "scholars" came together to determine if Jesus really said the things that the Bible says He said. They determined He did not say 80% of the things that the Bible says He said. They also denied the reality of His _____, His _____, and His _____.

## Faith & Reason Made Simple (Part 7) – The Person of Jesus Christ!

* In this session we will look at external evidences beyond the Bible that confirm the reality of Jesus' life, death and resurrection. We will look at the impact He has had upon the world. We will also look at Who the Bible says Jesus Christ is and what He has done.

## Jesus Is Truly a Historical Person!

Some modern critics of Jesus say that He never existed but is a myth made up by early Christians. The Bible certainly presents Jesus as an historical person. We have already seen confirming evidences that the Bible is the Word of God in parts 5 and 6. Note how Luke gives historical perspective to the life of Jesus in Luke 1:1-5. He says he is compiling an accurate account of public events as witnessed by eyewitnesses. In verse 5 he begins by dating the time to "the days of Herod, king of Judea." He later will give many other historical details in his account of the life of Jesus.

> Luke 1:1-5 NASB  Inasmuch as many have undertaken to compile an account of the things accomplished among us, (2) just as they were handed down to us by those who from the beginning were eyewitnesses and servants of the word, (3) it seemed fitting for me as well, having investigated everything carefully from the beginning, to write *it* out for you in consecutive order, most excellent Theophilus; (4) so that you may know the exact truth about the things you have been taught. (5) In the days of Herod, king of Judea, there was a priest named Zacharias, of the division of Abijah; and he had a wife from the daughters of Aaron, and her name was Elizabeth.

### Jesus has impacted our world like no other person in history!
(Even our _____ points to Him!)(Our calendar divides all of history upon His birth!)
(Nations have been impacted)(Women's Rights have emerged)(Mercy & Justice in Legal Systems)
(Missionary work has been accomplished in His Name including the building of Orphanages and Hospitals)

The Historical Life of Jesus is confirmed by a number of historical sources outside the Bible!
(Here are a few)

## Tacitus (Roman Historian)
(While speaking of Nero's response to the fire of Rome)

Consequently, to get rid of the report, _____ fastened the guilt and inflicted the most exquisite tortures on a class hated for their abominations, called Christians by the populace. Christus, from whom the name had its origin, suffered the extreme penalty during the reign of Tiberius at the hands of one of our procurators, Pontius Pilatus, and a most mischievous superstition, thus checked for the moment, again broke out not only in Judaea, the first source of the evil, but even in Rome, where all things hideous and shameful from every part of the world find their centre and become popular. ... Accordingly, an arrest was first made of all who pleaded guilty; then, upon their information, an immense multitude was convicted, not so much of the crime of firing the city, as of hatred against mankind. Mockery of every sort was added to their deaths. Covered with the skins of beasts, they were torn by dogs and perished, or were nailed to crosses, or were doomed to the flames and burnt, to serve as a nightly illumination, when daylight had expired. Nero offered his gardens for the spectacle, and was exhibiting a show in the circus, while he mingled with the people in the dress of a charioteer or stood aloft on a car. Hence, even for criminals who deserved extreme and exemplary punishment, there arose a feeling of compassion; for it was not, as it seemed, for the public good, but to glut one man's cruelty, that they were being destroyed. (Annals 15.44)

## (Josephus) (Jewish Historian) Antiquities 20.9.1
But the younger Ananus who, as we said, received the high priesthood, was of a bold disposition and exceptionally daring; he followed the party of the Sadducees, who are severe in judgment above all the Jews, as we have already shown. As therefore Ananus was of such a disposition, he thought he had now a good opportunity, as Festus was now dead, and Albinus was still on the road; so he assembled a council of judges, and brought before it the _____ of Jesus the so-called Christ, whose name was James, together with some others, and having accused them as law-breakers, he delivered them over to be stoned.

### (Josephus) Antiquities 18.3.3
Now there was about this time Jesus, a wise man, if it be lawful to call him a man, for he was a doer of wonderful works, a teacher of such men as receive the truth with pleasure. He drew over to him both many of the Jews, and many of the Gentiles. He was the Christ, and when Pilate, at the suggestion of the principal men among us, had condemned him to the cross, those that loved him at the first did not forsake him; for he appeared to them alive again the third day; as the divine prophets had foretold these and ten thousand other wonderful things concerning him. And the tribe of Christians so named from him are not extinct at this day.

## Pliny the Younger
**(a Lawyer, Author & Magistrate of 1st Century Rome)** (He speaks of Jesus & His followers)
Pliny the Younger, in Letters 10:96, recorded early Christian worship practices including the fact that Christians worshiped Jesus as God and were very _____, and he includes a reference to the love feast and _____ _____.

## Writings of the Sanhedrin speak of Jesus' crucifixion

The Babylonian Talmud (Sanhedrin 43a) confirms Jesus' crucifixion on the eve of Passover and the accusations against Him of practicing sorcery and encouraging Jewish apostasy –

"On the Eve of _____, they hung Jesus of Nazareth for sorcery and enticing Israel [to idolatry]."

## Lucian of Samosata (Second-Century Greek Writer)

Lucian admits that Jesus was worshiped by Christians, introduced new teachings, and was crucified for them. He said that Jesus' teachings included the brotherhood of believers, the importance of conversion, and the importance of denying other gods. Christians lived according to Jesus' laws, believed themselves to be immortal, and were characterized by contempt for death, voluntary self-devotion, and renunciation of material goods.

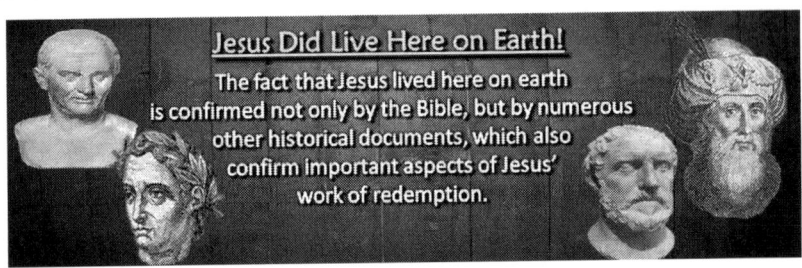

**Jesus Did Live Here on Earth!**
The fact that Jesus lived here on earth is confirmed not only by the Bible, but by numerous other historical documents, which also confirm important aspects of Jesus' work of redemption.

# The Biblical Account of Jesus is Not the Retelling of Ancient Deity Myths!

One of the accusations being promoted today by skeptics like Bill Maher is that the Biblical account of the birth, life, miracles, death and resurrection of Jesus is simply the retelling of one of numerous ancient deity myths that supposedly referred to the same details hundreds of years earlier. The idea that Jesus is a copy-cat deity was promoted by a few authors in the 18th & 19th centuries. Other authors have repeated these accusations in the 20th & 21st centuries. A careful examination of these claims reveals that many of the proposed details of myths regarding _____, Horus and others simply are not accurate. Also, many of the writings that show some details that are comparable to Jesus were written hundreds of years after the oldest New Testament manuscripts, showing that any striking similarities would actually indicate that pagan writers copied details of Jesus' life, not the other way around.

It is important to be aware of these accusations regarding the Biblical accounts of Jesus, since they are used by many critics of Christianity. Numerous helpful articles can be found on these subjects by going to **searchcreation.org** and typing in "Jesus vs. Mithras" or "Jesus vs. Horus".

# The Bodily Resurrection of Jesus is Confirmed in Many Ways!

The resurrection of Jesus Christ is the most important historical event in world history and is the centerpiece of all Christian teachings. _____ says - "that if you confess with your mouth Jesus as Lord, and believe in your heart that God raised Him from the dead, you will be saved". 1 Corinthians 15:14 reveals even further just how important the resurrection of Jesus is to the Christian faith.

> 1 Corinthians 15:14 NASB (14) and if Christ has not been raised, then our preaching is vain, your faith also is vain.

According to Romans 10:9-10, believing that God has raised Christ from the dead is a key part of salvation and being declared righteous by God! 1 Corinthians 15:14 tells us that our faith is vain, or useless if Christ did not rise from the dead. Let's look at evidences that support the biblical account of the bodily resurrection of Jesus Christ from the dead. To begin with look at the 9 facts listed by Dr. Gary Habermas concerning the resurrection of Jesus that contemporary _____ _____ agree to.

> **Dr. Gary Habermas (One of the world's foremost experts on the resurrection of Jesus) says most contemporary critical scholars agree to these 9 facts!**
>
> 1. The Disciples believed they had encounters with the risen Jesus!
> 2. The Disciples were transformed from fearful doubters to bold proclaimers!
> 3. Jesus' Tomb was empty!
> 4. The Resurrection message was central to early church teachings!
> 5. Jewish leaders could not disprove the disciples message!
> 6. The Resurrection was crucial to the church's birth & rapid spread!
> 7. Sunday became the primary day of worship!
> 8. James, (brother of Jesus) was transformed from skeptic to believer!
> 9. Paul (Saul) was transformed by his believed encounter with Christ!

## Eye Witnesses

The Bible presents the resurrection of Jesus Christ from the dead as historical fact that was witnessed by many eye witnesses that were still living at the time the New Testament writers were penning their accounts of the resurrection.

> 1 Corinthians 15:3-8 NASB (3) For I delivered to you as of first importance what I also received, that Christ died for our sins according to the Scriptures, (4) and that He was buried, and that He was raised on the third day according to the Scriptures, (5) and that He appeared to Cephas, then to the twelve. (6) After that He appeared to more than five hundred brethren at one time, most of whom remain until now, but some have fallen asleep; (7) then He appeared to James, then to all the apostles; (8) and last of all, as to one untimely born, He appeared to me also.

* 1 Corinthians is believed to be one of the first New Testament books written (apx. 55 A.D.) and this description of Christ's death, resurrection and appearance to more than _____ people was written while there were still many living witnesses who would have controverted it if it had not been true.
* Obviously, the Bible speaks much of the bodily resurrection of Jesus Christ from the dead!
* Paul, Mark, Luke and John all speak of eye witnesses who beheld the risen Christ!

## The Empty Tomb

When reading the accounts of the death and resurrection of Jesus in the gospels it is clear that the religious leaders who pushed to have Jesus crucified were concerned about his body being removed from the grave. They took extra measures to ensure that the body remained in the grave. (Extra Soldiers, Sealed the Tomb with a Large Stone, etc) Still the tomb was found empty a few days later! To squelch the Christian faith forever all they needed was the _____ of Jesus, but it was gone and the tomb was empty!

## Women Witnesses!

The Bible speaks of the fact that women were the first witnesses of the resurrection of Jesus Christ from the dead. Mary Magdalene is spoken of in more detail as a witness of the resurrection of Jesus on that first day that any other person. (Matthew 28:1-10) (Mark 16:1-11) (Luke 24:1-11) (John 20:1, 11-18)

> John 20:1 NASB Now on the first day of the week Mary Magdalene *came early to the tomb, while it *was still dark, and *saw the stone already taken away from the tomb.

> John 20:11-18 NASB But Mary was standing outside the tomb weeping; and so, as she wept, she stooped and looked into the tomb; (12) and she *saw two angels in white sitting, one at the head and one at the feet, where the body of Jesus had been lying. (13) And they *said to her, "Woman, why are you weeping?" She *said to them, "Because they have taken away my Lord, and I do not know where they have laid Him." (14) When she had said this, she turned around and *saw Jesus standing there, and did not know that it was Jesus. (15) Jesus *said to her, "Woman, why are you weeping? Whom are you seeking?" Supposing Him to be the gardener, she *said to Him, "Sir, if you have carried Him away, tell me where you have laid Him, and I will take Him away." (16) Jesus *said to her, "Mary!" She turned and *said to Him in Hebrew, "Rabboni!" (which means, Teacher). (17) Jesus *said to her, "Stop clinging to Me, for I have not yet ascended to the Father; but go to My brethren and say to them, 'I ascend to My Father and your Father, and My God and your God.'" (18) Mary Magdalene *came, announcing to the disciples, "I have seen the Lord," and that He had said these things to her.

At the time that Jesus rose from the dead, and at the time the Bible was written, women were not allowed to even _____ in a court of law. Certainly, in a culture like that, if people were attempting to make up a story about the resurrection of Jesus they would not have written that women were the first to witness His resurrection. Furthermore, they certainly would not have made the star witness, a former prostitute who had been previously delivered from demonic possession. The fact that the Bible records Mary Magdalene, along with other women as the first witnesses shows that the Bible is simply recording historical facts, not a made up story!

## The Changed Lives of the Disciples of Jesus!

The radically changed lives of the disciples of Jesus testify to the validity of the resurrection of Jesus Christ from the dead! These men were at first running scared, discouraged, confused and disillusioned. Within a few weeks of the crucifixion of Jesus they became bold, courageous, powerful witnesses of Jesus Christ! What changed them so drastically? The most obvious answer is that they beheld Jesus, risen from the dead! Eleven of the twelve died martyr's deaths for proclaiming the Gospel of Jesus Christ and the other was exiled to isolation for the same reason. They changed the world forever! Christianity is a modern day reality that goes back to these ___ _____ _____. Only the bodily resurrection of Jesus Christ can account for their radical change, powerful and effective witness, and their willingness to die for a crucified Savior!

# The Rise of Christianity Despite Great Persecution!

Not only were the first disciples of Jesus radically changed but so were the many who were transformed by responding to their message about Jesus Christ! In the first 250+ years of the Christian faith, Christians were _____ greatly! Many were crucified, burned alive, torn apart by wild beast, stoned, etc. for being Christian, yet Christianity continued to grow! I have personally been to the catacombs near Rome where many early Christians lived under the ground to escape the vicious persecution against Christians at that time. Only the resurrection of Jesus Christ can account for this, especially in the early years when many who accepted Christ were alive at the time He was crucified and resurrection. They would have known if He had not risen from the dead! There is no historical reason for the rise of Christianity other than the truth of the crucifixion and bodily resurrection of Jesus Christ!

# The Transformation of Millions of Lives Since the Resurrection!

What was seen in the commitment of the early Christians to their faith in Christ, has continued in true believers throughout the centuries and it continues today. Many Christians have endured persecution for their faith and many have died for their faith throughout the past nearly 2,000 years. The resurrection of Jesus Christ from the dead is the key to the power of the Christian faith to withstand even the greatest of persecutions. Christ is truly alive and He lives in the hearts of those who put their faith in Him and choose to follow Him!

## Jesus Christ is the Central Character of All of Scripture!

As we looked at the evidences which confirm that the Bible is the Word of God we touched on the fact that Jesus Christ is seen throughout the Bible, both New Testament and Old Testament! We will look at this fact here again as we peer deeper into who Jesus Christ really is.

### Understanding the term "_____"

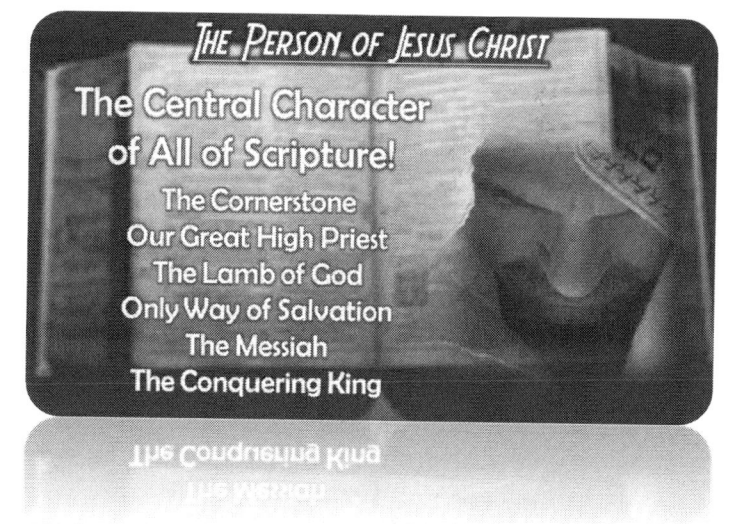

The terms "Scripture" or "Scriptures" are found many times in the New Testament. These terms refer to the sacred writings and the terms we use to speak of the writings that have been given to us by God. It is important to note though that when Jesus lived on earth the New Testament had not yet been written. For this reason we should understand that whenever we see the terms "Scripture" or "Scriptures" in the New Testament we should understand it to be speaking of the Old Testament. This is important because it will help us to see that Jesus Christ is not just the central character of the New Testament but He is very much the central character of the Old Testament as well. The terms "Scripture" or "Scriptures" are found ____ _____ in the New Testament (KJV). Many times we are told specifically that the Scriptures point to Jesus Christ. Note the following examples –

> **2 Timothy 3:15-16 KJV** And that from a child thou (Timothy) hast known the holy scriptures (of the Old Testament), which are able to make thee wise unto salvation through faith which is in Christ Jesus.
>
> (16) All scripture *is* given by inspiration of God, and *is* profitable for doctrine, for reproof, for correction, for instruction in righteousness:

> **John 5:39 NASB** "You search the Scriptures because you think that in them you have eternal life; it is these that testify about Me;

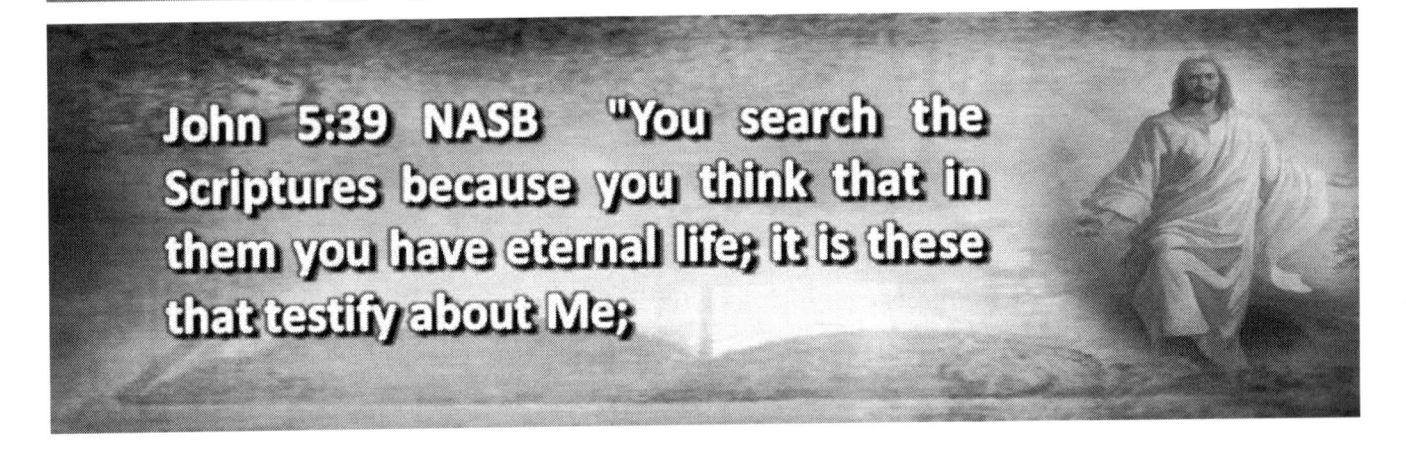

After Jesus rose from the dead He met 2 disciples on the road to Emmaus and spoke with them, giving them understanding of who He is and what He was accomplishing through His death and resurrection. They did not yet recognize Him as He spoke with them. Notice that He took them to the Old Testament to give them understanding about Himself.

> Luke 24:27 NASB  Then beginning with Moses and with all the prophets, He explained to them the things concerning Himself in all the Scriptures.

Paul also used the Old Testament to point people to Jesus Christ.

> Acts 17:2-3 NASB  And according to Paul's custom, he went to them, and for three Sabbaths reasoned with them from the Scriptures, (3) explaining and giving evidence that the Christ had to suffer and rise again from the dead, and saying, "This Jesus whom I am proclaiming to you is the Christ."

## The Old Testament Points to Jesus through many types and Shadows!

* **Melchizedek** (Genesis 14:18-20) (Psalm 110:4) (Hebrews 5,6 & 7)
* **The Brazen Serpent in the Dessert** (Numbers 21) (John 3:14-15) (Galatians 3:13)
* **The _____ Lamb** (Exodus 12) (1 Corinthians 5:7)

* **The Ark of Noah** (Covered with "pitch" – Same Hebrew word as "atonement")
* **Sin & Guilt Offerings of the Old Testament Law**
* **The _____** (Leviticus 16)
* **Rahab's Scarlet Cord**
* **_____** (Favored by his father) (Rejected by his brothers) (Sold for silver) (Raised from the pit (grave) to rule) (Walked in righteousness) (Falsely accused) (Became a servant) (Became a great deliverer of his people)
* **Moses/Joshua – The Promise Land**
   (Moses represents the law)
   ("Joshua" also is "_____" or "_____") (The law could not bring them into promised land (or God's promise of salvation) but Joshua could) (Galatians 3 says the law is not intended to save us but rather to lead us to Jesus, Who can save us)
* **Manna** (Exodus 16) (John 6) (Jesus is the living bread of life)
* **Water from the Rock** (Exodus 17:6) (Numbers 20:8)
   (Moses was to strike the rock in Exodus 17 so that life would flow from it)
   (Moses was to _____ ____ the rock in Numbers 20 so that life would flow from it)
   (1 Corinthians 10:4 tells us that the rock was a type of Jesus Christ)
   (Jesus Christ was striken once to bring us life – now we speak to Him to receive life)

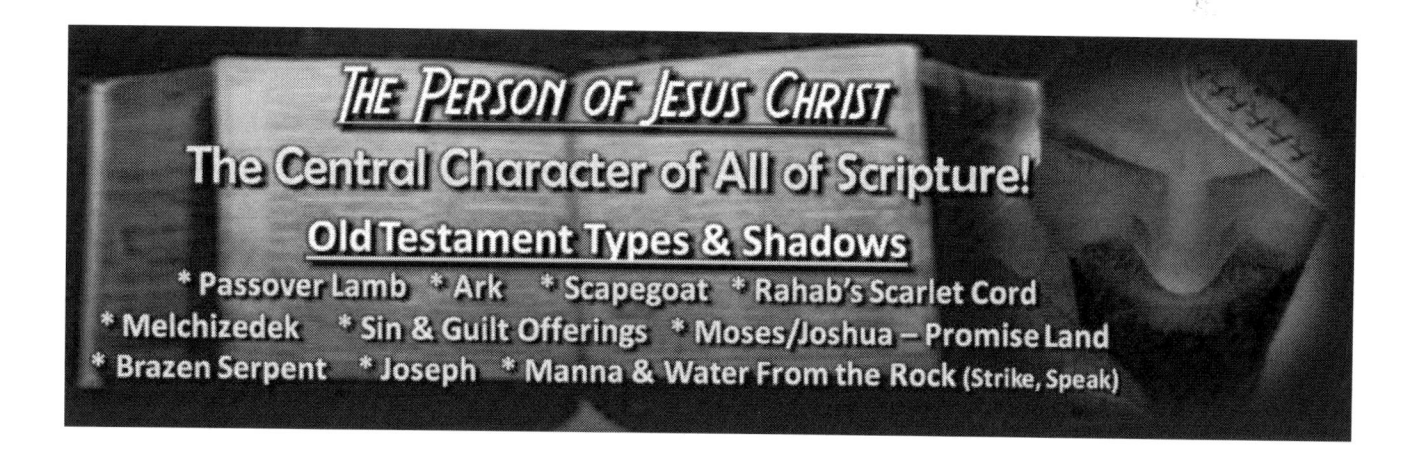

Evidence confirms that Jesus Christ was a real historical person. His death and resurrection from the dead are confirmed by numerous evidences. The radically changed lives of the disciples of Jesus and of the early New Testament believers are certainly among the evidences that confirm Jesus rose from the dead. Jesus is the central character of the entire Bible, not just the New Testament.

In the next session we look at the evidences confirming the deity of Jesus Christ and the evidences confirming that He is the Christ (Messiah).

# FAITH & REASON MADE SIMPLE — Part 7

## (The Person of Jesus Christ)

### Introduction – Review

We have looked at evidences which confirm that God created the heavens, the earth, and each of us!
We have looked at evidences which confirm that the Bible is the Word of God!
We will now approach the questions surrounding who Jesus Christ is with these issues in mind! Though we will look at external evidences beyond the Bible it is important to understand that the Bible is the Word of God and to look at what the Bible has to say about who Jesus Christ is! Note the progression of thought and inquiry listed here –

1. – Did God Create the Heavens & the Earth? - Yes
2. – Is God a Personal God Who Created Us in His Image? – Yes
3. – Is the Bible God's Word Given to Us to Reveal His Plans to Us? – Yes
4. – Is Jesus God, the Messiah (Christ), and the Savior of the World?
   (We look at this question after answering the first 3 as a basis.)

## The Identity of Jesus Christ is Attacked Today

### THE ATTACKS UPON THE IDENTITY OF JESUS CHRIST

**Challenge #1:** Scholars Are Uncovering a Radically Different Jesus through Ancient Documents (Gnostic Gospels) Just as Credible as the Four Gospels

**Challenge #2:** The Bible's Portrait of Jesus Can't Be Trusted Because the Church Tampered with the Text

**Challenge #3:** New Explanations Have Disproved Jesus' **Resurrection**

**Challenge #4:** Christianity's Beliefs about Jesus Were Copied from Pagan Religions

**Challenge #5:** Jesus Was an Impostor Who Failed to Fulfill the **Prophecies** about the Messiah

**Challenge #6:** People Should Be Free to Pick and Choose What to Believe about Jesus

(Note – These 6 challenges are addressed in Lee Stobel's book "The Case For the Real Jesus"

*****The DaVinci Code by Dan Brown** (Over 80 Million Copies Sold Worldwide) (Plus 2006 Blockbuster Movie) Portrays Jesus Christ as a mortal prophet who was **married** to Mary Magdalene. Claims that Jesus and Mary had children together and that their descendants are alive today. Also claims that the church has altered the story of Jesus to make him appear divine.

* **"Religulous" by Bill Maher** – (Documentary Movie – 2008)
    Among other things claims that the Christian narrative of Jesus in the Bible is a retelling of ancient deity myths from Persia, Egypt, etc., such as myths about "Mithras", "Horus" and others.

* **The Jesus Seminar** (Research Seminar by So-Called Scholars) (1985-1991)
    In 1985 numerous liberal "scholars" came together to determine if Jesus really said the things that the Bible says He said. They determined that He did not say 80% of the things that the Bible says He said. They also denied the reality of His **miracles**, His **resurrection**, and His **deity**.

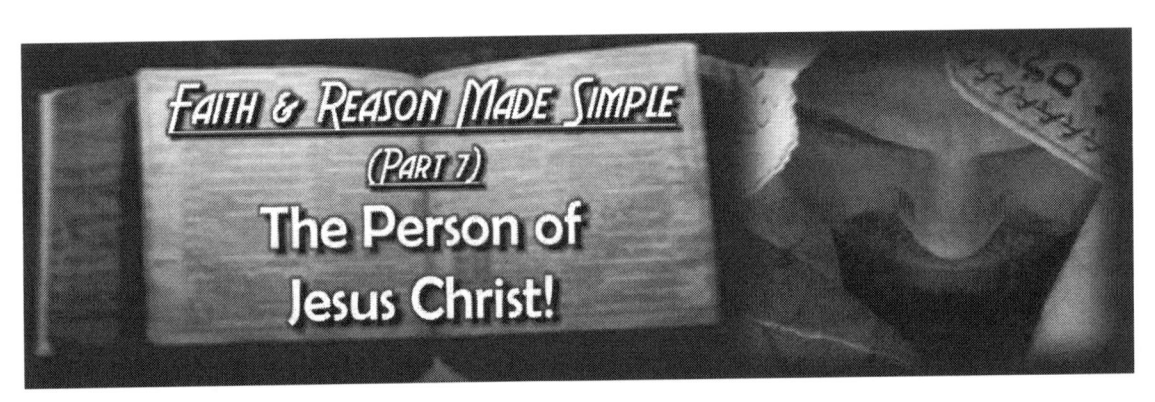

## Faith & Reason Made Simple (Part 7) — The Person of Jesus Christ!

* In this session we will look at external evidences beyond the Bible that confirm the reality of Jesus' life, death and resurrection. We will look at the impact He has had upon the world. We will also look at Who the Bible says Jesus Christ is and what He has done.

## Jesus Is Truly a Historical Person!

Some modern critics of Jesus say that He never existed but is a myth made up by early Christians. The Bible certainly presents Jesus as an historical person. We have already seen confirming evidences that the Bible is the Word of God in parts 5 and 6. Note how Luke gives historical perspective to the life of Jesus in Luke 1:1-5. He says he is compiling an accurate account of public events as witnessed by eyewitnesses. In verse 5 he begins by dating the time to "the days of Herod, king of Judea." He later will give many other historical details in his account of the life of Jesus.

> Luke 1:1-5 NASB  Inasmuch as many have undertaken to compile an account of the things accomplished among us, (2) just as they were handed down to us by those who from the beginning were eyewitnesses and servants of the word, (3) it seemed fitting for me as well, having investigated everything carefully from the beginning, to write *it* out for you in consecutive order, most excellent Theophilus; (4) so that you may know the exact truth about the things you have been taught. (5) In the days of Herod, king of Judea, there was a priest named Zacharias, of the division of Abijah; and he had a wife from the daughters of Aaron, and her name was Elizabeth.

### Jesus has impacted our world like no other person in history!
(Even our **calendar** points to Him!)(Our calendar divides all of history upon His birth!)
(Nations have been impacted)(Women's Rights have emerged)(Mercy & Justice in Legal Systems)
(Missionary work has been accomplished in His Name including the building of Orphanages and Hospitals)

The Historical Life of Jesus is confirmed by a number of historical sources outside the Bible!
(Here are a few)

## Tacitus (Roman Historian)
(While speaking of Nero's response to the fire of Rome)

Consequently, to get rid of the report, **Nero** fastened the guilt and inflicted the most exquisite tortures on a class hated for their abominations, called Christians by the populace. Christus, from whom the name had its origin, suffered the extreme penalty during the reign of Tiberius at the hands of one of our procurators, Pontius Pilatus, and a most mischievous superstition, thus checked for the moment, again broke out not only in Judaea, the first source of the evil, but even in Rome, where all things hideous and shameful from every part of the world find their centre and become popular. ... Accordingly, an arrest was first made of all who pleaded guilty; then, upon their information, an immense multitude was convicted, not so much of the crime of firing the city, as of hatred against mankind. Mockery of every sort was added to their deaths. Covered with the skins of beasts, they were torn by dogs and perished, or were nailed to crosses, or were doomed to the flames and burnt, to serve as a nightly illumination, when daylight had expired. Nero offered his gardens for the spectacle, and was exhibiting a show in the circus, while he mingled with the people in the dress of a charioteer or stood aloft on a car. Hence, even for criminals who deserved extreme and exemplary punishment, there arose a feeling of compassion; for it was not, as it seemed, for the public good, but to glut one man's cruelty, that they were being destroyed. (Annals 15.44)

## (Josephus) (Jewish Historian) Antiquities 20.9.1
But the younger Ananus who, as we said, received the high priesthood, was of a bold disposition and exceptionally daring; he followed the party of the Sadducees, who are severe in judgment above all the Jews, as we have already shown. As therefore Ananus was of such a disposition, he thought he had now a good opportunity, as Festus was now dead, and Albinus was still on the road; so he assembled a council of judges, and brought before it the **brother** of Jesus the so-called Christ, whose name was James, together with some others, and having accused them as law-breakers, he delivered them over to be stoned.

## (Josephus) Antiquities 18.3.3
Now there was about this time Jesus, a wise man, if it be lawful to call him a man, for he was a doer of wonderful works, a teacher of such men as receive the truth with pleasure. He drew over to him both many of the Jews, and many of the Gentiles. He was the Christ, and when Pilate, at the suggestion of the principal men among us, had condemned him to the cross, those that loved him at the first did not forsake him; for he appeared to them alive again the third day; as the divine prophets had foretold these and ten thousand other wonderful things concerning him. And the tribe of Christians so named from him are not extinct at this day.

## Pliny the Younger
**(a Lawyer, Author & Magistrate of 1st Century Rome)** (He speaks of Jesus & His followers)
Pliny the Younger, in Letters 10:96, recorded early Christian worship practices including the fact that Christians worshiped Jesus as God and were very **ethical**, and he includes a reference to the love feast and **Lord's Supper**.

## Writings of the Sanhedrin speak of Jesus' crucifixion

The Babylonian Talmud (Sanhedrin 43a) confirms Jesus' crucifixion on the eve of Passover and the accusations against Him of practicing sorcery and encouraging Jewish apostasy –
"On the Eve of **Passover**, they hung Jesus of Nazareth for sorcery and enticing Israel [to idolatry]."

## Lucian of Samosata (Second-Century Greek Writer)

Lucian admits that Jesus was worshiped by Christians, introduced new teachings, and was crucified for them. He said that Jesus' teachings included the brotherhood of believers, the importance of conversion, and the importance of denying other gods. Christians lived according to Jesus' laws, believed themselves to be immortal, and were characterized by contempt for death, voluntary self-devotion, and renunciation of material goods.

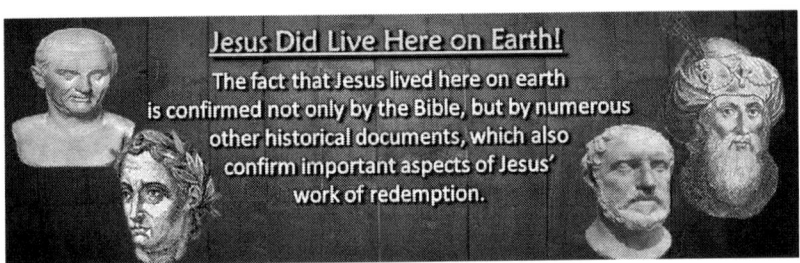

**Jesus Did Live Here on Earth!**
The fact that Jesus lived here on earth is confirmed not only by the Bible, but by numerous other historical documents, which also confirm important aspects of Jesus' work of redemption.

# The Biblical Account of Jesus is Not the Retelling of Ancient Deity Myths!

One of the accusations being promoted today by skeptics like Bill Maher is that the Biblical account of the birth, life, miracles, death and resurrection of Jesus is simply the retelling of one of numerous ancient deity myths that supposedly referred to the same details hundreds of years earlier. The idea that Jesus is a copy-cat deity was promoted by a few authors in the 18th & 19th centuries. Other authors have repeated these accusations in the 20th & 21st centuries. A careful examination of these claims reveals that many of the proposed details of myths regarding **Mithras**, **Horus** and others simply are not accurate. Also, many of the writings that show some details that are comparable to Jesus were written hundreds of years after the oldest New Testament manuscripts, showing that any striking similarities would actually indicate that pagan writers copied details of Jesus' life, not the other way around.

It is important to be aware of these accusations regarding the Biblical accounts of Jesus, since they are used by many critics of Christianity. Numerous helpful articles can be found on these subjects by going to **searchcreation.org** and typing in "Jesus vs. Mithras" or "Jesus vs. Horus".

# The Bodily Resurrection of Jesus is Confirmed in Many Ways!

The resurrection of Jesus Christ is the most important historical event in world history and is the centerpiece of all Christian teachings. **Romans 10:9** says - "that if you confess with your mouth Jesus as Lord, and believe in your heart that God raised Him from the dead, you will be saved". 1 Corinthians 15:14 reveals even further just how important the resurrection of Jesus is to the Christian faith.

> 1 Corinthians 15:14 NASB  (14) and if Christ has not been raised, then our preaching is vain, your faith also is vain.

According to Romans 10:9-10, believing that God has raised Christ from the dead is a key part of salvation and being declared righteous by God! 1 Corinthians 15:14 tells us that our faith is vain, or useless if Christ did not rise from the dead. Let's look at evidences that support the biblical account of the bodily resurrection of Jesus Christ from the dead. To begin with look at the 9 facts listed by Dr. Gary Habermas concerning the resurrection of Jesus that contemporary **critical scholars** agree to.

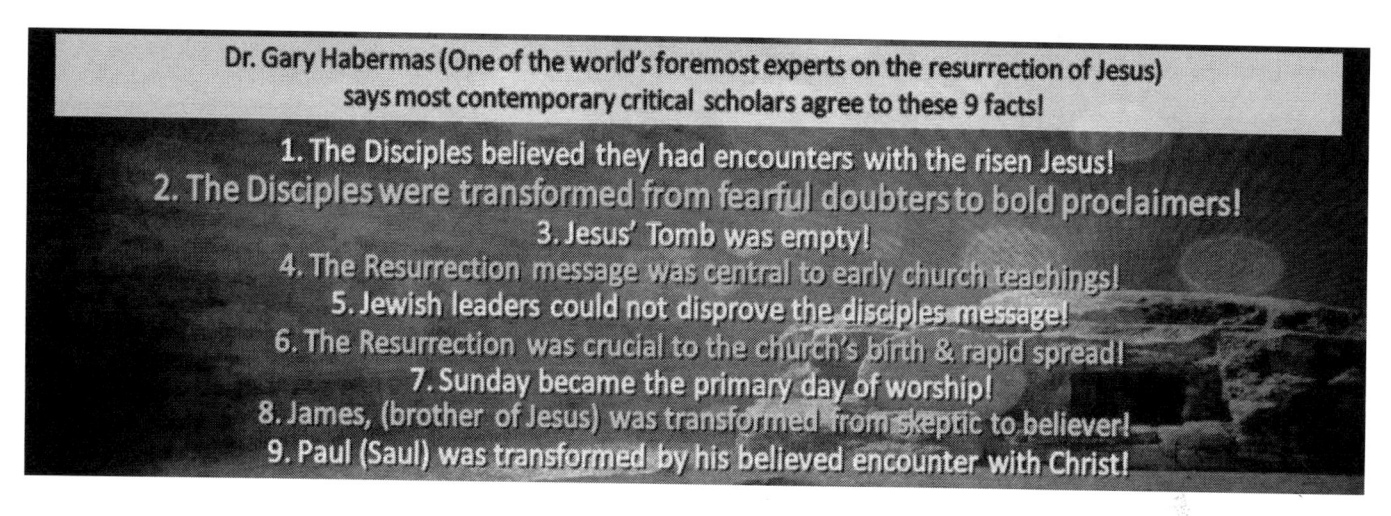

> **Dr. Gary Habermas (One of the world's foremost experts on the resurrection of Jesus) says most contemporary critical scholars agree to these 9 facts!**
>
> 1. The Disciples believed they had encounters with the risen Jesus!
> 2. The Disciples were transformed from fearful doubters to bold proclaimers!
> 3. Jesus' Tomb was empty!
> 4. The Resurrection message was central to early church teachings!
> 5. Jewish leaders could not disprove the disciples message!
> 6. The Resurrection was crucial to the church's birth & rapid spread!
> 7. Sunday became the primary day of worship!
> 8. James, (brother of Jesus) was transformed from skeptic to believer!
> 9. Paul (Saul) was transformed by his believed encounter with Christ!

## Eye Witnesses

The Bible presents the resurrection of Jesus Christ from the dead as historical fact that was witnessed by many eye witnesses that were still living at the time the New Testament writers were penning their accounts of the resurrection.

> 1 Corinthians 15:3-8 NASB (3) For I delivered to you as of first importance what I also received, that Christ died for our sins according to the Scriptures, (4) and that He was buried, and that He was raised on the third day according to the Scriptures, (5) and that He appeared to Cephas, then to the twelve. (6) After that He appeared to more than five hundred brethren at one time, most of whom remain until now, but some have fallen asleep; (7) then He appeared to James, then to all the apostles; (8) and last of all, as to one untimely born, He appeared to me also.

* 1 Corinthians is believed to be one of the first New Testament books written (apx. 55 A.D.) and this description of Christ's death, resurrection and appearance to more than **500** people was written while there were still many living witnesses who would have controverted it if it had not been true.
* Obviously, the Bible speaks much of the bodily resurrection of Jesus Christ from the dead!
* Paul, Mark, Luke and John all speak of eye witnesses who beheld the risen Christ!

## The Empty Tomb

When reading the accounts of the death and resurrection of Jesus in the gospels it is clear that the religious leaders who pushed to have Jesus crucified were concerned about his body being removed from the grave. They took extra measures to ensure that the body remained in the grave. (Extra Soldiers, Sealed the Tomb with a Large Stone, etc) Still the tomb was found empty a few days later! To squelch the Christian faith forever all they needed was the **body** of Jesus, but it was gone and the tomb was empty!

## Women Witnesses!

The Bible speaks of the fact that women were the first witnesses of the resurrection of Jesus Christ from the dead. Mary Magdalene is spoken of in more detail as a witness of the resurrection of Jesus on that first day that any other person. (Matthew 28:1-10) (Mark 16:1-11) (Luke 24:1-11) (John 20:1, 11-18)

> John 20:1 NASB  Now on the first day of the week Mary Magdalene *came early to the tomb, while it *was still dark, and *saw the stone already taken away from the tomb.

> John 20:11-18 NASB  But Mary was standing outside the tomb weeping; and so, as she wept, she stooped and looked into the tomb; (12) and she *saw two angels in white sitting, one at the head and one at the feet, where the body of Jesus had been lying. (13) And they *said to her, "Woman, why are you weeping?" She *said to them, "Because they have taken away my Lord, and I do not know where they have laid Him." (14) When she had said this, she turned around and *saw Jesus standing there, and did not know that it was Jesus. (15) Jesus *said to her, "Woman, why are you weeping? Whom are you seeking?" Supposing Him to be the gardener, she *said to Him, "Sir, if you have carried Him away, tell me where you have laid Him, and I will take Him away." (16) Jesus *said to her, "Mary!" She turned and *said to Him in Hebrew, "Rabboni!" (which means, Teacher). (17) Jesus *said to her, "Stop clinging to Me, for I have not yet ascended to the Father; but go to My brethren and say to them, 'I ascend to My Father and your Father, and My God and your God.'" (18) Mary Magdalene *came, announcing to the disciples, "I have seen the Lord," and that He had said these things to her.

At the time that Jesus rose from the dead, and at the time the Bible was written, women were not allowed to even **testify** in a court of law. Certainly, in a culture like that, if people were attempting to make up a story about the resurrection of Jesus they would not have written that women were the first to witness His resurrection. Furthermore, they certainly would not have made the star witness, a former prostitute who had been previously delivered from demonic possession. The fact that the Bible records Mary Magdalene, along with other women as the first witnesses shows that the Bible is simply recording historical facts, not a made up story!

## The Changed Lives of the Disciples of Jesus!

The radically changed lives of the disciples of Jesus testify to the validity of the resurrection of Jesus Christ from the dead! These men were at first running scared, discouraged, confused and disillusioned. Within a few weeks of the crucifixion of Jesus they became bold, courageous, powerful witnesses of Jesus Christ! What changed them so drastically? The most obvious answer is that they beheld Jesus, risen from the dead! Eleven of the twelve died martyr's deaths for proclaiming the Gospel of Jesus Christ and the other was exiled to isolation for the same reason. They changed the world forever! Christianity is a modern day reality that goes back to these **12 simple men**. Only the bodily resurrection of Jesus Christ can account for their radical change, powerful and effective witness, and their willingness to die for a crucified Savior!

## The Rise of Christianity Despite Great Persecution!

Not only were the first disciples of Jesus radically changed but so were the many who were transformed by responding to their message about Jesus Christ! In the first 250+ years of the Christian faith, Christians were **persecuted** greatly! Many were crucified, burned alive, torn apart by wild beast, stoned, etc. for being Christian, yet Christianity continued to grow! I have personally been to the catacombs near Rome where many early Christians lived under the ground to escape the vicious persecution against Christians at that time. Only the resurrection of Jesus Christ can account for this, especially in the early years when many who accepted Christ were alive at the time He was crucified and resurrection. They would have known if He had not risen from the dead! There is no historical reason for the rise of Christianity other than the truth of the crucifixion and bodily resurrection of Jesus Christ!

## The Transformation of Millions of Lives Since the Resurrection!

What was seen in the commitment of the early Christians to their faith in Christ, has continued in true believers throughout the centuries and it continues today. Many Christians have endured persecution for their faith and many have died for their faith throughout the past nearly 2,000 years. The resurrection of Jesus Christ from the dead is the key to the power of the Christian faith to withstand even the greatest of persecutions. Christ is truly alive and He lives in the hearts of those who put their faith in Him and choose to follow Him!

## Jesus Christ is the Central Character of All of Scripture!

As we looked at the evidences which confirm that the Bible is the Word of God we touched on the fact that Jesus Christ is seen throughout the Bible, both New Testament and Old Testament! We will look at this fact here again as we peer deeper into who Jesus Christ really is.

### Understanding the term "Scripture"

The terms "Scripture" or "Scriptures" are found many times in the New Testament. These terms refer to the sacred writings and the terms we use to speak of the writings that have been given to us by God. It is important to note though that when Jesus lived on earth the New Testament had not yet been written. For this reason we should understand that whenever we see the terms "Scripture" or "Scriptures" in the New Testament we should understand it to be speaking of the Old Testament. This is important because it will help us to see that Jesus Christ is not just the central character of the New Testament but He is very much the central character of the Old Testament as well. The terms "Scripture" or "Scriptures" are found **53 times** in the New Testament (KJV). Many times we are told specifically that the Scriptures point to Jesus Christ. Note the following examples –

> **2 Timothy 3:15-16 KJV** And that from a child thou (Timothy) hast known the holy scriptures (of the Old Testament), which are able to make thee wise unto salvation through faith which is in Christ Jesus.
>
> (16) All scripture *is* given by inspiration of God, and *is* profitable for doctrine, for reproof, for correction, for instruction in righteousness:

> **John 5:39 NASB** "You search the Scriptures because you think that in them you have eternal life; it is these that testify about Me;

After Jesus rose from the dead He met 2 disciples on the road to Emmaus and spoke with them, giving them understanding of who He is and what He was accomplishing through His death and resurrection. They did not yet recognize Him as He spoke with them. Notice that He took them to the Old Testament to give them understanding about Himself.

> Luke 24:27 NASB  Then beginning with Moses and with all the prophets, He explained to them the things concerning Himself in all the Scriptures.

Paul also used the Old Testament to point people to Jesus Christ.

> Acts 17:2-3 NASB  And according to Paul's custom, he went to them, and for three Sabbaths reasoned with them from the Scriptures,  (3)  explaining and giving evidence that the Christ had to suffer and rise again from the dead, and saying, "This Jesus whom I am proclaiming to you is the Christ."

## The Old Testament Points to Jesus through many types and Shadows!

* **Melchizedek** (Genesis 14:18-20) (Psalm 110:4) (Hebrews 5,6 & 7)
* **The Brazen Serpent in the Dessert** (Numbers 21) (John 3:14-15) (Galatians 3:13)
* **The Passover Lamb** (Exodus 12) (1 Corinthians 5:7)

* **The Ark of Noah** (Covered with "pitch" – Same Hebrew word as "atonement")
* **Sin & Guilt Offerings of the Old Testament Law**
* **The Scapegoat** (Leviticus 16)
* **Rahab's Scarlet Cord**
* **Joseph** (Favored by his father) (Rejected by his brothers) (Sold for silver) (Raised from the pit (grave) to rule) (Walked in righteousness) (Falsely accused) (Became a servant) (Became a great deliverer of his people)
* **Moses/Joshua – The Promise Land**
    (Moses represents the law)
    ("Joshua" also is "**Yeshua**" or "**Jesus**") (The law could not bring them into promised land (or God's promise of salvation) but Joshua could) (Galatians 3 says the law is not intended to save us but rather to lead us to Jesus, Who can save us)
* **Manna** (Exodus 16) (John 6) (Jesus is the living bread of life)
* **Water from the Rock** (Exodus 17:6) (Numbers 20:8)
    (Moses was to strike the rock in Exodus 17 so that life would flow from it)
    (Moses was to **speak to** the rock in Numbers 20 so that life would flow from it)
    (1 Corinthians 10:4 tells us that the rock was a type of Jesus Christ)
    (Jesus Christ was striken once to bring us life – now we speak to Him to receive life)

**THE PERSON OF JESUS CHRIST**
**The Central Character of All of Scripture!**
**Old Testament Types & Shadows**
* Passover Lamb  * Ark  * Scapegoat  * Rahab's Scarlet Cord
* Melchizedek  * Sin & Guilt Offerings  * Moses/Joshua – Promise Land
* Brazen Serpent  * Joseph  * Manna & Water From the Rock (Strike, Speak)

Evidence confirms that Jesus Christ was a real historical person. His death and resurrection from the dead are confirmed by numerous evidences. The radically changed lives of the disciples of Jesus and of the early New Testament believers are certainly among the evidences that confirm Jesus rose from the dead. Jesus is the central character of the entire Bible, not just the New Testament.

In the next session we look at the evidences confirming the deity of Jesus Christ and the evidences confirming that He is the Christ (Messiah).

# FAITH & REASON MADE SIMPLE — Part 8

## (The Person of Jesus Christ – Cont.)

## Jesus Is The Christ (Messiah)!

"Messiah" is the Hebrew word for "_____ _____". "Christ" is the equivalent Greek word for "Anointed One". The word "Messiah" is only found thirty nine times in the Old Testament and is usually translated "anointed". It is only translated Messiah twice in the Old Testament (Daniel 9:25 & 9:26). Still, the message of the coming Messiah was clearly transmitted throughout the Old Testament in many ways. The word "Christ" is found in the New Testament over _____ times, referencing Jesus of Nazareth as the "Anointed One" Who has come in fulfillment of all the Old Testament messianic prophecies.

Jesus is clearly and boldly presented as "The Christ" in the New Testament in many passages.

> John 20:31 NASB  but these have been written so that you may believe that Jesus is the Christ, the Son of God; and that believing you may have life in His name.

> Matthew 16:13-18 NASB  Now when Jesus came into the district of Caesarea Philippi, He was asking His disciples, "Who do people say that the Son of Man is?" (14) And they said, "Some *say* John the Baptist; and others, Elijah; but still others, Jeremiah, or one of the prophets." (15) He *said to them, "But who do you say that I am?" (16) Simon Peter answered, "You are the Christ, the Son of the living God." (17) And Jesus said to him, "Blessed are you, Simon Barjona, because flesh and blood did not reveal *this* to you, but My Father who is in heaven. (18) "I also say to you that you are Peter, and upon this rock I will build My church; and the gates of Hades will not overpower it.

Examples of Old Testament Messianic Passages – Psalm 2:2, Isaiah 53; Isaiah 9:6-7; Psalm 22; Isaiah 7:14; Daniel 9:25-26; Daniel 7:13

### The Suffering Messiah

The Jewish image of a conquering, ruling Messiah often misses the fact that the Old Testament clearly portrayed the Messiah as one who would _____ and _____ on behalf of those he would come to redeem. The prophetic emphasis on a Messiah that would be victorious is certainly strong but it does not negate the strong indication of other prophetic passages that the Messiah would first suffer for our sin. Note these passages from Psalm 22 and Isaiah 53.

Psalms 22:1-18 NASB My God, my God, why have You forsaken me? ... (7) All who see me sneer at me; They separate with the lip, they wag the head, saying, (8) "Commit yourself to the LORD; let Him deliver him; Let Him rescue him, because He delights in him." ... (12) Many bulls have surrounded me; Strong bulls of Bashan have encircled me. (13) They open wide their mouth at me, As a ravening and a roaring lion. (14) I am poured out like water, And all my bones are out of joint; My heart is like wax; It is melted within me. (15) My strength is dried up like a potsherd, And my tongue cleaves to my jaws; And You lay me in the dust of death. (16) For dogs have surrounded me; A band of evildoers has encompassed me; They pierced my hands and my feet. (17) I can count all my bones. They look, they stare at me; (18) They divide my garments among them, And for my clothing they cast lots.

Isaiah 53:3-12 NASB (3) He was despised and forsaken of men, A man of sorrows and acquainted with grief; And like one from whom men hide their face He was despised, and we did not esteem Him. (4) Surely our griefs He Himself bore, And our sorrows He carried; Yet we ourselves esteemed Him stricken, Smitten of God, and afflicted. (5) But He was pierced through for our transgressions, He was crushed for our iniquities; The chastening for our well-being fell upon Him, And by His scourging we are healed. (6) All of us like sheep have gone astray, Each of us has turned to his own way; But the LORD has caused the iniquity of us all To fall on Him. (7) He was oppressed and He was afflicted, Yet He did not open His mouth; Like a lamb that is led to slaughter, And like a sheep that is silent before its shearers, So He did not open His mouth. (8) By oppression and judgment He was taken away; And as for His generation, who considered That He was cut off out of the land of the living For the transgression of my people, to whom the stroke was due? (9) His grave was assigned with wicked men, Yet He was with a rich man in His death, Because He had done no violence, Nor was there any deceit in His mouth. (10) But the LORD was pleased To crush Him, putting Him to grief; If He would render Himself as a guilt offering, He will see His offspring, He will prolong His days, And the good pleasure of the LORD will prosper in His hand. (11) As a result of the anguish of His soul, He will see it and be satisfied; By His knowledge the Righteous One, My Servant, will justify the many, As He will bear their iniquities. (12) Therefore, I will allot Him a portion with the great, And He will divide the booty with the strong; Because He poured out Himself to death, And was numbered with the transgressors; Yet He Himself bore the sin of many, And interceded for the transgressors.

So the foretelling of the suffering of the Messiah to become an offering for the sins of the people is clear! It is unfortunate that many have missed this and only looked for a Messiah that will conquer his enemies and rule. Jesus Christ fulfilled the prophetic passages of a suffering Messiah as well as the prophetic passages of a Messiah who would rise up in victory to rule forever!

* One of the strongest images of the Messiah in the Old Testament is found in _____ where Daniel sees "One like a Son of Man" coming to the Ancient of Days. He is given a kingdom and everlasting dominion.

> Daniel 7:13-14 NASB  "I kept looking in the night visions, And behold, with the clouds of heaven One like a Son of Man was coming, And He came up to the Ancient of Days, And was presented before Him. (14) "And to Him was given dominion, Glory and a kingdom, That all the peoples, nations and *men of every* language Might serve Him. His dominion is an everlasting dominion Which will not pass away; And His kingdom is one Which will not be destroyed.

Because of this passage the title "_____ __ _____" became synonymous with "Messiah" to the Jews who were waiting for their victorious Messiah to come and establish His kingdom. As we will see here, Jesus is referred to many times in the New Testament as "Son of Man", including when He is judged by the religious leaders for saying " ... and you shall see the Son of Man sitting at the _____ _____ of power, and coming with the clouds of heaven." (Mark 14:62)

**Jesus Is The Christ (Messiah)**
**Jesus is Referred to "Son of Man"**
(85 Times in the Gospels & Acts)
Matthew (31xs) - Mark (14xs) - Luke (26xs) - John (13xs)
Important to Remember "Son of Man" Refers to the Messiah

> Mark 14:62 NASB  And Jesus said, "I am; and you shall see THE SON OF MAN SITTING AT THE RIGHT HAND OF POWER, and COMING WITH THE CLOUDS OF HEAVEN."

> Acts 7:55-56 NASB  But being full of the Holy Spirit, he gazed intently into heaven and saw the glory of God, and Jesus standing at the right hand of God; (56) and he said, "Behold, I see the heavens opened up and the Son of Man standing at the right hand of God."

When Jesus spoke of His _____ _____ He used this term "Son of Man" to indicate that He will come in glory as the victorious Messiah. He actually is referencing Daniel 7:13-14.

> Matthew 24:30 NASB  "And then the sign of the Son of Man will appear in the sky, and then all the tribes of the earth will mourn, and they will see the SON OF MAN COMING ON THE CLOUDS OF THE SKY with power and great glory.

**\* Jesus fulfilled over _____ Old Testament prophecies about the coming Messiah!**
**This proves, without question that He is the Messiah, the Christ!**

**Jesus Is The Messiah (The Christ)**
Over 300 Messianic Prophecies Fulfilled by Jesus Christ
* Genesis 3:15 (Seed of Woman)
* Isaiah 7:14, Micah 5:2 (Birth)
* Isaiah 53, Psalm 22 (Cross)
* Psalm 78:2 (Parables) * Zechariah 9:9 (Donkey)
* Zechariah 11:12-13 (Silver) * Psalm 22:18 (Garments)

**Jesus fulfilled 300 Old Testament Prophecies about the Coming Messiah!  (Here are some examples)**
* Seed of a Woman to Conquer the _____ of Old  (Genesis 3:15)
* His Suffering Upon the Cross (Many Details)  (Psalm 22 & Isaiah 53)
* His Birth in _____  (Micah 5:2)
* He Would Be Born of a Virgin  (Isaiah 7:14) (Also on His Birth – Isaiah 9:6-7)
* He Would Teach in _____  (Psalm 78:2)
* He Would Ride Into Jerusalem on a _____  (Zechariah 9:9)
* He Would Be Betrayed For 30 Pieces of Silver  (Zechariah 11:12-13)
* His _____ Would be Divided by the Soldiers  (Psalm 22:18)
* Soldiers Would Cast Lots for His Cloak  (Psalm 22:18)

In his book "Science Speaks", Dr. Peter Stoner explains a research project that he and students at Pasadena City College, where he was a professor, did to estimate the probability of one person fulfilling various Old Testament Messianic prophecies. "When multiplied together it was found that even using these very conservative estimates, there would be a 1 in $10^{28}$ chance of someone fulfilling just __ Messianic prophecies."

"That number looks like this when written out.
10,000,000,000,000,000,000,000,000,000."

To illustrate how large the number $10^{28}$ is Dr. Stoner gives this illustration. Image covering the entire state of _____ 2' thick with silver dollars. Then mark one of the silver dollars and put anywhere in the state of Texas randomly. Now send a blind man into the state of Texas and have him pick one silver dollar from anywhere in the state. The chances of him picking the marked silver dollar are about 1 in $10^{28}$.

Remember that Jesus did not just fulfill 8 of the Old Testament prophecies concerning the Messiah (the Christ). He fulfilled over 300 of them!!! Jesus is the Messiah (the Christ)! The New Testament refers to Jesus as the Christ over 500 times! Jesus of Nazareth is the Christ!

## **The Deity of Jesus Christ**

### **Seen in The Gospel of John**

(The Gospel of _____ is Dedicated to Presenting Jesus Christ as the Divine Son of God!)

> John 1:1 NASB  In the beginning was the Word, and the Word was with God, and **the Word was God.**  (Note – V. 14 says the Word became flesh and dwelt among us)

> John 20:31 NASB  but these have been written so that you may believe that Jesus is the Christ, **the Son of God**; and that believing you may have life in His name.

The Gospel of John is unique in many ways. This is because of its stated purpose found in John 20:31. It is written so that we would believe that Jesus is (1) _____ _____, and (2) _____ _____ ___ _____, and so that believing we might have life in His name! One of the ways that the Gospel of John does this is by using "__ ____" statements referring to Jesus. These statements are not found in Matthew, Mark or Luke. They are unique to the Gospel of John. To understand the significance of these statements we have to go back to Exodus 3:14-15 where Moses is conversing with God at the burning bush. God is sending Moses back to Egypt to deliver the people and Moses is asking God how he should respond when people ask him "Who sent you?" Notice God's answer to Moses.

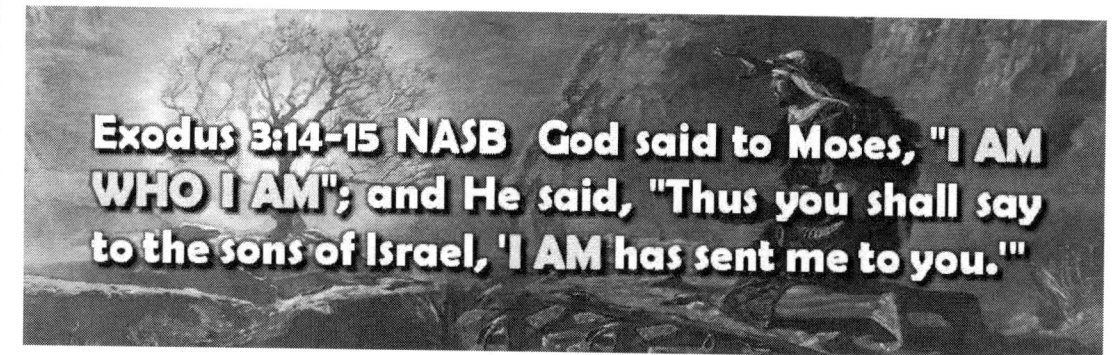

**Exodus 3:14-15 NASB** God said to Moses, "I AM WHO I AM"; and He said, "Thus you shall say to the sons of Israel, 'I AM has sent me to you.'"

Exodus 3:15 NASB God, furthermore, said to Moses, "Thus you shall say to the sons of Israel, 'The LORD, the God of your fathers, the God of Abraham, the God of Isaac, and the God of Jacob, has sent me to you.' This is My name forever, and this is My memorial-name to all generations.

God reveals Himself as "I Am". This title refers to the fact that God is the self-existent One. In verse 15 God gives more information to Moses. He says that He shall also be called "The LORD" which in the Hebrew is "Yahweh" or "Jehovah" and which means the _____ One. So God is "I Am" or "The LORD", the self-existent One. Often times in the Old Testament the name "Yahweh" or "Jehovah" was then connected with a descriptive term to communicate characteristics of God such as "Jehovah Shalom" which means "The LORD our peace" or "Jehovah Jireh" which means "The LORD our provider.

In the Gospel of John we see this same pattern used with reference now to Jesus Christ, showing His deity. Note the following examples from the _____ "I Am" statements in the Gospel of John.

**The 23 "I Am" Statements in the Gospel of John!**

"I Am the Bread of Life" (John 6:35) - "I Am the Door" (John 10:9)
"I Am the Good Shepherd" (John 10:11)
"I Am the Resurrection & the Life" (John 11:25)
"I Am the Way, the Truth & the Life" (John 14:6)

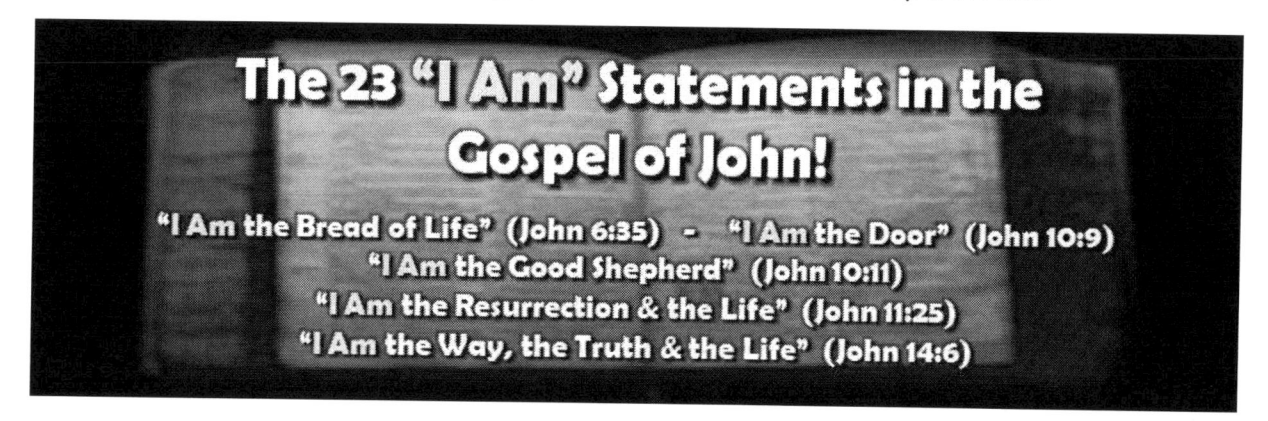

In addition to the times when the "I Am" statements include descriptive terms with reference to Jesus there are a number of places where "I Am" is used to refer to Jesus without descriptive terms added. Note the following examples –

> John 8:24 NASB "Therefore I said to you that you will die in your sins; for unless you believe that **I am** *He,* you will die in your sins." (Note – "He" is added by the translators)

> John 8:58 NASB Jesus said to them, "Truly, truly, I say to you, before Abraham was born, **I am.**"

> John 18:4-6 NASB So Jesus, knowing all the things that were coming upon Him, went forth and *said to them, "Whom do you seek?" (5) They answered Him, "Jesus the Nazarene." He *said to them, "**I am** *He.*" And Judas also, who was betraying Him, was standing with them. (6) So when He said to them, "**I am** *He,*" they drew back and fell to the ground.
> (Note – "He is added by the translators – It was note found in the original language)

The Gospel of John is dedicated to revealing the deity of Jesus. The very first verse declares His deity directly. The 23 "I Am" statements also reveal His deity. A number of times we read of people picking up stones to stone Him when He made statements declaring Himself to be "I Am" like John 8:58-59.

The deity of Jesus Christ is also seen in other places throughout the New Testament.

## The Deity of Jesus Christ Seen Throughout the Remaining New Testament

> Philippians 2:5-8 NASB Have this attitude in yourselves which was also in Christ Jesus, (6) who, although He existed in the form of God, did not regard equality with God a thing to be grasped, (7) but emptied Himself, taking the form of a bond-servant, *and* being made in the likeness of men. (8) Being found in appearance as a man, He humbled Himself by becoming obedient to the point of death, even death on a cross.

Compare Joel 2:32 which speaks of _____ with Romans 10:9-13 which speaks of _____.

> Joel 2:32 NASB "And it will come about that whoever calls on the name of the LORD Will be delivered (saved) …"

> Romans 10:9-13 NASB that if you confess with your mouth Jesus as Lord, and believe in your heart that God raised Him from the dead, you will be saved; (10) for with the heart a person believes, resulting in righteousness, and with the mouth he confesses, resulting in salvation … (13) for "WHOEVER WILL CALL ON THE NAME OF THE LORD WILL BE SAVED."

Here are a few more examples.

> Titus 2:13 NASB looking for the blessed hope and the appearing of the glory of our great God and Savior, Christ Jesus,

> Hebrews 1:6-8 NASB And when He again brings the firstborn into the world, He says, "AND LET ALL THE ANGELS OF GOD WORSHIP HIM." (7) And of the angels He says, "WHO MAKES HIS ANGELS WINDS, AND HIS MINISTERS A FLAME OF FIRE." (8) But of the Son *He says,* "YOUR THRONE, O GOD, IS FOREVER AND EVER, AND THE RIGHTEOUS SCEPTER IS THE SCEPTER OF HIS KINGDOM.

> Colossians 2:9 NASB For in Him all the fullness of Deity dwells in bodily form,

**Jesus taught with _____ _____** (This also reveals His deity) At the end of the Sermon on the Mount, "the crowds were astonished at his teaching, for he was teaching them as one who had authority, and not as their scribes" (Matt. 7:28–29) The teachers of the law in Jesus' day had no authority of their own. Their authority came from their use of earlier authorities. Even Moses and the other OT prophets and authors did not speak in their own authority, but would say, "This is what the Lord says." Jesus, on the other hand, interprets the law by saying, "You have heard that it was said. . . . But I say to you" (see Matt. 5:22, 28, 32, 34, 39, 44). (Also see Matthew 7:24-29) This divine authority is shown with staggering clarity when he speaks of himself as the Lord who will judge the whole earth and will say to the wicked, "I never knew you; depart from me, you workers of lawlessness" (Matt. 7:23). No wonder the crowd was amazed at the authority with which Jesus spoke.

Jesus recognized that his words carried divine weight. He acknowledged the permanent authority of ____ _____ (Matt. 5:18) and put his words on an equal plane with it:

> "For truly, I say to you, until heaven and earth pass away, not an iota, not a dot, will pass from the Law until all is accomplished" (Matt. 5:18);

> "Heaven and earth will pass away, but my words will not pass away" (Matt. 24:35).

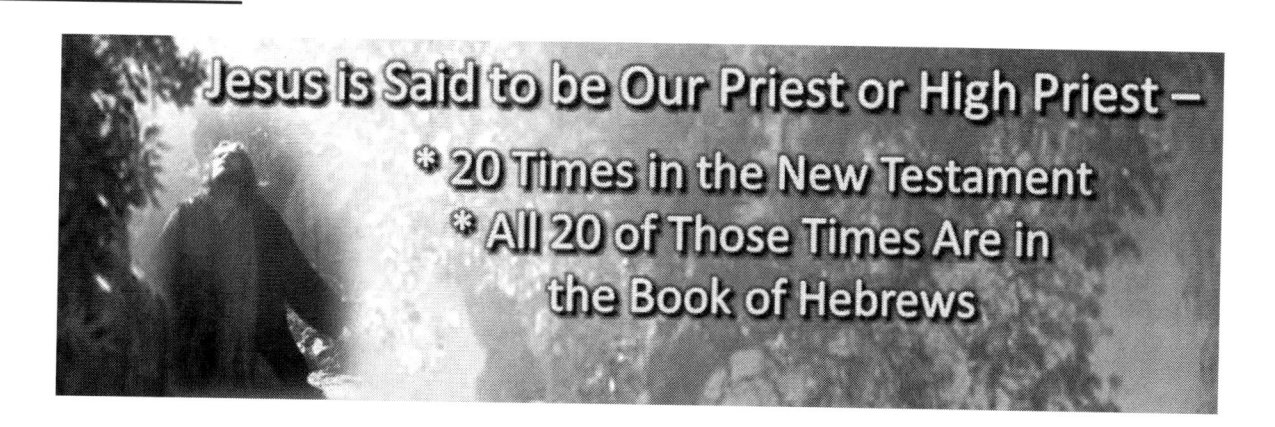

## Jesus is Our Great High Priest!

The book of Hebrews presents Jesus as our Great High Priest! It shows Him to be superior to the angels, to Moses, and to the Levitical priests. It also shows that the new covenant He has come to establish is superior to the old covenant! Jesus is seen to be a priest after the order of _____.

Jesus is Said to be Our Priest or High Priest –
* 20 Times in the New Testament
* All 20 of Those Times Are in the Book of Hebrews

The Book of Hebrews is focused on presenting Jesus Christ as our Great High Priest. In the first 4 verses of the book we see Jesus referenced as the _____ ___ _____, the _____ of everything, and introduced as our Great High Priest Who made purification for our sins and then sat down at the right hand of God the Father, where He always lives to make intercession for us.

> Hebrews 1:1-3 NASB  God, after He spoke long ago to the fathers in the prophets in many portions and in many ways, (2) in these last days has spoken to us in His Son, whom He appointed heir of all things, through whom also He made the world. (3) And He is the radiance of His glory and the exact representation of His nature, and upholds all things by the word of His power. When He had made purification of sins, He sat down at the right hand of the Majesty on high,

Jesus is presented in the Book of Hebrews as being greater than _____, greater than _____, and greater than the Old Testament _____. As a greater priest He is seen to have established a better covenant, of which we can now enter into by faith in Him.

Jesus is shown to have a priesthood that is greater than the _____ priesthood of the Old Testament. The Levitical priests were weak because of their own sin and because of the fact that they died and had to be replaced. Jesus is shown to be a priest, not after the order of Levi, but after the order of Melchizedek by virtue of an unending life.

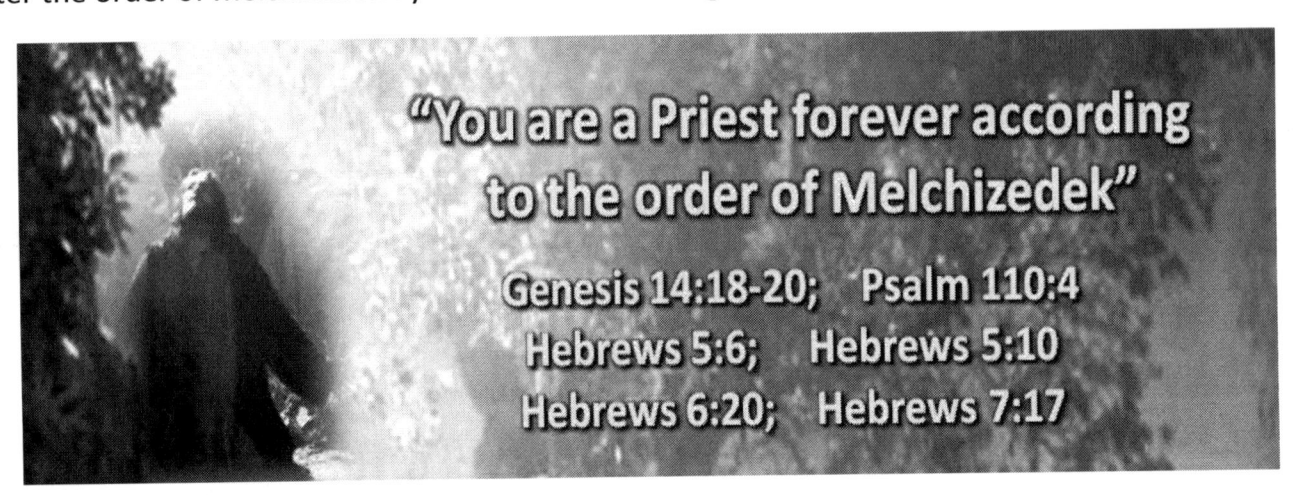

"You are a Priest forever according to the order of Melchizedek"

Genesis 14:18-20;   Psalm 110:4
Hebrews 5:6;   Hebrews 5:10
Hebrews 6:20;   Hebrews 7:17

The beginning of Hebrews 7 gives us much information about Melchizedek, showing that he was certainly a type of Christ in the Old Testament, and probably an actual Old Testament appearance of Christ. Maybe the pinnacle of the Book of Hebrews is found in Hebrews 7:24-25 which reveals why this all so important; "He is able to save _____ those who draw near to god through Him!"

> Hebrews 7:24-25 NASB  but Jesus, on the other hand, because He continues forever, holds His priesthood permanently. (25) Therefore He is able also to save forever those who draw near to God through Him, since He always lives to make intercession for them.

This presentation of Jesus as our Great High Priest continues in chapter 8-10. Note the following examples.

> Hebrews 8:1 NASB  Now the main point in what has been said is this: we have such a high priest, who has taken His seat at the right hand of the throne of the Majesty in the heavens,

> Hebrews 9:11-12 NASB  But when Christ appeared as a high priest of the good things to come, He entered through the greater and more perfect tabernacle, not made with hands, that is to say, not of this creation;  (12)  and not through the blood of goats and calves, but through His own blood, He entered the holy place once for all, having obtained eternal redemption.

## Jesus Christ is the Only Way of Salvation!

The Bible does not hesitate to proclaim that Jesus Christ is the only way of salvation. This is offensive to many today. We should not be surprised at this. Jesus told us that He is the rock that would cause many to stumble. The idea that there are many paths to heaven is very popular today but it is not what the Bible tells to be true! Notice these examples of Scripture -

> John 14:6 NASB  Jesus *said to him, "I am the way, and the truth, and the life; no one comes to the Father but through Me.

> Acts 4:12 NASB  "And there is salvation in no one else; for there is no other name under heaven that has been given among men by which we must be saved."

Consider for a moment the idea that there are many ways to heaven in light of what Jesus did for us in order to offer us forgiveness, reconciliation and eternal life. Can we imagine that God the Father would say to His Son, "Hey Son, even though there are many ways for people to get to heaven, why don't you become a man and allow them to spit on you, mock you, reject you, beat you, scourge you, put a crown of thorns on your head, drive nails in your hands and feet, and crucify you so there will be one more way among the many ways for people to make it to heaven." It doesn't make sense does it. If there are many ways to be saved and to make it to heaven Jesus would not have come and suffered all that He did in order to save us from our sin!

## We must believe in Jesus to be Saved!
(John 20:31; Romans 10:9-10; Acts 16:31; John 3:16)

There are many places in the New Testament where we see the need to believe upon Jesus Christ in order to be saved. The Gospel of John in particular emphasizes this truth. Remember that the purpose statement of the book is found in John 20:31 and it states that, "these have been written _____ _____ _____ _____ that Jesus is the Christ, the Son of God; and _____ _____ you may have life in His name."

Note the unique emphasis on Jesus' words "_____, _____ I say unto you" that is found in the Gospel of John. This in essence is a call to believe in what He has said about Himself and in His teachings, realizing that His words are true.

### Another Example of the Gospel of John's Emphasis on Believing

The phrase "truly, truly I say unto you" is found 25 times in the N.T.

* **Every one of them is in the Gospel of John**
* Each time the phrase is spoken by Jesus
* When Jesus said "truly, truly I say unto you" He was emphasizing that the things He proclaimed to His followers were absolutely true and trustworthy

NIV - "Very truly I tell you"   NKJV - "Most assuredly I say to you"

The Gospel of John's emphasis on the need to believe in Jesus goes far beyond the purpose statement in 20:31. Note the following picture showing this remarkable emphasis on believing.

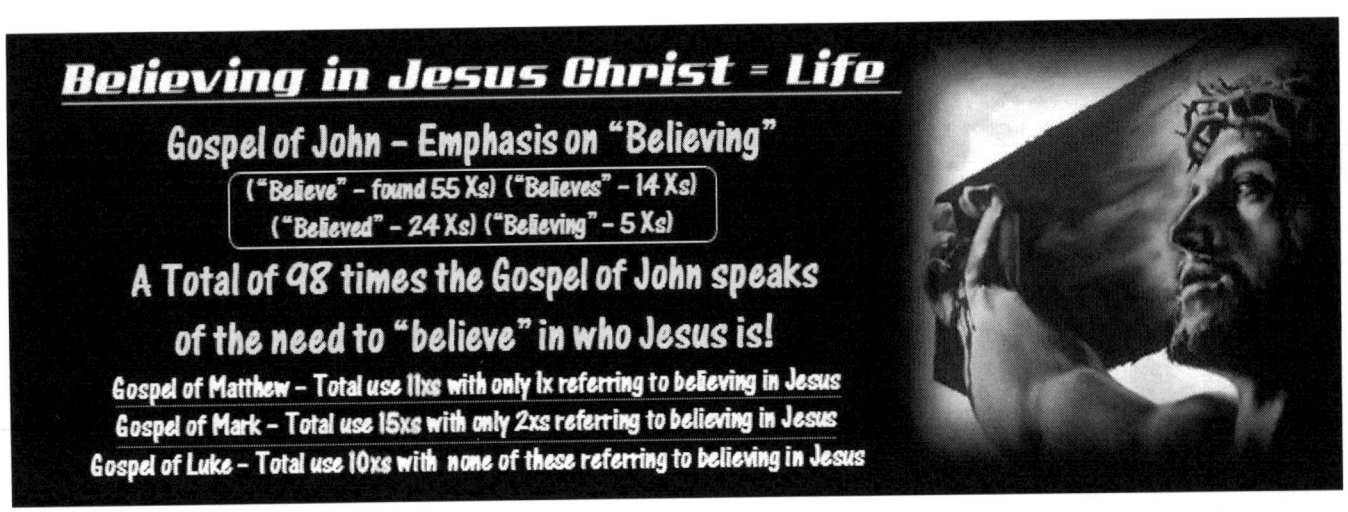

### Believing in Jesus Christ = Life

Gospel of John – Emphasis on "Believing"

("Believe" – found 55 Xs) ("Believes" – 14 Xs)
("Believed" – 24 Xs) ("Believing" – 5 Xs)

A Total of 98 times the Gospel of John speaks of the need to "believe" in who Jesus is!

Gospel of Matthew – Total use 11xs with only 1x referring to believing in Jesus
Gospel of Mark – Total use 15xs with only 2xs referring to believing in Jesus
Gospel of Luke – Total use 10xs with none of these referring to believing in Jesus

Believing in Jesus is critical for salvation. Understanding Who Jesus Is, Is the Most Important Thing in Life!

## Closing Thoughts for Faith & Reason Made Simple (Parts 1-8)

We've seen evidence that
**(1) We are Created by God, Not a Result of Evolution,
(2) The Bible is the Word of God, and
(3) Jesus is the Christ, the Son of God & the Savior!**

We must always be ready to give a defense for the hope within us – 1 Peter 3:15
We must in faith face the Goliath of our day!
We must help our children, grandchildren and others in the area of apologetics!

# FAITH & REASON MADE SIMPLE
## Part 8

## (The Person of Jesus Christ – Cont.)

### Jesus Is The Christ (Messiah)!

"Messiah" is the Hebrew word for "**Anointed One**". "Christ" is the equivalent Greek word for "Anointed One". The word "Messiah" is only found thirty nine times in the Old Testament and is usually translated "anointed". It is only translated Messiah twice in the Old Testament (Daniel 9:25 & 9:26). Still, the message of the coming Messiah was clearly transmitted throughout the Old Testament in many ways. The word "Christ" is found in the New Testament over **500** times, referencing Jesus of Nazareth as the "Anointed One" Who has come in fulfillment of all the Old Testament messianic prophecies.

Jesus is clearly and boldly presented as "The Christ" in the New Testament in many passages.

> John 20:31 NASB but these have been written so that you may believe that Jesus is the Christ, the Son of God; and that believing you may have life in His name.

> Matthew 16:13-18 NASB Now when Jesus came into the district of Caesarea Philippi, He was asking His disciples, "Who do people say that the Son of Man is?" (14) And they said, "Some say John the Baptist; and others, Elijah; but still others, Jeremiah, or one of the prophets." (15) He *said to them, "But who do you say that I am?" (16) Simon Peter answered, "You are the Christ, the Son of the living God." (17) And Jesus said to him, "Blessed are you, Simon Barjona, because flesh and blood did not reveal this to you, but My Father who is in heaven. (18) "I also say to you that you are Peter, and upon this rock I will build My church; and the gates of Hades will not overpower it.

Examples of Old Testament Messianic Passages – Psalm 2:2, Isaiah 53; Isaiah 9:6-7; Psalm 22; Isaiah 7:14; Daniel 9:25-26; Daniel 7:13

**The Suffering Messiah**

The Jewish image of a conquering, ruling Messiah often misses the fact that the Old Testament clearly portrayed the Messiah as one who would **suffer** and **die** on behalf of those he would come to redeem. The prophetic emphasis on a Messiah that would be victorious is certainly strong but it does not negate the strong indication of other prophetic passages that the Messiah would first suffer for our sin. Note these passages from Psalm 22 and Isaiah 53.

Psalms 22:1-18 NASB My God, my God, why have You forsaken me? ... (7) All who see me sneer at me; They separate with the lip, they wag the head, saying, (8) "Commit yourself to the LORD; let Him deliver him; Let Him rescue him, because He delights in him." ... (12) Many bulls have surrounded me; Strong bulls of Bashan have encircled me. (13) They open wide their mouth at me, As a ravening and a roaring lion. (14) I am poured out like water, And all my bones are out of joint; My heart is like wax; It is melted within me. (15) My strength is dried up like a potsherd, And my tongue cleaves to my jaws; And You lay me in the dust of death. (16) For dogs have surrounded me; A band of evildoers has encompassed me; They pierced my hands and my feet. (17) I can count all my bones. They look, they stare at me; (18) They divide my garments among them, And for my clothing they cast lots.

Isaiah 53:3-12 NASB (3) He was despised and forsaken of men, A man of sorrows and acquainted with grief; And like one from whom men hide their face He was despised, and we did not esteem Him. (4) Surely our griefs He Himself bore, And our sorrows He carried; Yet we ourselves esteemed Him stricken, Smitten of God, and afflicted. (5) But He was pierced through for our transgressions, He was crushed for our iniquities; The chastening for our well-being fell upon Him, And by His scourging we are healed. (6) All of us like sheep have gone astray, Each of us has turned to his own way; But the LORD has caused the iniquity of us all To fall on Him. (7) He was oppressed and He was afflicted, Yet He did not open His mouth; Like a lamb that is led to slaughter, And like a sheep that is silent before its shearers, So He did not open His mouth. (8) By oppression and judgment He was taken away; And as for His generation, who considered That He was cut off out of the land of the living For the transgression of my people, to whom the stroke was due? (9) His grave was assigned with wicked men, Yet He was with a rich man in His death, Because He had done no violence, Nor was there any deceit in His mouth. (10) But the LORD was pleased To crush Him, putting Him to grief; If He would render Himself as a guilt offering, He will see His offspring, He will prolong His days, And the good pleasure of the LORD will prosper in His hand. (11) As a result of the anguish of His soul, He will see it and be satisfied; By His knowledge the Righteous One, My Servant, will justify the many, As He will bear their iniquities. (12) Therefore, I will allot Him a portion with the great, And He will divide the booty with the strong; Because He poured out Himself to death, And was numbered with the transgressors; Yet He Himself bore the sin of many, And interceded for the transgressors.

So the foretelling of the suffering of the Messiah to become an offering for the sins of the people is clear! It is unfortunate that many have missed this and only looked for a Messiah that will conquer his enemies and rule. Jesus Christ fulfilled the prophetic passages of a suffering Messiah as well as the prophetic passages of a Messiah who would rise up in victory to rule forever!

* One of the strongest images of the Messiah in the Old Testament is found in **Daniel 7:13-14** where Daniel sees "One like a Son of Man" coming to the Ancient of Days. He is given a kingdom and everlasting dominion.

> Daniel 7:13-14 NASB "I kept looking in the night visions, And behold, with the clouds of heaven One like a Son of Man was coming, And He came up to the Ancient of Days, And was presented before Him. (14) "And to Him was given dominion, Glory and a kingdom, That all the peoples, nations and *men of every* language Might serve Him. His dominion is an everlasting dominion Which will not pass away; And His kingdom is one Which will not be destroyed.

Because of this passage the title "**Son of Man**" became synonymous with "Messiah" to the Jews who were waiting for their victorious Messiah to come and establish His kingdom. As we will see here, Jesus is referred to many times in the New Testament as "Son of Man", including when He is judged by the religious leaders for saying " ... and you shall see the Son of Man sitting at the **right hand** of power, and coming with the clouds of heaven." (Mark 14:62)

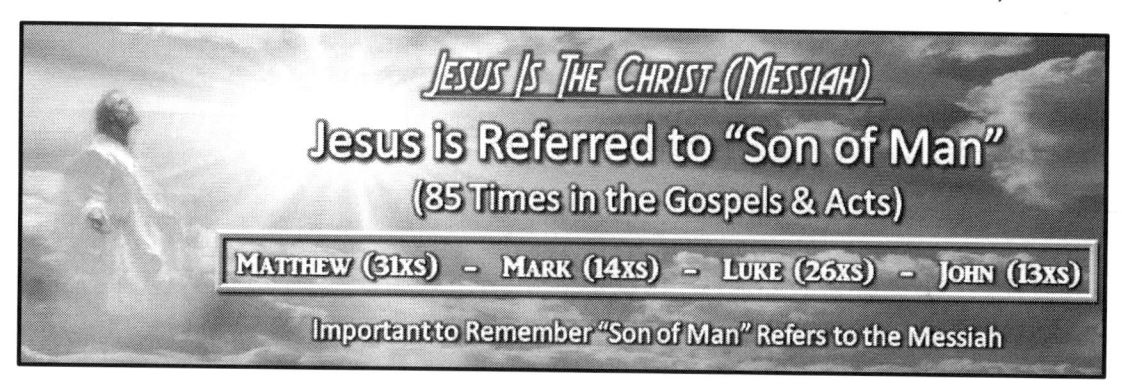

**Jesus Is The Christ (Messiah)**
**Jesus is Referred to "Son of Man"**
(85 Times in the Gospels & Acts)
Matthew (31xs) – Mark (14xs) – Luke (26xs) – John (13xs)
Important to Remember "Son of Man" Refers to the Messiah

> Mark 14:62 NASB And Jesus said, "I am; and you shall see THE SON OF MAN SITTING AT THE RIGHT HAND OF POWER, and COMING WITH THE CLOUDS OF HEAVEN."

> Acts 7:55-56 NASB But being full of the Holy Spirit, he gazed intently into heaven and saw the glory of God, and Jesus standing at the right hand of God; (56) and he said, "Behold, I see the heavens opened up and the Son of Man standing at the right hand of God."

When Jesus spoke of His **2ⁿᵈ Coming** He used this term "Son of Man" to indicate that He will come in glory as the victorious Messiah. He actually is referencing Daniel 7:13-14.

> Matthew 24:30 NASB "And then the sign of the Son of Man will appear in the sky, and then all the tribes of the earth will mourn, and they will see the SON OF MAN COMING ON THE CLOUDS OF THE SKY with power and great glory.

**\* Jesus fulfilled over 300 Old Testament prophecies about the coming Messiah!**
**This proves, without question that He is the Messiah, the Christ!**

**Jesus Is The Messiah (The Christ)**
Over 300 Messianic Prophecies Fulfilled by Jesus Christ
* Genesis 3:15 (Seed of Woman)
* Isaiah 7:14, Micah 5:2 (Birth)
* Isaiah 53, Psalm 22 (Cross)
* Psalm 78:2 (Parables) * Zechariah 9:9 (Donkey)
* Zechariah 11:12-13 (Silver) * Psalm 22:18 (Garments)

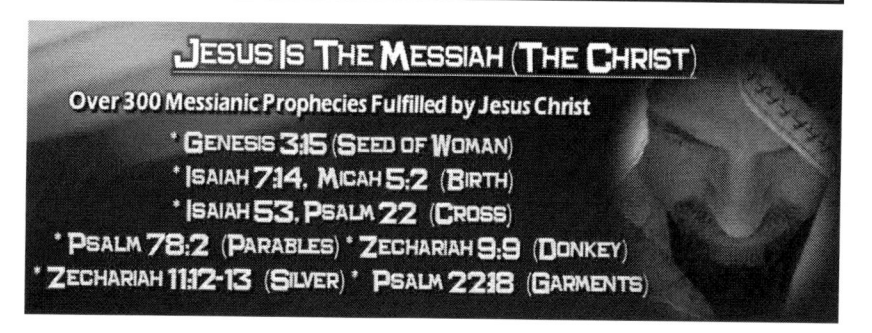

**Jesus fulfilled 300 Old Testament Prophecies about the Coming Messiah! (Here are some examples)**
- * Seed of a Woman to Conquer the **Serpent** of Old  (Genesis 3:15)
- * His Suffering Upon the Cross (Many Details) (Psalm 22 & Isaiah 53)
- * His Birth in **Bethlehem**  (Micah 5:2)
- * He Would Be Born of a Virgin  (Isaiah 7:14) (Also on His Birth – Isaiah 9:6-7)
- * He Would Teach in **Parables**  (Psalm 78:2)
- * He Would Ride Into Jerusalem on a **Donkey**  (Zechariah 9:9)
- * He Would Be Betrayed For 30 Pieces of Silver  (Zechariah 11:12-13)
- * His **Garments** Would be Divided by the Soldiers (Psalm 22:18)
- * Soldiers Would Cast Lots for His Cloak  (Psalm 22:18)

In his book "Science Speaks", Dr. Peter Stoner explains a research project that he and students at Pasadena City College, where he was a professor, did to estimate the probability of one person fulfilling various Old Testament Messianic prophecies. "When multiplied together it was found that even using these very conservative estimates, there would be a 1 in $10^{28}$ chance of someone fulfilling just **8** Messianic prophecies."
"**That number looks like this when written out.**
10,000,000,000,000,000,000,000,000,000."

To illustrate how large the number $10^{28}$ is Dr. Stoner gives this illustration. Image covering the entire state of **Texas** 2' thick with silver dollars. Then mark one of the silver dollars and put anywhere in the state of Texas randomly. Now send a blind man into the state of Texas and have him pick one silver dollar from anywhere in the state. The chances of him picking the marked silver dollar are about 1 in $10^{28}$.

Remember that Jesus did not just fulfill 8 of the Old Testament prophecies concerning the Messiah (the Christ). He fulfilled over 300 of them!!! Jesus is the Messiah (the Christ)! The New Testament refers to Jesus as the Christ over 500 times! Jesus of Nazareth is the Christ!

## The Deity of Jesus Christ

### Seen in The Gospel of John

(The Gospel of **John** is Dedicated to Presenting Jesus Christ as the Divine Son of God!)

> John 1:1 NASB  In the beginning was the Word, and the Word was with God, and **the Word was God.**  (Note – V. 14 says the Word became flesh and dwelt among us)

> John 20:31 NASB  but these have been written so that you may believe that Jesus is the Christ, **the Son of God**; and that believing you may have life in His name.

The Gospel of John is unique in many ways. This is because of its stated purpose found in John 20:31. It is written so that we would believe that Jesus is (1) **the Christ**, and (2) **the Son of God**, and so that believing we might have life in His name! One of the ways that the Gospel of John does this is by using "**I Am**" statements referring to Jesus. These statements are not found in Matthew, Mark or Luke. They are unique to the Gospel of John. To understand the significance of these statements we have to go back to Exodus 3:14-15 where Moses is conversing with God at the burning bush. God is sending Moses back to Egypt to deliver the people and Moses is asking God how he should respond when people ask him "Who sent you?" Notice God's answer to Moses.

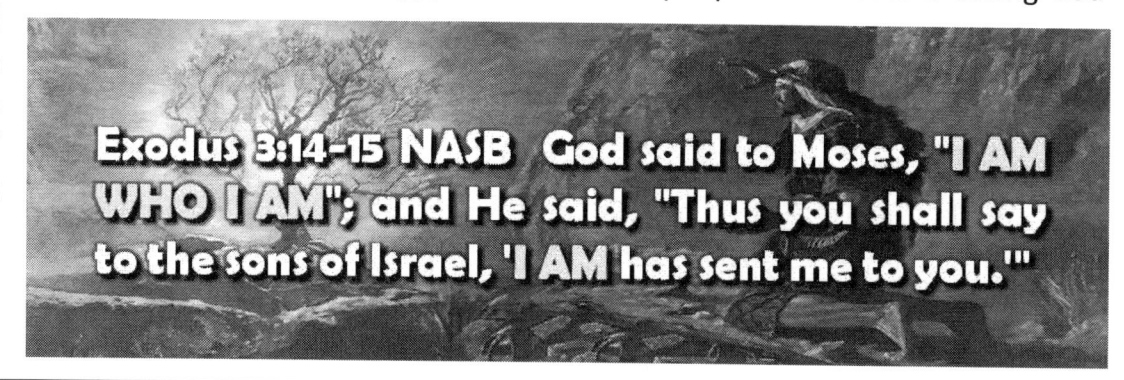

Exodus 3:14-15 NASB God said to Moses, "I AM WHO I AM"; and He said, "Thus you shall say to the sons of Israel, 'I AM has sent me to you.'"

Exodus 3:15 NASB God, furthermore, said to Moses, "Thus you shall say to the sons of Israel, 'The LORD, the God of your fathers, the God of Abraham, the God of Isaac, and the God of Jacob, has sent me to you.' This is My name forever, and this is My memorial-name to all generations.

God reveals Himself as "I Am". This title refers to the fact that God is the self-existent One. In verse 15 God gives more information to Moses. He says that He shall also be called "The LORD" which in the Hebrew is "Yahweh" or "Jehovah" and which means the **self-existent** One. So God is "I Am" or "The LORD", the self-existent One. Often times in the Old Testament the name "Yahweh" or "Jehovah" was then connected with a descriptive term to communicate characteristics of God such as "Jehovah Shalom" which means "The LORD our peace" or "Jehovah Jireh" which means "The LORD our provider.

In the Gospel of John we see this same pattern used with reference now to Jesus Christ, showing His deity. Note the following examples from the **23** "I Am" statements in the Gospel of John.

### The 23 "I Am" Statements in the Gospel of John!

"I Am the Bread of Life" (John 6:35) - "I Am the Door" (John 10:9)
"I Am the Good Shepherd" (John 10:11)
"I Am the Resurrection & the Life" (John 11:25)
"I Am the Way, the Truth & the Life" (John 14:6)

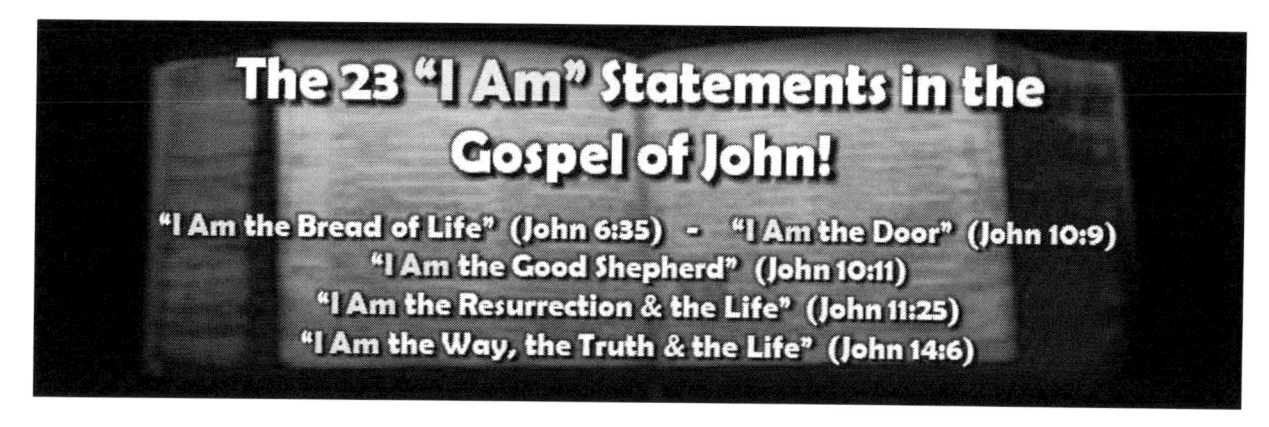

In addition to the times when the "I Am" statements include descriptive terms with reference to Jesus there are a number of places where "I Am" is used to refer to Jesus without descriptive terms added. Note the following examples –

> John 8:24 NASB  "Therefore I said to you that you will die in your sins; for unless you believe that **I am** *He,* you will die in your sins."   (Note – "He" is added by the translators)

> John 8:58 NASB  Jesus said to them, "Truly, truly, I say to you, before Abraham was born, **I am.**"

> John 18:4-6 NASB  So Jesus, knowing all the things that were coming upon Him, went forth and *said to them, "Whom do you seek?" (5) They answered Him, "Jesus the Nazarene." He *said to them, "**I am** *He.*" And Judas also, who was betraying Him, was standing with them. (6) So when He said to them, "**I am** *He,*" they drew back and fell to the ground.
> (Note – "He is added by the translators – It was note found in the original language)

The Gospel of John is dedicated to revealing the deity of Jesus. The very first verse declares His deity directly. The 23 "I Am" statements also reveal His deity. A number of times we read of people picking up stones to stone Him when He made statements declaring Himself to be "I Am" like John 8:58-59.

The deity of Jesus Christ is also seen in other places throughout the New Testament.

## The Deity of Jesus Christ Seen Throughout the Remaining New Testament

> Philippians 2:5-8 NASB  Have this attitude in yourselves which was also in Christ Jesus, (6) who, although He existed in the form of God, did not regard equality with God a thing to be grasped, (7) but emptied Himself, taking the form of a bond-servant, *and* being made in the likeness of men. (8) Being found in appearance as a man, He humbled Himself by becoming obedient to the point of death, even death on a cross.

Compare Joel 2:32 which speaks of **Jehovah** with Romans 10:9-13 which speaks of **Jesus**.

> Joel 2:32 NASB  "And it will come about that whoever calls on the name of the LORD Will be delivered (saved) …"

> Romans 10:9-13 NASB  that if you confess with your mouth Jesus as Lord, and believe in your heart that God raised Him from the dead, you will be saved; (10) for with the heart a person believes, resulting in righteousness, and with the mouth he confesses, resulting in salvation … (13) for "WHOEVER WILL CALL ON THE NAME OF THE LORD WILL BE SAVED."

Here are a few more examples.

> Titus 2:13 NASB  looking for the blessed hope and the appearing of the glory of our great God and Savior, Christ Jesus,

> Hebrews 1:6-8 NASB  And when He again brings the firstborn into the world, He says, "AND LET ALL THE ANGELS OF GOD WORSHIP HIM." (7) And of the angels He says, "WHO MAKES HIS ANGELS WINDS, AND HIS MINISTERS A FLAME OF FIRE." (8) But of the Son *He says,* "YOUR THRONE, O GOD, IS FOREVER AND EVER, AND THE RIGHTEOUS SCEPTER IS THE SCEPTER OF HIS KINGDOM.

> Colossians 2:9 NASB  For in Him all the fullness of Deity dwells in bodily form,

**Jesus taught with <u>divine</u> <u>authority</u>** (This also reveals His deity) At the end of the Sermon on the Mount, "the crowds were astonished at his teaching, for he was teaching them as one who had authority, and not as their scribes" (Matt. 7:28–29) The teachers of the law in Jesus' day had no authority of their own. Their authority came from their use of earlier authorities. Even Moses and the other OT prophets and authors did not speak in their own authority, but would say, "This is what the Lord says." Jesus, on the other hand, interprets the law by saying, "You have heard that it was said. . . . But I say to you" (see Matt. 5:22, 28, 32, 34, 39, 44). (Also see Matthew 7:24-29) This divine authority is shown with staggering clarity when he speaks of himself as the Lord who will judge the whole earth and will say to the wicked, "I never knew you; depart from me, you workers of lawlessness" (Matt. 7:23). No wonder the crowd was amazed at the authority with which Jesus spoke.

Jesus recognized that his words carried divine weight. He acknowledged the permanent authority of **<u>the law</u>** (Matt. 5:18) and put his words on an equal plane with it:

> "For truly, I say to you, until heaven and earth pass away, not an iota, not a dot, will pass from the Law until all is accomplished" (Matt. 5:18);

> "Heaven and earth will pass away, but my words will not pass away" (Matt. 24:35).

## Jesus is Our Great High Priest!

The book of Hebrews presents Jesus as our Great High Priest! It shows Him to be superior to the angels, to Moses, and to the Levitical priests. It also shows that the new covenant He has come to establish is superior to the old covenant! Jesus is seen to be a priest after the order of **<u>Melchizedek</u>**.

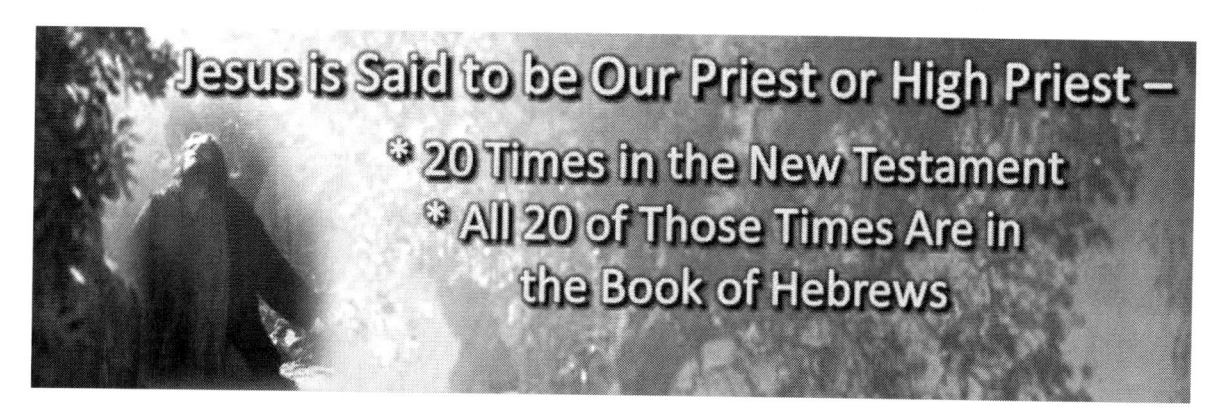

> Jesus is Said to be Our Priest or High Priest –
> * 20 Times in the New Testament
> * All 20 of Those Times Are in the Book of Hebrews

The Book of Hebrews is focused on presenting Jesus Christ as our Great High Priest. In the first 4 verses of the book we see Jesus referenced as the **Son of God**, the **creator** of everything, and introduced as our Great High Priest Who made purification for our sins and then sat down at the right hand of God the Father, where He always lives to make intercession for us.

> Hebrews 1:1-3 NASB  God, after He spoke long ago to the fathers in the prophets in many portions and in many ways,  (2)  in these last days has spoken to us in His Son, whom He appointed heir of all things, through whom also He made the world.  (3)  And He is the radiance of His glory and the exact representation of His nature, and upholds all things by the word of His power. When He had made purification of sins, He sat down at the right hand of the Majesty on high,

Jesus is presented in the Book of Hebrews as being greater than **angels**, greater than **Moses**, and greater than the Old Testament **priests**. As a greater priest He is seen to have established a better covenant, of which we can now enter into by faith in Him.

Jesus is shown to have a priesthood that is greater than the **Levitical** priesthood of the Old Testament. The Levitical priests were weak because of their own sin and because of the fact that they died and had to be replaced. Jesus is shown to be a priest, not after the order of Levi, but after the order of Melchizedek by virtue of an unending life.

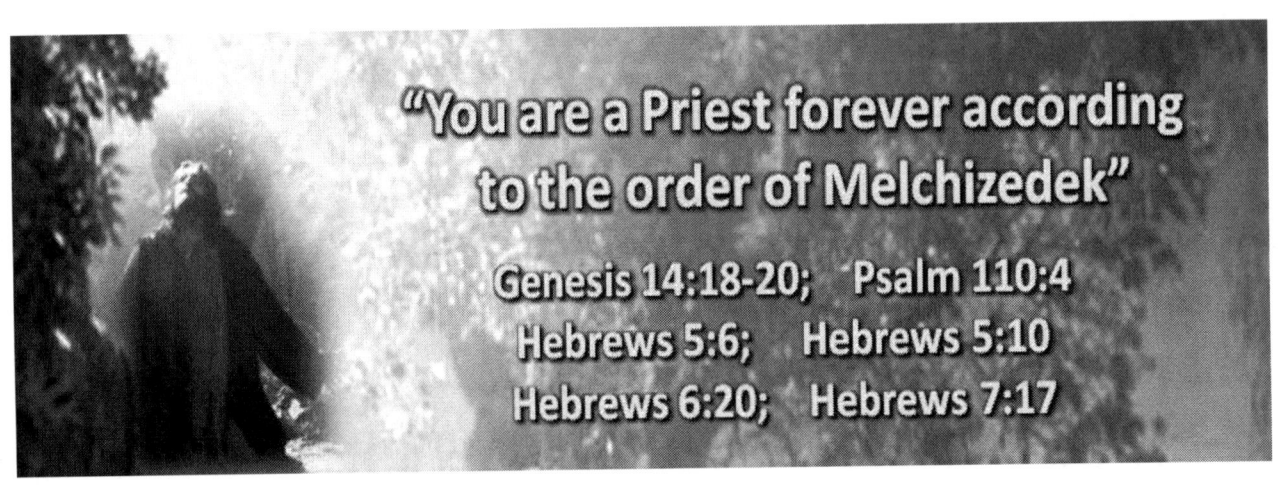

"You are a Priest forever according to the order of Melchizedek"

Genesis 14:18-20;   Psalm 110:4
Hebrews 5:6;    Hebrews 5:10
Hebrews 6:20;   Hebrews 7:17

The beginning of Hebrews 7 gives us much information about Melchizedek, showing that he was certainly a type of Christ in the Old Testament, and probably an actual Old Testament appearance of Christ. Maybe the pinnacle of the Book of Hebrews is found in Hebrews 7:24-25 which reveals why this all so important; "He is able to save **forever** those who draw near to god through Him!"

> Hebrews 7:24-25 NASB  but Jesus, on the other hand, because He continues forever, holds His priesthood permanently.  (25)  Therefore He is able also to save forever those who draw near to God through Him, since He always lives to make intercession for them.

This presentation of Jesus as our Great High Priest continues in chapter 8-10. Note the following examples.

> Hebrews 8:1 NASB  Now the main point in what has been said is this: we have such a high priest, who has taken His seat at the right hand of the throne of the Majesty in the heavens,

> Hebrews 9:11-12 NASB  But when Christ appeared as a high priest of the good things to come, He entered through the greater and more perfect tabernacle, not made with hands, that is to say, not of this creation; (12) and not through the blood of goats and calves, but through His own blood, He entered the holy place once for all, having obtained eternal redemption.

## Jesus Christ is the Only Way of Salvation!

The Bible does not hesitate to proclaim that Jesus Christ is the only way of salvation. This is offensive to many today. We should not be surprised at this. Jesus told us that He is the rock that would cause many to stumble. The idea that there are many paths to heaven is very popular today but it is not what the Bible tells to be true! Notice these examples of Scripture -

> John 14:6 NASB  Jesus *said to him, "I am the way, and the truth, and the life; no one comes to the Father but through Me.

> Acts 4:12 NASB  "And there is salvation in no one else; for there is no other name under heaven that has been given among men by which we must be saved."

Consider for a moment the idea that there are many ways to heaven in light of what Jesus did for us in order to offer us forgiveness, reconciliation and eternal life. Can we imagine that God the Father would say to His Son, "Hey Son, even though there are many ways for people to get to heaven, why don't you become a man and allow them to spit on you, mock you, reject you, beat you, scourge you, put a crown of thorns on your head, drive nails in your hands and feet, and crucify you so there will be one more way among the many ways for people to make it to heaven." It doesn't make sense does it. If there are many ways to be saved and to make it to heaven Jesus would not have come and suffered all that He did in order to save us from our sin!

## We must believe in Jesus to be Saved!
(John 20:31; Romans 10:9-10; Acts 16:31; John 3:16)

There are many places in the New Testament where we see the need to believe upon Jesus Christ in order to be saved. The Gospel of John in particular emphasizes this truth. Remember that the purpose statement of the book is found in John 20:31 and it states that, "these have been written **that you may believe** that Jesus is the Christ, the Son of God; and **that believing** you may have life in His name."

Note the unique emphasis on Jesus' words "**Truly, truly** I say unto you" that is found in the Gospel of John. This in essence is a call to believe in what He has said about Himself and in His teachings, realizing that His words are true.

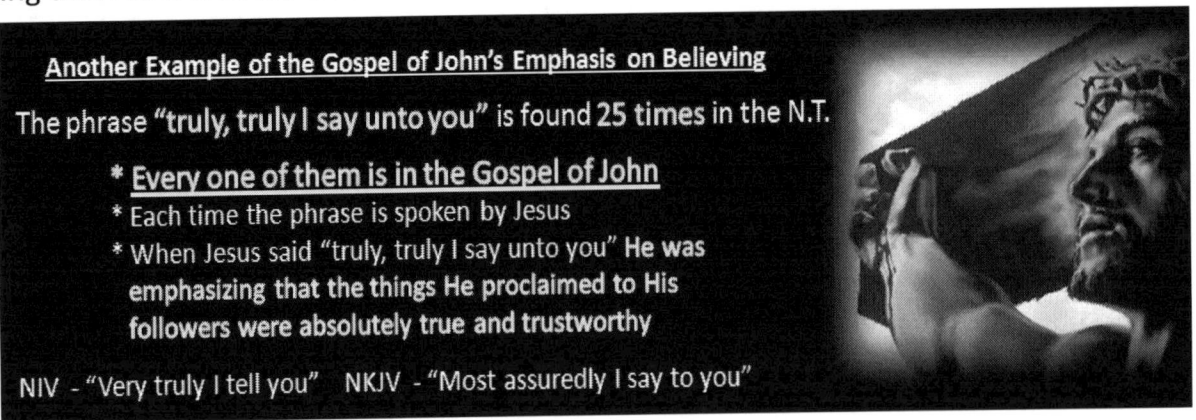

> **Another Example of the Gospel of John's Emphasis on Believing**
>
> The phrase "truly, truly I say unto you" is found 25 times in the N.T.
> * **Every one of them is in the Gospel of John**
> * Each time the phrase is spoken by Jesus
> * When Jesus said "truly, truly I say unto you" He was emphasizing that the things He proclaimed to His followers were absolutely true and trustworthy
>
> NIV - "Very truly I tell you"    NKJV - "Most assuredly I say to you"

The Gospel of John's emphasis on the need to believe in Jesus goes far beyond the purpose statement in 20:31. Note the following picture showing this remarkable emphasis on believing.

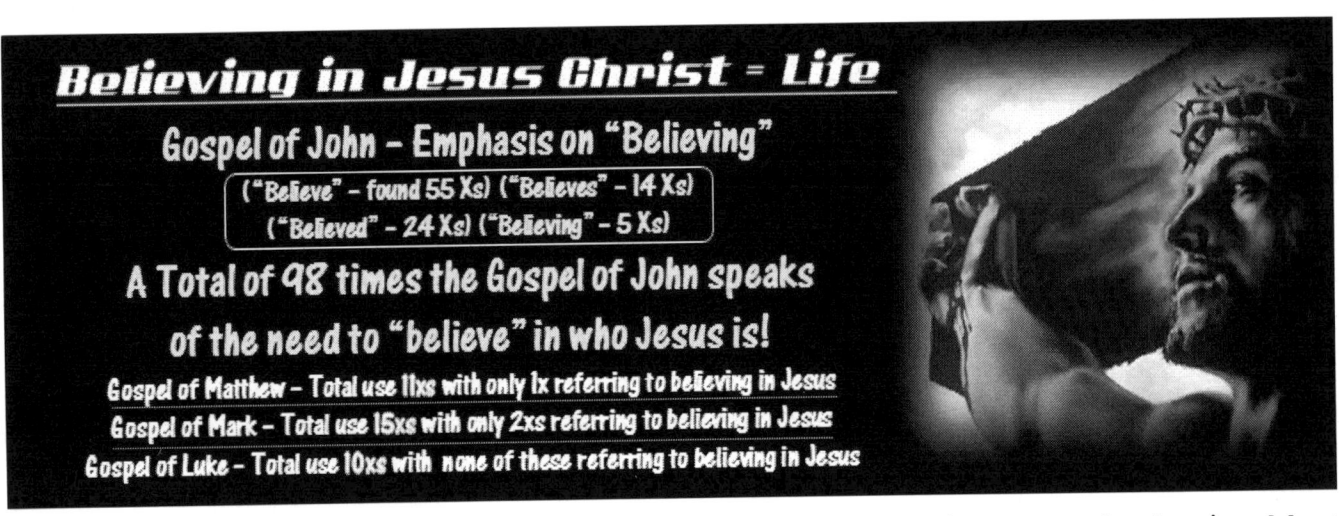

> **Believing in Jesus Christ = Life**
>
> Gospel of John – Emphasis on "Believing"
> ("Believe" - found 55 Xs) ("Believes" - 14 Xs)
> ("Believed" - 24 Xs) ("Believing" - 5 Xs)
>
> A Total of 98 times the Gospel of John speaks of the need to "believe" in who Jesus is!
>
> Gospel of Matthew – Total use 11xs with only 1x referring to believing in Jesus
> Gospel of Mark – Total use 15xs with only 2xs referring to believing in Jesus
> Gospel of Luke – Total use 10xs with none of these referring to believing in Jesus

Believing in Jesus is critical for salvation. Understanding Who Jesus Is, Is the Most Important Thing in Life!

## Closing Thoughts for Faith & Reason Made Simple (Parts 1-8)

We've seen evidence that
**(1) We are Created by God, Not a Result of Evolution,
(2) The Bible is the Word of God, and
(3) Jesus is the Christ, the Son of God & the Savior!**

We must always be ready to give a defense for the hope within us – 1 Peter 3:15
We must in faith face the Goliath of our day!
We must help our children, grandchildren and others in the area of apologetics!

# FAITH & REASON
## MADE SIMPLE
### Memory Cards

### (Memory Cards)

The memory cards shown here in this section are designed to assist you in memorizing the main points of the 8 sessions of this training course. To download and print out free color versions of these cards go to **LOCALCHURCHAPOLOGETICS.ORG**. There are 6 cards for the 6 scientific flaws of the theory of evolution. There are 12 cards for the 8 levels of evidence of a creator. There are 12 cards for the evidences confirming that the Bible is the Word of God and there are 12 cards for the evidences regarding the person of Jesus Christ.

## 6 Scientific Flaws With the "Theory" of Evolution

**1 – The Theory of Evolution Violates the 2nd Law of Thermodynamics**

The amount of usable energy in any closed system always decreases (Things move from order to chaos, Not from chaos to order) ("Entropy")

**2 – The Theory of Evolution Violates the Law of Bio-Genesis**

Life only comes from life! The idea of "spontaneous generation" which is life coming from non-life has been tested and proven to be false!

**3 – The Theory of Evolution Purposely Confuses Micro-Evolution w/Macro Evolution (New Kind)**

Micro-Evolution (adaptation within a kind) can be observed & verified scientifically. Macro-Evolution (one kind evolving into a new kind) has <u>never</u> been observed in nature or by scientific discovery!

**4 – The Theory of Evolution Contradicts The Fossil Record**

If the theory of evolution were true the fossil record would be filled with "transitional" life forms. It is not! Also, fossils found in rock layers give evidence that rock layers were formed quickly!

**5 – The Theory of Evolution Contradicts the fact that Mutations Do Not Bring Increased Genetic Information!**

For more complex life forms to evolve from simpler life forms an increase of genetic information would be needed. Mutations are the result of missing genetic information!

**6 – The Theory of Evolution contradicts the Order, Design, Beauty & Information we observe in the Universe!**

Everywhere from the vast universe, to the planet earth, to the living creatures we observe, to the microscopic world & the human cell we observe tremendous amounts of order, design, beauty & information!

# Scientific Evidence That Confirms Creation

## EVIDENCES OF A CREATOR - GOD
### FINELY TUNED UNIVERSE!
"Design - Designer"
"Information - Intelligence"

Scientists now know that the universe is held together by precisely set laws of physics (constants) such as "the law of gravity" & "the speed of light". If these constants were set just slightly different, galaxies, stars and planets would not exist! This precision shows great design and confirms the involvement of a designer!

(1)

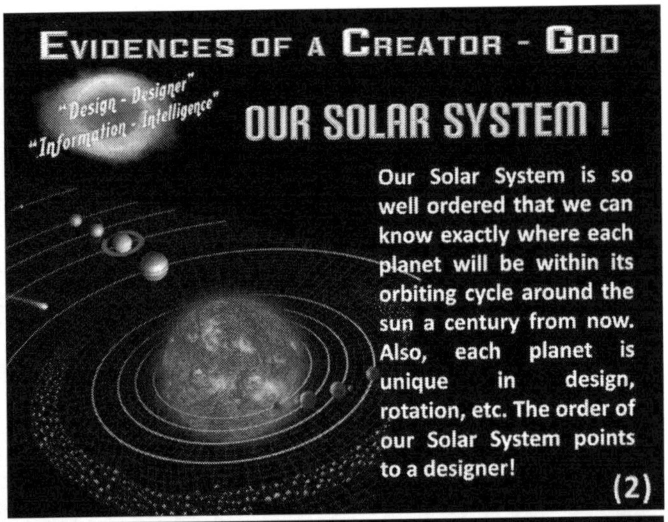

## EVIDENCES OF A CREATOR - GOD
### OUR SOLAR SYSTEM!
"Design - Designer"
"Information - Intelligence"

Our Solar System is so well ordered that we can know exactly where each planet will be within its orbiting cycle around the sun a century from now. Also, each planet is unique in design, rotation, etc. The order of our Solar System points to a designer!

(2)

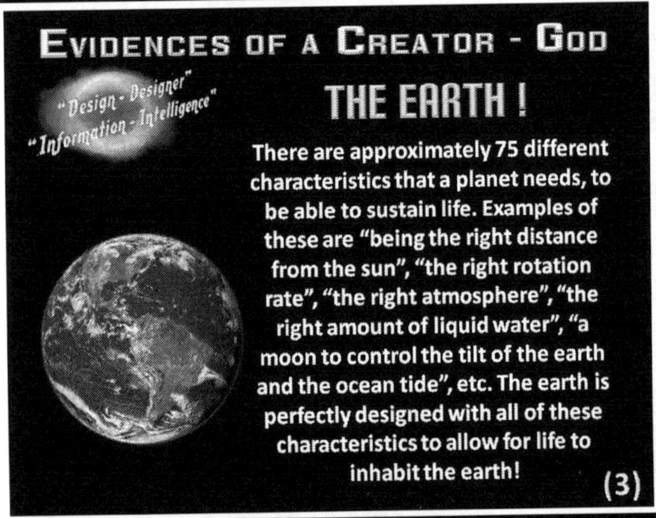

## EVIDENCES OF A CREATOR - GOD
### THE EARTH!
"Design - Designer"
"Information - Intelligence"

There are approximately 75 different characteristics that a planet needs, to be able to sustain life. Examples of these are "being the right distance from the sun", "the right rotation rate", "the right atmosphere", "the right amount of liquid water", "a moon to control the tilt of the earth and the ocean tide", etc. The earth is perfectly designed with all of these characteristics to allow for life to inhabit the earth!

(3)

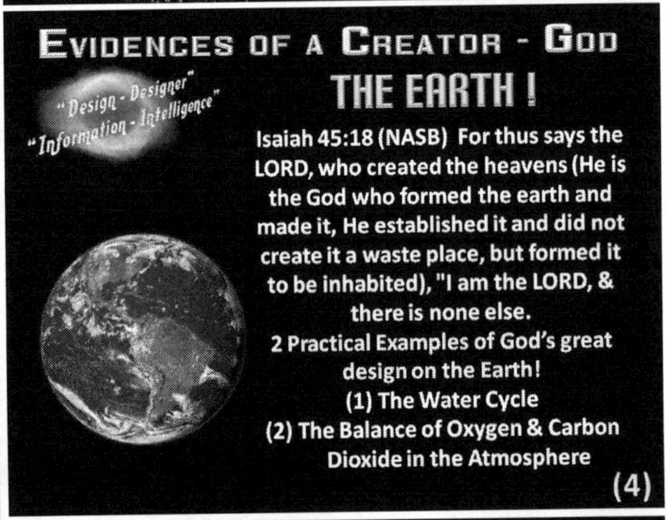

## EVIDENCES OF A CREATOR - GOD
### THE EARTH!
"Design - Designer"
"Information - Intelligence"

Isaiah 45:18 (NASB) For thus says the LORD, who created the heavens (He is the God who formed the earth and made it, He established it and did not create it a waste place, but formed it to be inhabited), "I am the LORD, & there is none else.
2 Practical Examples of God's great design on the Earth!
(1) The Water Cycle
(2) The Balance of Oxygen & Carbon Dioxide in the Atmosphere

(4)

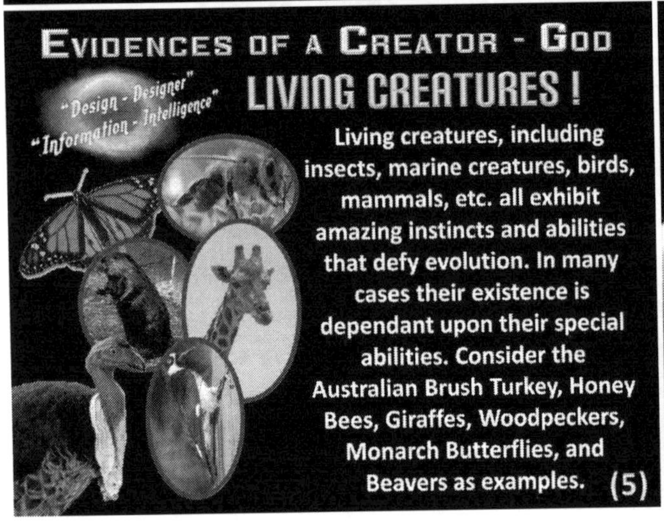

## EVIDENCES OF A CREATOR - GOD
### LIVING CREATURES!
"Design - Designer"
"Information - Intelligence"

Living creatures, including insects, marine creatures, birds, mammals, etc. all exhibit amazing instincts and abilities that defy evolution. In many cases their existence is dependant upon their special abilities. Consider the Australian Brush Turkey, Honey Bees, Giraffes, Woodpeckers, Monarch Butterflies, and Beavers as examples.

(5)

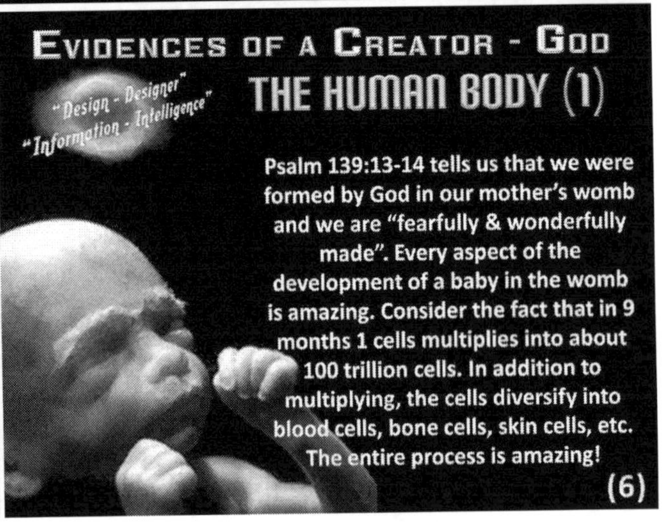

## EVIDENCES OF A CREATOR - GOD
### THE HUMAN BODY (1)
"Design - Designer"
"Information - Intelligence"

Psalm 139:13-14 tells us that we were formed by God in our mother's womb and we are "fearfully & wonderfully made". Every aspect of the development of a baby in the womb is amazing. Consider the fact that in 9 months 1 cells multiplies into about 100 trillion cells. In addition to multiplying, the cells diversify into blood cells, bone cells, skin cells, etc. The entire process is amazing!

(6)

# Scientific Evidence That Confirms Creation (Cont.)

## EVIDENCES OF A CREATOR - GOD
### THE HUMAN BODY (2)

"Design - Designer"
"Information - Intelligence"

The human body shows a multitude of design features that reflect what Psalm 139:13-14 says. Every one of the systems of the body (digestive, respiratory, etc.) function with staggering amounts of precision design. The organs of the body also are each incredible in function. The eyes & ears in particular cannot be explained by mere chance and time, but rather, point to a designer!

(7)

## EVIDENCES OF A CREATOR - GOD
### MICROSCOPIC WORLD !

"Design - Designer"
"Information - Intelligence"

The microscopic world reveals tremendous amounts of complex design that points to a designer. E.G. - The tail of a single celled bacteria (called a "flagellum") involves 40 different microscopic parts, each functioning with a specified purpose allowing the flagellum to move the bacteria in various directions. If even 1 of the parts were missing the flagellum could not function. (Irreducible Complexity)

(8)

## EVIDENCES OF A CREATOR - GOD
### THE HUMAN CELL (1)

"Design - Designer"
"Information - Intelligence"

The approximately 5 million parts of a Boeing 747 that work together to allow the jet to function show great amounts of undeniable design. The human cell actually has billions of parts that all work together to allow the cell to function, and the human body to live. The cell clearly shows evidence of a designer. The cell has manufacturing plants, power plants, transportation systems, a postal service, quality control systems, security systems, communication systems, etc.

(9)

## EVIDENCES OF A CREATOR - GOD
### THE HUMAN CELL (2)

"Design - Designer"
"Information - Intelligence"

The function of human cells clearly points to an intelligent designer! Consider the fact that on average, each of the 100 trillion cells of the human body produces 2,000 proteins per second! (The process of producing even 1 protein is nothing short of remarkable & amazing.)
Also, on average, each of the 100 trillion cells of the body produces 10 million ATP energy molecules per second. (The ATP synthase motors producing ATP rotate at apx. 1,000 rpms!)

(10)

## EVIDENCES OF A CREATOR - GOD
### INFORMATION (DNA) (1)

"Design - Designer"
"Information - Intelligence"

Information is evidence of intelligence because it takes a source of intelligence to produce usable information. DNA, found in the cells of living creatures, (and living plants) is most densely packed source of information found in the known universe! The amount of information found in 1 gram of DNA is equivalent to the amount of information found in 1 trillion CDs!

(11)

## EVIDENCES OF A CREATOR - GOD
### INFORMATION (DNA) (2)

"Design - Designer"
"Information - Intelligence"

An illustration of how information points to a source of intelligence is seen by considering 3 simple words written in the sand; "I love you". Any person who would see these 3 words scratched in the sand would instinctively know that someone with intelligence had been there and had scratched the words in the sand. In the same way, the information in DNA tells us clearly that an intelligent being has placed the information there for a purpose.

(12)

# Confirming Evidence That The Bible is God's Word

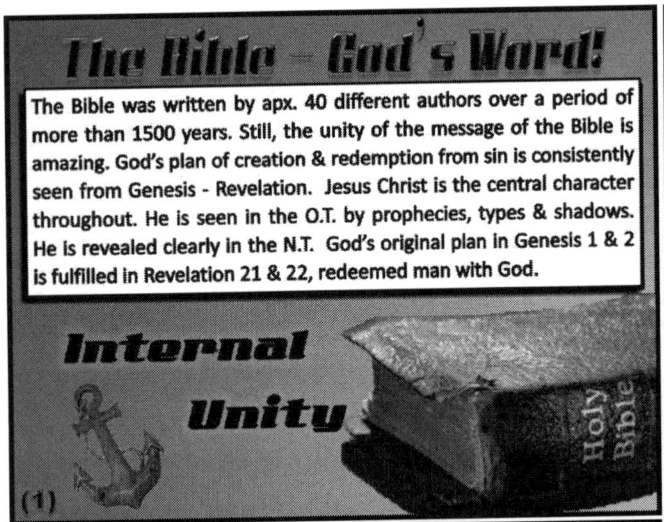

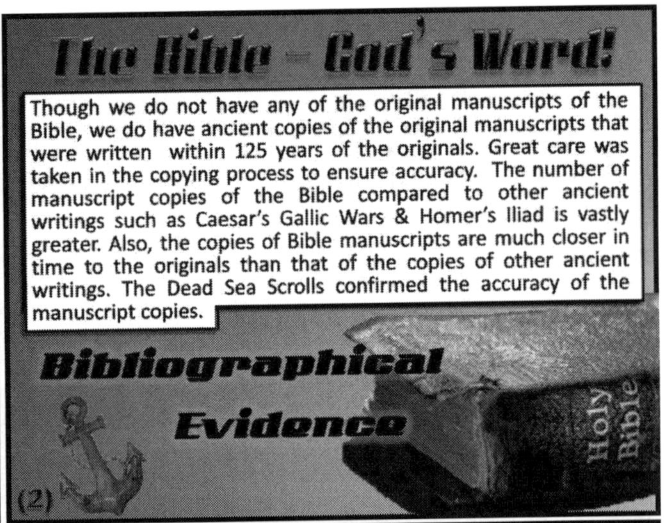

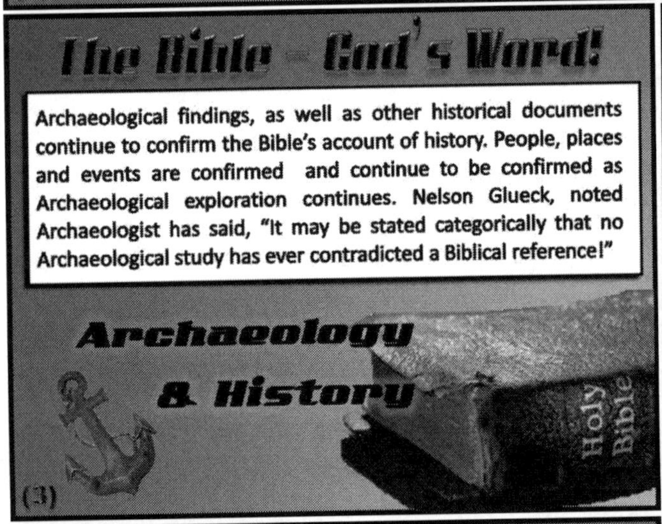

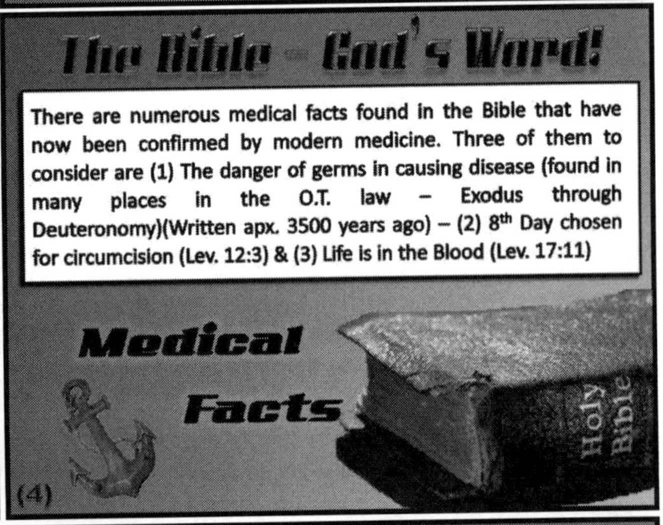

## (1) The Bible – God's Word! — Internal Unity

The Bible was written by apx. 40 different authors over a period of more than 1500 years. Still, the unity of the message of the Bible is amazing. God's plan of creation & redemption from sin is consistently seen from Genesis - Revelation. Jesus Christ is the central character throughout. He is seen in the O.T. by prophecies, types & shadows. He is revealed clearly in the N.T. God's original plan in Genesis 1 & 2 is fulfilled in Revelation 21 & 22, redeemed man with God.

## (2) The Bible – God's Word! — Bibliographical Evidence

Though we do not have any of the original manuscripts of the Bible, we do have ancient copies of the original manuscripts that were written within 125 years of the originals. Great care was taken in the copying process to ensure accuracy. The number of manuscript copies of the Bible compared to other ancient writings such as Caesar's Gallic Wars & Homer's Iliad is vastly greater. Also, the copies of Bible manuscripts are much closer in time to the originals than that of the copies of other ancient writings. The Dead Sea Scrolls confirmed the accuracy of the manuscript copies.

## (3) The Bible – God's Word! — Archaeology & History

Archaeological findings, as well as other historical documents continue to confirm the Bible's account of history. People, places and events are confirmed and continue to be confirmed as Archaeological exploration continues. Nelson Glueck, noted Archaeologist has said, "It may be stated categorically that no Archaeological study has ever contradicted a Biblical reference!"

## (4) The Bible – God's Word! — Medical Facts

There are numerous medical facts found in the Bible that have now been confirmed by modern medicine. Three of them to consider are (1) The danger of germs in causing disease (found in many places in the O.T. law – Exodus through Deuteronomy)(Written apx. 3500 years ago) – (2) 8th Day chosen for circumcision (Lev. 12:3) & (3) Life is in the Blood (Lev. 17:11)

## (5) The Bible – God's Word! — Scientific Facts

There are scientific facts in the Bible, now confirmed by modern science. For example Is. 40:22 reveals that the earth is round & that the heavens are being stretched out. Also, Job 38:31 speaks of star constellations, "the Pleiades" & "Orion". The Bible reveals that the stars of "Pleiades" are gravitationally bound while the stars of "Orion" are not.

## (6) The Bible – God's Word! — Fulfilled Prophecy (a)

The Bible includes detailed prophecies concerning the destruction of ancient cities such as Petra, Tyre and Babylon. History books and encyclopedias reveal the accuracy of these Biblical prophecies which not only spoke of the destruction of these cities in general but in some cases gave details of how they would be destroyed.

# Confirming Evidence That The Bible is God's Word (Cont.)

## The Bible – God's Word!

The Bible includes prophecies of the <u>World Empires</u> from the time of Daniel (apx. 600 B.C.) through today. In Daniel 2, 7 & 8 the Bible prophesies that there would be (1) the Babylonian Empire, (2) the Medo-Persian Empire, (3) the Greek Empire, and (4) the Roman Empire. It also speaks of an End Time World Empire that is now referred to often as "The New World Order."

**Fulfilled Prophecy (b)**

(7)

## The Bible – God's Word!

The Bible includes over 300 Messianic prophecies in the O.T. that are fulfilled by Jesus Christ in the N.T. through His birth, life, ministry, death & resurrection. These fulfilled prophecies attest to the fact that the Bible is the Word of God & are another example of the unity of the message throughout the Bible. They also confirm that Jesus Christ is the Messiah!

**Fulfilled Prophecy (c)**

(8)

## The Bible – God's Word!

The Bible includes amazing prophecies concerning the <u>scattering of the Jewish people</u> into the nations of the world (e.g. – Deut. 28:64) <u>and the regathering of the Jewish people</u> from the nations of the world back to Israel in the last days. (e.g. – Ez. 36:23-24 & Ez. 37:21-22) It is also prophesied that the land will become fruitful again (Ez. 36:6-12) & Israel will become a nation (Is. 66:8)

**Fulfilled Prophecy (d)**

(9)

## The Bible – God's Word!

The Bible includes detailed prophecies concerning the <u>end times</u> (or last days) that are being fulfilled before our eyes. Of these (increase of immorality, wars & rumors of wars, movement toward a new world order, attention to Jerusalem, etc.) the most specific seems to be the use of the number 666 (Rev. 13:16-18) which is now used in the Universal Product Code on products.

**Fulfilled Prophecy (e)**

(10)

## The Bible – God's Word!

The changed lives of millions and millions of people who have accepted and followed the message of the Bible bears witness to the Bible being the Word of God. For centuries, including today, people all around the world give testimony of the dramatic change (for the good) that they have experienced when obeying the words of Scripture and putting their faith in Jesus Christ!

**Changed Lives**

(11)

## The Bible – God's Word!

The Bible has been attacked by kings, emperors and "intellectual" skeptics for centuries but has stood through every attack. All the while, the Bible has continued to be the undisputed leader when it comes to the number of copies produced and distributed, year after year after year!

**Indestructibility & Distribution**

(12)

# Jesus Christ (His Deity)(Historicity)(Etc.)

## The Person of Jesus Christ

### The Cornerstone!

Jesus Christ is said to be the Cornerstone that the church is built upon in numerous passages. Along with this, He is said to be the Stone that the builders rejected & the Stone of Stumbling!

Psalm 118:22-23, 1 Peter 2:6-8
Acts 4:10-12, Luke 20:17-18

(1)

## The Person of Jesus Christ

### His Deity (Pt.1)

Jesus Christ is presented in the Gospel of John as God! His deity is expressed in the 1st verse, "In the beginning was the Word, & the Word was with God, & the Word was God!" His deity is also seen through the 23 "I Am" Statements in John's Gospel.

John 1:1, John 20:31
John 8:24, John 8:58

(2)

## The Person of Jesus Christ

### His Deity (Pt.2)

Jesus Christ is presented as Lord & God throughout the N.T. Note - Rom. 10 refers to Jesus as the fulfillment of Joel's prophecy about "The LORD". Other N.T. passages show Jesus as having deity & receiving worship!

Phil. 2:5-8, Titus 2:13, Heb. 1:6-8
Joel 2:32 & Rom. 10:9-10, Col. 2:9

(3)

## The Person of Jesus Christ

### Our Great High Priest

In the book of Hebrews Jesus Christ is presented as our Great Eternal High Priest! He is seen as both the blood sacrifice and the High Priest Who offers His blood for us in heaven. He is author of our faith & of the New Covenant between God & His people!

The Book of Hebrews

(4)

## The Person of Jesus Christ

### Only Way of Salvation

Jesus Christ is clearly seen in the Bible as the only way of Salvation! Numerous passages speak of this. Also, Jesus Christ is the focus of all the Bible; in the O.T. by types, shadows & prophesies, and in the N.T. by direct statements.

John 14:6, 1 Timothy 2:5-6
Acts 4:12, Romans 10:9-10

(5)

## The Person of Jesus Christ

### God Incarnate!

Jesus Christ is fully God but He also became fully man so He might be the sacrifice for our sin and our Great High Priest forever. As God Incarnate He became "Immanuel" which is "God with us". While here in the flesh He laid aside His deity.

Matt. 1:23, Phil 2:5-8
Heb. 2:14-18, Is. 9:6-7

(6)

# Jesus Christ (His Deity)(Historicity)(Etc.)(Cont.)

## The Person of Jesus Christ

### The Christ (Messiah)

Jesus fulfilled all of the O.T. messianic prophesies (over 300 of them) showing that He is "Messiah" (Hebrew) or "Christ" (Greek). This means that He is the "Anointed One" Who would bring salvation & victory!

Is. 53, Is. 9:6-7, Ps. 22, Is. 7:14
John 20:31, Matt. 16:13-17

(7)

## The Person of Jesus Christ

### The Lamb of God

Jesus is introduced by John the Baptist in John 1 as "The Lamb of God Who takes away the sins of the world". The book of Revelation applied the term "The Lamb" to Jesus 9xs including a reference to the "Marriage Supper of the Lamb".

John 1:29 & 36, Rev. 5:6 & 6:9
Rev. 7:17 & 19:9 & 21:23

(8)

## The Person of Jesus Christ

### Conquering (Victorious King)

Jesus has defeated Satan through His death & resurrection. Hebrews says "He destroyed him who has the power of death." He has conquered death. He sits at the right hand of the Father awaiting final victory over all of His enemies.

Heb. 2:14, Col. 2:13-15, Rev. 19:11-21
1 Cor. 15:23-28, Eph. 1:20-22

(9)

## The Person of Jesus Christ

### Life = Believing in Jesus!

The purpose of John's gospel is pronounced in John 20:31, "... that you may believe that Jesus is the Christ, the Son of God, and that believing you may have life in His Name". Believing upon Jesus for salvation is seen in other scriptures also.

John 20:31, Romans 10:9-10
Acts 16:31, John 3:16

(10)

## The Person of Jesus Christ

### Historical Person!

Some question if Jesus really lived on earth as the Bible declares. The life of Jesus is confirmed by Roman historians and the Jewish historian Josephus. The impact of Jesus upon people & nations is undeniable. Even our calendars date back to His birth! The gospels tell of His earthly life.

Luke 1:1-4, Acts 1:1-2

(11)

## The Person of Jesus Christ

### Confirmed Resurrection!

Some question Jesus' bodily resurrection. There are many evidences of Jesus' resurrection. The bold witness of His disciples who had previously been fearful confirms the resurrection. They were willing now to die for their faith. The empty tomb, plus the rise of Christianity also confirm that He rose from the dead!

1 Corinthians 15:3-8

(12)

# Additional Resources Available

Additional Memory Cards are Available for Other Subjects Such As "Creation Verses", "Answering the Questions of Skeptics" and "Sharing The Plan of Salvation" at LOCALCHURCHAPOLOGETICS.ORG

The Book "Faith & Reason Made Simple" that is the basis for this training series is available at LOCALCHURCHAPOLOGETICS.ORG

The video series "Faith & Reason Made Simple" which consists of 8 (28 minute) sessions is available at LOCALCHURCHAPOLOGETICS.ORG

A Teacher's Manual for this series is also available at LOCALCHURCHAPOLOGETICS.ORG

Additional Helpful Apologetics Materials are also available at LOCALCHURCHAPOLOGETICS.ORG

For help in researching apologetics questions go to the extremely helpful website found at SEARCHCREATION.ORG

Contact Rick McGough for Speaking Engagements at LOCALCHURCHAPOLOGETICS.ORG or at 309-738-4863 or at rick@lcapologetics.org